WOMEN & CATHOLICISM

D1598628

WOMEN & CATHOLICISM
GENDER, COMMUNION, AND AUTHORITY

Phyllis Zagano

palgrave
macmillan

WOMEN & CATHOLICISM

First published in 2011 by PALGRAVE MACMILLAN® in the United States—a division of St. Martin's Press LLC, 175 Fifth Avenue, New York, NY 10010.

Where this book is distributed in the UK, Europe and the rest of the world, this is by Palgrave Macmillan, a division of Macmillan Publishers Limited, registered in England, company number 785998, of Houndmills, Basingstoke, Hampshire RG21 6XS.

Palgrave Macmillan is the global academic imprint of the above companies and has companies and representatives throughout the world.

Palgrave® and Macmillan® are registered trademarks in the United States, the United Kingdom, Europe and other countries.

ISBN: 978-0-230-11163-9 (hardback)

ISBN: 978-0-230-11164-6 (paperback)

Library of Congress Cataloging-in-Publication Data

Zagano, Phyllis.
   Women & Catholicism : gender, communion, and authority / Phyllis Zagano.
      p. cm.
   1. Women in the Catholic Church. 2. Catholic Church—Doctrines. I. Title. II. Title: Women and Catholicism.

   BX2347.8.W6Z34 2011
   262'.02—dc22   2010049031

Design by Scribe, Inc.

First edition: June 2011

D 10 9 8 7 6 5 4 3 2

Printed in the United States of America.

Contents

ACKNOWLEDGMENTS

To whom am I indebted? The question turns over in my mind as I close this book with more questions than answers. The trajectory of the past 15 years or so of my academic work and writing has led me into deeper corridors of the Catholic Church, looking always for answers to its apparent problems with women. Eleven years ago I published *Holy Saturday: An Argument for the Restoration of the Female Diaconate in the Catholic Church* (Crossroad, 2000); that book suggested additional writings, mostly in academic journals, as well as talks, conference papers, and even a few newspaper columns. The issue will not go away, nor should it, as its underlying questions remain unresolved.

Much of what I discovered while writing *Holy Saturday* propels the discussion here presented. This work, like *Holy Saturday*, was undertaken neither lightly nor quickly. I am indebted to various editors and friends who first gave me the opportunity to explore bits and pieces of the topic at various levels, beginning with David Gibson (*Politics Daily*), Kevin Eckstrom (Religion News Service), and John Jones (Crossroad Publishing) who suggested the overall schema of the book. Terrence Tilley (Fordham University), Margaret Farley (Yale Divinity School), and Kevin F. Burke, SJ (Jesuit School of Theology, Berkeley) supported its publication, and Burke Gerstenschlager (Palgrave Macmillan) believed in it and brought it to publication.

The substance of the work relies on the assistance of many persons who generously took time to converse with me about both issues and facts, including William T. Ditewig (St. Leo University), Dennis Doyle (University of Dayton), Paul Lakeland (Fairfield University), Gerard Mannion (University of San Diego), Most Rev. John Myers (Archdiocese of Newark), and the many others who took the time for brief conversations along the way.

Those who kindly assisted me in the first part, on jurisdiction and Bishop Bruskewitz, included Sister Jeannine Gramick, SL (New

Ways Ministry); Sister Teresa Kane, RSM (Mercy College); James A. McShane, PhD (Call to Action—Nebraska); Elizabeth Peterson (CALL); Monsignor Timothy J. Thorburn (Diocese of Lincoln); and the officers and staffs of Call to Action, especially Jim FitzGerald and Nicole Sotelo, and of the Dioceses of Grand Island and Lincoln, Nebraska, and of the Archdiocese of Omaha, and of the US Conference of Catholic Bishops, especially Teresa Kettlekamp and Sister Mary Ann Walsh, RSM.

For the second part, on sacramental power and Archbishop Milingo, help came from many quarters: from Sister Sheila Browne, RSM (Diocese of Rockville Centre); from Peter Paul Brennan (Married Priests USA); from Rev. Dennis McManus (Archdiocese of Mobile), and from officers and staff of CORPUS, especially William Manseau and Anthony Padovano; of the Imani Temple (Washington, DC), of the Archdioceses of Newark, New York, and of Washington, of the Diocese of Rockville Centre, and of the US Conference of Catholic Bishops.

For the third part, on women's ordination, those who assisted included Monsignor Donald McE. Beckmann (Diocese of Rockville Centre); Dagmar Celeste (Roman Catholic Womenpriests); Monsignor George Graham (Diocese of Rockville Centre); Dorothy Irwin (Roman Catholic Womenpriests); Rev. Ronald G. Roberson, CSP (US Conference of Catholic Bishops); Sister Christine Schenk, CSJ (FutureChurch); the officers and staffs of the Archdiocese of St. Louis and the Archdiocese of New York; and the many scholars and friends who worked with me on *Holy Saturday*.

That so many distinct and even distant parts of the church genuinely assisted me speaks more of their commonalities than of their differences.

Throughout, I am indebted to many professionals who assisted with fact checking, especially the editorial staffs of the *National Catholic Reporter*, the *National Catholic Register*, *Catholic News Service*, and *The Pilot*.

And where would I be without libraries? I am most indebted to the libraries of St. Joseph's Seminary, Yonkers, and of Hofstra University. Hofstra's Interlibrary Loan staff and its Religion Librarian, David Woolwine, assisted in innumerable ways throughout the conduct of my research. I am grateful as well to Hofstra College of Liberal Arts and Sciences Dean Bernard E. Firestone, who has encouraged and supported my research and writing on this and other topics since 2002. Portions of my research for this book were supported by a

Hofstra Faculty Research and Development Grant. Hofstra's Faculty Computing Support Center and its Help Desk Staff provided regular and reliable technical assistance: I am particularly grateful to Monica Yatsyla, whose suggestions and assistance with word processing troubles moved this project to its final stages. To Joanne Herlihy and the student assistants of the Department of Religion, I remain indebted for their routine and cheerful assistance with copying and printing.

Burke Gerstenschlager, Kaylan Connally, Erin Ivy, and many others at Palgrave Macmillan brought this book to speedy publication, and for their attention to detail and cheerful assistance I am most grateful.

Finally, without the criticism and editorial assistance of Rev. John E. Fanning (Archdiocese of New York) and of Peter J. Houle, PhD, I would not have been able to confidently put forth this work. Their many years of cheerful commentary have lighted many of my intellectual paths, and I am deeply thankful for their generosity.

Needless to say, any errors of fact or interpretation belong to me. To each and all, especially those colleagues I have inadvertently overlooked and those of my relatives and personal friends who remain unnamed here, I give thanks.

On to the next event!

INTRODUCTION

The Catholic Church is in trouble. Depending on which side of the altar rail you sit, women are either part of the problem or part of the solution. That's too broad a brush stroke, but it often seems that way.

Hyperbole aside, most levels of church membership see different facets of the global meltdown of internal communion and external authority as rooted in questions of gender. Questions of where and how women may participate in church liturgy, structure, and ritual circle the globe. Can women be ordained? Can women participate in governance? Can women have authority? Tellingly, the question, "Can priests be married?" circles back to both cause and effect of some of the scandals.

This book investigates three distinct yet interrelated situations in the Catholic Church, each of which has further theological and ecclesiological implications. Each of the three situations—one might call them case studies—is reflective of the problems in various parts of the global church and presents questions and some answers to be shared.

In the Catholic Church, communion and authority formally understood are by definition and by law inextricably bound, each reflecting on the other in support of official, or "magisterial," teaching. Each alone and both together form the frame of analysis for these three Catholic "cases," one each focused on questions of juridical authority and communion, of sacramental authority and communion, and the breaking away from both the juridical and sacramental in the matter of women's ordination. Each, in turn, presents distinct situations with larger implications and reflects on the other, presenting similar theological, canonical, sociological, historical, and practical questions.

The three representative cases from around the globe are viewed through an admittedly American lens. The stories move from the United States, to Zambia and South Korea, to Central and Western Europe, and back to North America. The thread of women in the church weaves through the tapestry of stories, as questions regarding women either surface or are self-evident in each of the cases. Each sheds light on the Catholic Church's perceived need for hierarchically imposed laws and sanctions designed to keep women at a distance from the holy, whether as liturgical ministers, as wives of priests, or as priests themselves.

JURIDICAL AUTHORITY AND COMMUNION

The Catholic Diocese of Lincoln, Nebraska, is inarguably the most conservative, tightly controlled diocese in the United States. In 1996, Lincoln Bishop Fabian W. Bruskewitz decreed automatic excommunication for members of any of 12 organizations: 10 non-Catholic and 2—Call to Action–Nebraska and the National Call to Action—for all intents and purposes "Catholic." While each group, Catholic or not, attacks, skirts, or departs from Catholic teachings, there seems an underlying animus on the part of the bishop and his clerical lieutenants toward anyone who questions authority, and, especially, toward women. Such may account for the depth of anger with which Bruskewitz wielded his authority, even denying communion to some members of his flock. While Bishop Bruskewitz appears to have had the tacit approval of Rome, some of his methods may be extracanonical, that is, beyond the boundaries of the Code of Canon Law.

Simultaneously, Bishop Bruskewitz steadfastly refused to cooperate with the US Conference of Catholic Bishops (USCCB), which (with Rome's approval) established a reporting system to gauge and address the still-smoldering crisis of priestly sexual abuse of minors. In each prong of the Lincoln situation, the bishop claimed his direct authority in communion with the See of Peter and the requirement that he need only respond to the bidding of Rome independent of what the US Conference of Catholic Bishops does or says.

So long as he complies with canon law, the diocesan bishop is the end of juridical authority within his diocese. His preferences and predilections set the tone of the diocese, of diocesan structure, and of diocesan practice. If he does not want women to serve in legitimate liturgical roles, he can ban them. If he does not want married men ordained to the diaconate, he can refuse them.

The question, however, becomes this: at what point does a bishop's insistence on policy cause a break with the people of his diocese and with the rest of the bishops of his territory? Is he "in communion" with the church, or has he removed himself from it? Clearly, he can legally—as far as canon law is concerned—do pretty much whatever he wishes. But sometimes canonical rights collide with common sense and with the needs and desires of the church at large.

SACRAMENTAL AUTHORITY AND COMMUNION

In 1983, Archbishop Emmanuel Milingo was forced to retire as archbishop of Lukasa in Zambia. As archbishop, Milingo was juridically in control of Lukasa. The Zambian people he served sought his faith healing more than his leadership, and when that ministry incorporated African practices, his largely white European clergy effectively rebelled. Did he actually move beyond what the Vatican considered "Catholic"? Was his involvement in faith healing too "African" and not close enough to European Catholicism? Or was he denied his diocese because he sought to serve (and speak out on behalf of) the poor? The question is moot, as Milingo was given one option: retire to Rome, where he lived for several years.

Milingo did travel back to Africa during his forced retirement to Rome, always under the watchful eye of a priest from the Vatican's Congregation for the Doctrine of the Faith. Then, in 2001 he surfaced in New York, at a group marriage blessing ceremony presided over by Rev. Sun Myung Moon, leader of the Unification Church (now the Universal Peace Federation).[1] After his marriage to a Korean acupuncturist, Milingo created a movement entitled "Married Priests Now!" and ordained four married men as bishops and two married men as priests in the United States. Now both excommunicated and laicized, for a time Milingo, as a validly consecrated bishop, performed arguably valid sacraments. But he has no jurisdiction—no legal authority rooted in territorial authority over a diocese—and so performs sacraments and acts outside any level of church jurisdiction or approval.

Since Milingo's break with Rome, his various organizations have claimed worldwide membership of thousands of resigned, married priests who wish to (and in some cases do) minister publicly. In the United States, his support grew but waned as his connection to Moon became more apparent. Yet, despite his Moon funding, Milingo's worldwide efforts on behalf of a wider married priesthood have touched several continents and continue, now apparently from both Africa and South Korea.

Milingo is definite in his argument for a married clergy—he refuses to ordain celibates in his new church—and he blames celibacy for every clerical problem imaginable, always circling back to homosexuality and pederasty. His argument (if not his reasoning) for married priests resonates with longstanding Catholic tradition and teaching about married clergy. Today, as throughout history, Eastern Catholic Churches routinely ordain married men as priests. The Western, or Roman Catholic Church by exception allows ordination of married men—usually former Anglican or Protestant clergy—as priests, and married men as deacons. Neither East nor West has allowed married bishops in modern times except in the most limited circumstances.

While the Vatican's 2005 Synod of Bishops on the Eucharist considered and discussed the married priests in the Western or Latin Church (the Roman Catholic Church), celibacy as the norm was reaffirmed by Pope Benedict XVI in *Sacramentum Caritatis,* his January 2007 synod report.[2] More recent calls, both from bishops and from the faithful, have raised awareness but resulted in nothing. The message is clear: men who touch the sacred should not touch women.

JURIDICAL AUTHORITY, SACRAMENTAL AUTHORITY, AND WOMEN'S ORDINATION

In 2002, members of the Roman Catholic Womenpriests movement were ordained as priests on a Danube River tour boat by an Argentine Catholic priest, Romulo Antonio Braschi, who had been twice ordained bishop by men claiming legitimate and valid provenance of episcopal orders. Later, two members of the movement were ordained as bishops in Europe, possibly by a valid Catholic bishop. They have subsequently held ordination ceremonies in various North American locations.

While the first women ordained were formally excommunicated by the Vatican, little action against the others was taken against women ordained subsequently, with the notable exception of Archbishop (now Cardinal) Raymond L. Burke's excommunication of Roman Catholic Womenpriests bishop Patricia Fresen and two women she ordained in St. Louis in 2007.[3] Later, the Congregation for the Doctrine of the Faith issued a declaration that anyone who participates in ordination ceremonies for women—both those ordained and those who ordain—are automatically excommunicated. More recently, the Congregation's decree has been entered into canon law.

Positions on both sides have hardened. While the Vatican continues to rail against women's ordination, the Roman Catholic Womenpriests movement boasts a large formation program, and its ordinations continue.

The juridical and sacramental questions surrounding the Roman Catholic Womenpriests phenomenon point to other, perhaps less complex situations. What about priests and deacons in other groups displaying various combinations and permutations of Vatican-recognized communion and authority? What about the breakaway Society of Saint Pius X, founded in 1970 by Archbishop Marcel-François Lefebvre? What about the Czech underground church, headed by Bishop Felix Maria Davídek? How about the Vatican's new outreach to priests and bishops of the Anglican Communion? And what about women ordained as deacons in churches fully recognized by Rome as having valid sacraments?

The three topics interwoven here attempt to answer some of these questions and ask others. Juridical authority means the bishop can essentially do as he wishes and substantiates the liceity (lawfulness) of his actions. Sacramental authority means a validly ordained bishop can perform valid sacraments, even without juridical authority. If validity does not depend on liceity, what is the status of the ordained women of the various churches and communions under investigation here? Are they "ordained"? They certainly are, in the eyes of their individual communions and churches. But what ordinations would (or could) Rome recognize? And will it?

Each of these three cases calls into question the relationship of the local church and the diocesan bishop with Rome. Together, the three cases ask fundamental ecclesial questions about juridical authority, sacramental authority, and church: what does it mean to be in communion with the "Chair of Peter"? What comprises church?

PART I

———⟡———

JURIDICAL AUTHORITY

BISHOP BRUSKEWITZ, THE BISHOPS' CONFERENCE, AND CALL TO ACTION

The best lesson that can be learned from everything that has happened is that one finds happiness, joy and satisfaction in obedience to the Church.

—Fabian W. Bruskewitz, Bishop of Lincoln, Nebraska[1]

The Catholic Church does not have an easily understood organizational model. While the pope is its "head," he gains his status from his first title: Bishop of Rome. Some of his other titles are honorific: Vicar of Jesus Christ, Successor of the Prince of the Apostles, Servant of the Servants of God. Others of his titles imply a leadership or jurisdictional role: Supreme Pontiff of the Universal Church, Primate of Italy, Archbishop and Metropolitan of the Roman Province, Sovereign of the State of Vatican City.

As Bishop of Rome, the pope has ecclesiastical jurisdiction over church matters within the diocese, which are actually handled by his Cardinal Vicar (called a Vicar General in other dioceses) and diocesan staff.

As Archbishop and Metropolitan of the Roman Province, the pope has additional ecclesiastical jurisdiction, most ordinarily exercised in appeals from lower diocesan courts (in the Province of Rome) to the Metropolitan Tribunal.

As Primate of Italy, the pope is considered as first among equals within the context of all the diocesan archbishops and bishops of Italy.

As Supreme Pontiff of the Universal Church, he has a coordinating role, overseeing policy and, to a certain extent, procedure, for the entire Catholic Church. This, his most recognized role, is carried out by the members of the Holy See (or Apostolic See), which is in many respects the Church's central government. The shorthand denotation of "the Vatican" refers to this governing arm of the Holy See, and to the several curial offices and judicial bodies that function under this title. Diplomatically, other nations are accredited to the Holy See, which also has permanent observer status at the United Nations.

As Sovereign of the State of Vatican City, the pope is the ultimate civil authority for the Vatican's territories, now 109 acres of Vatican City State set squarely in the middle of Rome.

The rest of the Catholic Church operates similarly, but on a much smaller scale. Dioceses are territories overseen by diocesan bishops. Importantly, individual diocesan bishops "report" only to the pope, who holds ultimate authority because of and on behalf of the others (bishops and people) who act "in communion" with Rome.

Relatively speaking, women have little if any jurisdiction in Catholic Church structures.

COMMUNION AND AUTHORITY

In communion with Rome are approximately 2,800 dioceses in the Roman Catholic Church, each with its own diocesan bishop, and 22 Eastern Catholic Churches coordinated through the Vatican's Congregation for the Oriental Churches, a curial office. There are individual eparchies (dioceses) in the Eastern Catholic Churches, each with its own ecclesiastical head.

In addition, Western or Latin Rite dioceses typically have a territorial conference of bishops that serves to coordinate policy and procedure on a national level.

In theory, at least, it all works well. Juridical and doctrinal determinations serve to coordinate (and often accommodate) the various cultural milieux in which the Catholic Church operates. Sometimes, however, individual bishops do not wish to ascribe to particular determinations. Often (as with the inclusion of women as altar servers) the bishop is expressly permitted to decide whether the innovation or change would serve his particular diocese.

In other instances, bishops simply refuse to cooperate with norms established by their territorial bishops' conference because it has no juridical standing or authority over an individual bishop. Sometimes an individual bishop will interpret canon law in such a fashion that he can go beyond it.

Questions of communion and authority often arise in dioceses where diocesan bishops for whatever reason choose to become—or at least exercise—law unto themselves. Such situations are particularly difficult in countries where democratic freedom is a protected right of all citizens and where personal achievements are both unfettered and valued. The problem of autocracy is not new in the Catholic Church, but when it collides with legitimate lay rights and illegitimate notions of democracy, episcopal autocracy presents reminders of earlier times in church history when the Christian faithful had even fewer rights and responsibilities than today and when bishops were literally the rulers of their territories, rarely, if ever, answerable to anyone. Today, autocracy grinds most noisily against the earliest traditions of the church, which traditions display a far more collegial attitude among and between not only the bishops but all the members of the church.

It is one thing for Catholics to defend the faith from forces without—the very real and virulent forces that they find criticize and bowdlerize Christian belief and practice for comedic or for darker, more nefarious reasons and goals. But when Catholicism is rightly criticized from within, that is, when groups of Christian faithful or national bishops' conferences attempt to correct apparent malfeasance or situations of inequality, Catholic teaching and tradition recognize that the church as a whole (and the diocesan bishop) can and should take note. Both can enter into respectful dialogue where disagreement lies.

Such is not always the case. From the time he took over his diocese, one diocesan bishop, Fabian W. Bruskewitz (b. 1935), eighth Catholic bishop of Lincoln, Nebraska, entered into contentious relationships not only with loyal members of his diocese and with non-Catholic and apparently anti-Catholic groups but with the US Conference of Catholic Bishops (USCCB) as well. Bruskewitz regularly criticized those he found beyond the Catholic pale in and out of his diocese since he left Milwaukee in 1992—possibly as a surprise to his own archbishop—to take possession of the Lincoln diocese.[2]

WHO IS FABIAN BRUSKEWITZ?

Fabian Wendelein Bruskewitz[3] was born in Milwaukee on September 6, 1935, attended St. Wenceslaus parochial school there, and then entered St. Lawrence Seminary at Mount Calvary, Wisconsin, when he was about 14. He continued his priestly formation and training at St. Francis Seminary in Milwaukee, Wisconsin, then at the Pontifical North American College and the Gregorian University, both in Rome.

Bishop Bruskewitz's training brackets Vatican II. He was ordained a priest on July 17, 1960, in Rome, at the Church of the Twelve Apostles by Cardinal Luigi Traglia (1895–1977), then-Cardinal Vicar of the Diocese of Rome.[4] Bruskewitz served as an assistant pastor in parishes near Milwaukee and then pursued a doctorate in dogmatic theology at the Pontifical Gregorian University in Rome, receiving his degree in 1969. He taught briefly at St. Francis Seminary in Milwaukee, then headed back to Rome to a staff job in the Congregation for Catholic Education, where he remained for 11 years. From 1980 to 1992 he was pastor of St. Bernard of Clairvaux in Wauwatosa, Wisconsin, a Milwaukee suburb.

Meanwhile, Bruskewitz's clerical advancement continued apace. He was named Papal Chamberlain with the title of Monsignor in 1976 and a Prelate of Honor in 1980. He was consecrated a bishop and installed in the Cathedral of the Risen Christ in Lincoln, on May 13, 1992.[5]

Succeeding retiring Lincoln Bishop Glennon Patrick Flavin (1916–1995), Bruskewitz soon set his sights on pro-abortion groups, liturgical reformers, and the lay church reform group Call to Action. Eventually, he began to do battle with the USCCB over the "Dallas Charter," which the US bishops passed in 2001 as an initial corporate response to the priest sex abuse crisis within the continental United States.

Bishop Bruskewitz's extreme conservative—some would say rigid—stance raised the profile of his now 95,000-member diocese, which he appeared to rule in a straight arrow, take-no-prisoners fashion. Replete with traditional Catholic groups—from the Catholic Daughters of America and the Knights of Columbus, to the Legion of Mary and the Catholic Boy Scouts—Lincoln claims no priest shortage. Its enviable ratio of one priest per six hundred Catholics does not make Bruskewitz a hero to his fellow bishops at the USCCB or to the more liberal Catholics within his diocese and across the nation.[6] Nor does the apparent plethora of priests point to total happiness among the faithful of his diocese, which stretches west across the Nebraska plains south of the Platte River, complementing the two other Catholic dioceses in the state of Nebraska—the Archdiocese of Omaha and the Diocese of Grand Island.[7]

Collisions within and without the Diocese of Lincoln—often on what might be viewed as "women's issues"—sculpt in sharp relief the relationships between a diocesan bishop and his people and with the national bishops' conference. They also underscore what a bishop can do relative to the sacramental life of his diocese, independent of any consultation or agreement with his metropolitan (the archbishop of his province) or the national conference of bishops. While technically an ordinary can act independently, in the larger picture Bishop Bruskewitz appears as an episcopal Lone Ranger of the American Midwest.

THE US CONFERENCE OF CATHOLIC BISHOPS

The USCCB is the national bishops' conference of the United States and the US Virgin Islands. It is a direct descendant of the National Catholic War Council, which was established in 1917 to provide funds, recreational services, and spiritual care to US military personnel. In 1919, the National Catholic Welfare Council was established as an administrative committee to handle matters between plenary meetings of US bishops; the Welfare Council was joined three years later by the National Catholic Welfare Conference, which addressed national questions of education, immigration, and social policy. In 1966, the National Conference of Catholic Bishops (NCCB) and the United States Catholic Conference (USCC) were established. The former met the mandate of the Second Vatican Council that bishops "jointly exercise their pastoral office,"[8] and comprised bishops' committees and their full-time staff; the latter comprised committees that included bishops, other clergy, and lay persons.

On July 1, 2001, the NCCB and the USCC joined to form the USCCB. The USCCB now comprises the 424 or so active and retired bishops, auxiliary bishops, and eparchs from the 195 (arch)dioceses and one apostolic exarchate in the United States.[9] Its approximately three hundred Washington-based staffers—the number was reduced to offset dropping income—work from a modern five-story building near the campus of Catholic University of America completed in 1989 at a cost of $24 million. Self-defined as "an assembly of the Catholic Church hierarchy who work together to unify, coordinate, promote, and carry on Catholic activities in the United States," the conference meets twice annually: in Washington, DC, in November and in another major city in June. Since 2006, however, and at least to 2013, its fall meetings are in Baltimore, the premier see of the United States.[10]

The Vatican II Decree Concerning the Pastoral Office of Bishops in the Church, *Christus Dominus* (October 28, 1965), suggested that every national or regional grouping of bishops meets regularly—typically interpreted as at least annually—to discuss matters of common concern.[11] The Decree states,

> In these days especially bishops frequently are unable to fulfill their office effectively and fruitfully unless they develop a common effort involving constant growth in harmony and closeness of ties with other bishops. Episcopal conferences already established in many nations have furnished outstanding proofs of a more fruitful apostolate. Therefore, this sacred synod considers it to be supremely fitting that everywhere bishops belonging to the same nation or region form an association which would meet at fixed times. Thus, when the insights of prudence and experience have been shared and views exchanged, there will emerge a holy union of energies in the service of the common good of the churches.[12]

Christus Dominus, which appeared thirty years before the general introduction of the Internet and email, and the concomitant increased ease of communication, addressed the need for increased communication among bishops within given national or regional boundaries. That is, the advent of widespread telecommunications via television and radio within nation-states created a further need for bishops to accommodate their own public pronouncements one to another, since public media often serve multiple dioceses and since national media theoretically serve all dioceses. Without coordination, the bishops within given countries risked presenting a disjointed and confusing collective front. The Decree continues: "An episcopal conference is, as it were, a council in which the bishops of a given nation or territory jointly exercise their pastoral office to promote the greater good which the Church offers mankind, especially through the forms and methods of the apostolate fittingly adapted to the circumstances of the age."[13]

The potentiality of episcopal conferences to coordinate ordinary matters—for example, admissions criteria to seminaries or the ages at which sacraments are to be received—may have been uppermost in the minds of the writers of *Christus Dominus*. As episcopal conferences progressed and grew in stature and staff, other tasks came to be theirs, especially the writing of statements signed onto (by vote) of the episcopal conference as a body.

In the United States, the US Catholic Bishops' Pastoral Letter on War and Peace, "The Challenge of Peace: God's Promise and Our Response" (May 3, 1983), was the first such major statement, one that went through several drafts and several rounds of national publicity before it was finally promulgated.[14] The Pastoral Letter and others like it fulfill the conciliar determination of *Christus Dominus* that bishops "exercise their pastoral office . . . through the forms and methods of the apostolate fittingly adapted to the circumstances of the age."[15]

Christus Dominus further presents detail about voting membership (essentially active diocesan bishops and auxiliaries of dioceses within the national or regional territory) and states that materials for the care of souls within the given territory be prepared by the episcopal conference of that territory: "This sacred synod also prescribes that general directories be prepared treating of the care of souls for the use of both bishops and pastors. Thus they will be provided with certain methods which will help them to discharge *their own* pastoral office with greater ease and effectiveness."[16]

Bishops' conferences around the world responded with "general directories"—sets of instructions—regarding varied and sundry items on their respective agendas. The USCCB developed several national directories in accord with the general directories issued by Rome including, for example, the *National Directory for the Formation, Ministry and Life of Permanent Deacons* (2005) and the *National Directory for Catechesis* (2005).

In the United States, USCCB staff provide guidance and help craft both policy statements and directories. Both major and minor public issues have routinely been discussed and debated among the US Catholic bishops and from time to time the USCCB has issued pastoral letters addressing both external and internal policy matters. These statements, usually developed by committees, are typically written by a single writer and vetted by bishop members, then approved by conference votes. Just as a committee of bishops wrote "The Challenge of Peace: God's Promise and Our Response," the 1983 pastoral letter on war and peace in response to a growing national interest in disarmament, perhaps sparked by the United Nations' Second Special Session on Disarmament (SSOD II) held in New York from June 7 to 10, 1982, other pressing social issues have led the bishops' conference to organize the drafting of and agree to the promulgation of multiple statements more or less respected (or read) by the varied layers of church membership.[17]

Despite their effectiveness in coordinating policy statements and specific pastoral practices, episcopal conferences (created and operating in response to the obvious need to conform policies and practices between and among dioceses, at least within national territorial boundaries), continue to receive mixed theological reviews. The predictable conflict is between the rights of a diocesan bishop within his diocese as against the perceived will of the national episcopal conference in matters both large and small. A good part of the conflict is administrative in nature, but it is theological as well. That is, because the conference exists as an essentially administrative convenience for the assembled bishops of a national territory—serving more to coordinate than to mandate—it risks becoming, or being understood as, more than an administrative and consultative body because its coordinating functions are often confused with true juridical authority.

Further, despite the obvious administrative advantages of bishops' conferences, there is no historical-theological basis for them in the Catholic Church. Despite the time, effort, and money devoted to their coordinating functions, they are an anomaly in the Church's juridical structure, a fact recognized at the highest levels. When interviewed while head of the Congregation for the Doctrine of the Faith some years ago, Pope Benedict XVI said "The decisive new emphasis on the role of the bishops is in reality restrained or actually risks being smothered by the insertion of bishops into episcopal conferences . . . [which] have no theological basis."[18]

Even so, bishops' conferences are most often defended as examples of the collegiality provided for—actually required—in canon law. Collective determinations made by the bishops are sent to Rome for a *"recognitio,"* and some documents are returned for "clarification" before they are approved. While the bishops' conferences have no ecclesial legal power, they do exert power by means of their collective moral authority.

One way of understanding the Catholic Church's juridical structure is by analogy. Various dioceses form a collective of juridical structures "in communion" with but not tied to Rome in civil law. Each diocese is in large respect a fiefdom whose aims are tied to the larger church, but whose governance and funding are specifically internal. The corporate analogy would be that a diocese operates more like a territorial franchise.

What is central to any view of "church" in Catholicism is the papacy, which has caused a dual development of the notion of ecclesiology. The papacy functions concurrently as a locus of communion and leadership and as the pinnacle of jurisdictional and organizational structure. These disparate understandings spawn two views. When the papacy is seen as the locus of communion and leadership, collegiality among the pope and bishops follows. When the papacy is seen as the pinnacle of jurisdictional and organizational structure, collaboration with the pope on the part of the bishops follows. The challenge—and the difficulty—is in the balance of these two views of "church."[19]

Granting traditional structures and the obvious tensions between views, the wider ecclesiological considerations—including what does the church do, who is the church, where does authority rest, and how should the church be governed?—typically begin and end with the role of the bishop. Contrasting models of ecclesiology set the "communal" (collegial, ecclesial) model against the "juridical" (collaborative, political) model. The "communal" model finds the best decision making in communal and collegial give-and-take within ecclesial boundaries, be they parochial or diocesan, and is kinder to bishops' conferences.

The "juridical" model is more top-down, and while members of a given parish or diocese may collaborate, decision making is reserved to the pastor, bishop, or pope. The latter model more strictly (and correctly) applies a collaborative, as opposed to authoritative, role to bishops' conferences (and, by extension, to parochial or diocesan committees and similar structures).

Successive pontificates have interpreted the relative weight of "communal" versus "juridical" models. In modern times, however, the coalescence of power to the Roman Curia has lent itself more to the "juridical" model and created an obvious tension between episcopal conferences and Rome and among individual bishops, who in reality "report" only to the Pope.[20] That is, whereas the "communal" model lends itself toward collegial decision making on the part of assembled bishops and sees the papacy more as a coordinator, the "juridical" model lends itself more to independent decision making on the part of individual bishops who see the papacy as a direct manager. Each model has elements of reality; it is the specific emphasis that causes the problems.

On the national level, the "communal" coordinating function of a bishops' conference becomes increasingly consultative (and therefore nonbinding) when it comes up against the juridical rights and authority of an individual diocesan bishop or pastor.

While the precise status of Catholic bishops' conferences remains fodder for theological speculation, the conferences still serve a coordinating and advisory function. This is especially true in the United States, where the USCCB remains relatively well funded, primarily because it holds the copyright to approved scripture translations for liturgical use. The USCCB as an organization and the assembled bishops have no juridical authority over anyone in and of themselves, including and especially any bishop member, although combined they can wield a certain amount of moral authority. Sometimes—only rarely—bishops' conferences are conceded authority by Rome, and when conceded, the authority is real. This would be in the case of specific directories or other documents that Rome approves as particular law for their given territories, as noted earlier.

The USCCB and the Sex Abuse Scandal

Perhaps the most widely publicized matter of common concern on which the assembled bishops have coordinated policy efforts and the USCCB staff have provided support is clerical sexual abuse of minors. The troubles have been commented on and catalogued by authors both friendly and unfriendly to the Catholic Church and Catholicism.[21] After simmering for nearly twenty years behind closed chancery doors and in the pages of Catholic journals, the widespread pattern of sex abuse of minors and concurrent cover-up by church officials burst into national view on January 6, 2002, when *The Boston Globe* began its exposé of priest pederasty and cover-up within the Archdiocese of Boston.

The following June, the USCCB met at Dallas to pass the "Dallas Charter," or the "Charter for the Protection of Children and Young People," outlining procedures for dealing with accusations, called for a National Review Board to gather diocesan statistics, and provided for the establishment of an Office for Child and Youth Protection.[22] Concurrently, the USCCB also voted on "Essential Norms for Diocesan/Eparchial Policies Dealing with Allegations of Sexual Abuse of Minors by Priests or Deacons," which were approved by the Congregation for Bishops in 2002 as particular law for the Catholic Church in the United States. The Norms require that individual dioceses have and report their policies for dealing with sexual abuse of minors by priests or deacons (but not by bishops) to the USCCB.

In 2004, the USCCB published a separate double blind sex abuse study conducted at its request by John Jay College, which examined the problem of sex abuse by Catholic priests and deacons in the United

States for the period 1950–2002. The mandate for the study was to (1) examine allegations by number and nature, (2) collect information about alleged abusers, (3) collect information about the alleged victims, and (4) accumulate information about the financial impact of the abuse on the Church.[23] Separate studies for by the Center for Applied Research in the Apostolate surveyed additional accusations and the accumulating financial impact on the Church and are published within the annual reports for the Office of Child and Youth Protection, the National Review Board, and the USCCB.[24]

In 2005, the assembled US bishops approved a new charter, and sent revised Norms for the United States to Rome. The revised Norms reworded sections regarding presumption of innocence of accused priests and deacons and the removal of the accused from ministry. The revised Norms also strengthened references to canon law procedure and specified procedures for transferring accused clerics (especially priests and deacons who are members of religious orders). These revised Norms were promulgated as particular law of the Catholic Church in the United States in May 2006.[25]

This appears to be the final revision of the US Norms, although in 2010 the norms of John Paul II's apostolic letter *Sacramentorum Sanctitatis Tutela* (April 30, 2001) were expanded by the Congregation for the Doctrine of the Faith with the approval of Benedict XVI. These caused a revisiting of the USCCB's Norms and Charter.[26]

Bishops who were not predators themselves, but who managed past cover-ups, were not sanctioned, nor have they been sanctioned since. Neither are bishops specifically mentioned or included in the Charter or the Norms, which in this respect fall short of the requirements of canon law that include all clerics (C. 1395). That is, the bishops themselves seem exempt from their own determinations and therefore from the particular law for the United States. Some argue that since all bishops are priests they are included in the Charter and Norms. Others argue that bishops answer only to Rome, where episcopal crimes automatically go. Still others argue that the bishops themselves remain in denial regarding their role in the abuse scandal and consequent cover-ups.[27] This last point is increasingly obvious, at least in individual cases, as more and more dioceses face bankruptcy while their bishops deny responsibility for the fiscal collapse of these corporations—for which these very bishops are the "corporation sole."[28] The 2007 settlement with 175 persons reached by the Archdiocese of Portland, Oregon, is a case in point. Barbara Blaine, president of Survivors Network of those Abused by Priests (SNAP) "blasted Archbishop John Vlazny, accusing him of using the bankruptcy system 'to keep a lid on the Catholic hierarchy's cover-up of horrific child sex crimes.'"[29] Many other dioceses face similar criticisms.

A key element of the "Charter for the Protection of Children and Young People" was the establishment of an independent National Review Board, headed by Francis Anthony "Frank" Keating, Governor of Oklahoma from 1995 to 2003. Approximately one year after the bishops called for the board, on June 16, 2003, Keating resigned as its head. Keating submitted his resignation shortly after Cardinal Roger M. Mahony, then Archbishop of Los Angeles, criticized him for comparing actions of some bishops to those of the Mafia. In his resignation letter, Keating, a former Special Agent for the Federal Bureau of Investigation, wrote: "My remarks, which some Bishops found offensive, were deadly accurate. I make no apology . . . To resist Grand Jury subpoenas, to suppress the names of offending clerics, to deny, to obfuscate, to explain away; that is the model of a criminal organization, not my church."[30] It must be underscored that Keating is a former federal agent, well schooled in the workings of the underworld. His ringing indictment did little to change matters and additional improprieties and cover-ups have come to light since, in the United States and around the world.

The well-documented pattern of secretiveness and nonresponse to problems of sexual impropriety among Catholic clergy highlighted by Keating and typified by the Boston cases grew from misuse of diocesan secret archives, to which only the diocesan bishop may have access (C. 490), and which became repositories for information that would damage the diocese in civil or criminal legal actions.[31]

Secret archives are maintained and kept closed by dioceses (and by the Vatican) until such time as all those named may be reasonably thought to have died. Currently, with the exception of the archives surrounding Vatican I and Vatican II and some other records, the Vatican Secret Archives prior to February 1939 (death of Pius XI) are closed.[32] But the use of Secret Archives to hide pederasts is an obvious abuse of the concept.

In the nineteenth century, Pope Pius IX mandated secrecy for all cases involving sexual solicitation in the confessional. Thereafter the Vatican repeatedly reasserted official secrecy regarding clergy sexual misconduct in the confessional through regulatory documents in 1922, 1962, and, most recently, in 2001. The logic of secrecy regarding the confessional is understandable. Cases of sexual solicitation or similar misconduct in the confessions involved communications with the Apostolic Penitentiary about "internal forum" matters, such as matters of conscience, and were rightly secreted. That is, these documents in one way or another were concerned with matters privileged through the seal of confession and sealed in protection of the penitent. However, the concurrent protection of the abuser is possible where the abuser was the confessor.

It seems fairly well documented that bishops used their secret archives to protect themselves and their diocesan checkbooks. As the child abuse scandal brewed and grew, and civil authorities sought information about pederasty and abuse outside the confessional in "external forum" cases, bishops improperly placed documents in the secret archives claiming that they were necessarily secreted for protection of the victim. That is, the bishops misused the secret archives to protect the crimes of their clerics, rather than the penitential privacy of individuals.[33]

The twin engines of avoidance of scandal and preservation of patrimony (money and property) drove these bishops' actions, and there appears little distinction in the ways records about different types of sexual misconduct by clerics came to be handled. That is, both "internal forum" cases (usually sexual solicitation within the confessional) and "external forum" cases (the large majority of pederasty and other clerical abuse cases) were locked away, and only the bishop had the key. Despite the promulgation of the Charter and the Norms and the existence of a National Review Board and a professional staff at the USCCB, diocesan bishops continue to conceal documents and refuse transparency where lawsuits and criminal cases are concerned.

Activist groups such as BishopAccountability.org and SNAP (Survivor's Network of those Abused by Priests) continue to publicize the hidden recidivism among the bishops through websites, conferences, public appearances, and direct mail.

Clearly, 2002 was the most public year of allegations and, in retrospect, the most public year of episcopal reaction, as hundreds of priests were placed on leave pending investigations. Then, as local media followed developing scandals in individual dioceses, on a national level the Catholic lay group Call to Action joined the charge against clergy sex abuse and concomitant cover-ups. SNAP and BishopAccountability.org were active. The Boston-based lay group Voice of the Faithful was the most vocal critic, but Call to Action became another voice in the growing cacophony of criticisms.

BISHOP BRUSKEWITZ AND CALL TO ACTION

There have been relatively few known cases of clerical impropriety among the priests of the Diocese of Lincoln, Nebraska since Fabian Bruskewitz became its bishop. Two Lincoln priests were convicted and imprisoned and one other Lincoln priest was accused by two men, who reached an out-of-court settlement with the diocese for an undisclosed sum.[34] Call to Action–Nebraska (CTA-N), founded in 1996, after Bishop Bruskewitz came to Lincoln, roundly criticized the diocese's preference for secrecy. As noted earlier, he continually refused to participate in USCCB annual audits.[35] Of his actions, Dr. Patricia O'Donnell Ewers, second chair of the National Review Board for the Protection of Children and Young People, whose term ended in October 2007, called Bruskewitz "unwilling to participate in the one measure of public scrutiny that assures the Catholic lay faithful that the Church is taking every means possible to reach out to those who have been harmed by individuals in the service of the Church and to promote the safety and well being of the children entrusted to its care."[36]

Bishop Bruskewitz's preference for secrecy—a hallmark of clericalism—may stem from his Roman training and connections. His resume includes sufficient staff time at the Vatican's Congregation for Catholic Education, in addition to student days at the prestigious North American College (the seminary for up-and-coming US seminarians) and at the Pontifical Gregorian University, for him to develop important connections well beyond Milwaukee. If rumors are to be believed, he returned to Milwaukee as a surprise to Archbishop Weakland, and as mentioned earlier, Weakland was allegedly surprised again by Bruskewitz's 1992 appointment to Lincoln. What is not surprising is that these events took place during the increasingly centralized pontificate of John Paul II, when the Curia's power expanded markedly.

While Bruskewitz was still in Rome, the people—and especially the women—of the Diocese of Lincoln chafed under the conservative outlook of their outgoing bishop, Glennon P. Flavin (1916–1995), who had attended all four sessions of Vatican II but did not seem to touched by it. The women's complaints were mainly over women's legitimate participation in liturgy, which was disallowed in Lincoln.

In response to Bishop Flavin's reportedly wooden management style and refusal to include women in legitimate ministries in the diocese, Catholics for an Active Liturgical Life (CALL) developed in the Lincoln diocese in 1988 and attempted to encourage Bishop Flavin to accept some of the spirit of Vatican II. CALL challenged

Bishop Flavin over diocesan regulations denying women liturgical and ministerial services—specifically as lectors, Eucharistic ministers, and altar servers—and attempted to convince him to include women in these ministries.

The most tendentious issue was women altar servers. By 1992, only the Dioceses of Lincoln, Nebraska and Arlington, Virginia did not allow women or girls to serve as acolytes, despite explicit provision in canon law—fully resolved by the Pontifical Commission for the Interpretation of Legislative Texts—that women and girls were permitted to serve at the altar.[37] Arlington eventually allowed female altar servers; Bishop Bruskewitz continues to forbid them.[38]

CALL had other issues with Bishop Flavin, particularly regarding the 1984 diocesan-wide collection of funds for the Campaign for Human Development, which he directed be taken up on Sunday, November 18, 1984. While funds were collected, in two letters to CALL leadership the national director of the Campaign for Human Development in Washington reported no funds were received from the Lincoln diocese. Apparently the Lincoln official responsible for the collection twice denied to the Washington director any collection had been taken up, a denial disputed (and disproved) by CALL. The CALL newsletter for September/October 1985 lists the amounts four parishes reported sending to the Lincoln chancery as the results of their Campaign for Human Development collections.[39]

The same issue of the CALL newsletter noted that Bishop Flavin refused to participate in grievance procedures of the Conciliation and Arbitration Committee of the National Conference of Catholic Bishops (USCCB's predecessor organization), adopted in the United States and approved by the Vatican in 1979. Ten persons signed the grievance: Diana McCown, a speech professor; Gordon Peterson, an attorney; Elizabeth Peterson (no relation), a housewife; Kay Haley, a secretary; Gerald Johnson, a mathematics professor; Joan Johnson, his wife, a hospital administrator; James McShane, an English professor; Carol McShane, his wife, a registered nurse; Marilyn Seiker, a farmwife; and Desmond Wheeler, a chemistry professor. The grievance asserted that Bishop Flavin (1) refuses to communicate with laity about his policies; (2) established regulations for service as lector that effectively eliminate all women as well as parents whose children attend public schools; (3) neglected CCD education for public school children; (4) refuses to allow anyone, including installed acolytes, to bring Eucharist to the homebound and those in nursing homes; (5) refuses to engage in ecumenical activities; and (6) refuses lay participation in the life of the Church.⁴⁰

Soon, CALL was gaining notoriety. At least two local newspapers (the *Lincoln Journal* and the *Western Nebraska Register*) and two Iowa newspapers (the *Davenport Catholic Messenger* and the *Sioux City Globe*) reported on the six requests. In time, both the Left-liberal *National Catholic Reporter* and the Right-conservative *Wanderer* published their reportage.

Meanwhile, three weeks after the CALL newsletter published its story of the missing funds, a Lincoln diocese check for $20,724 arrived at the Washington office of the Campaign for Human Development without explanation. CALL published a question: "Since 25% of the collection remains in the diocese (approximately $7,000) and some interest accumulated on the $20,724, CALL asks again, 'How are funds used?'"⁴¹

Concurrently, the group continued to discuss the role of women in the church and eventually spread its concerns outside diocesan boundaries. After considering a draft of the US bishops' pastoral letter on women (a project eventually abandoned by the NCCB), in early 1988, CALL both published its responses and sent them along to the pastoral letter's committee chair, Bishop Joseph L. Imesch, then Bishop of Joliet, Illinois. The suggestions were mild by contemporary standards, but apparently not by those of Bishop Flavin: (1) the bishops' pastoral should be for all lay people, not just women; (2) the Church needs the input of women; (3) the Church must formulate nonsexist theological terms; (4) Church tasks should be assigned according to gifts and regardless of gender; (5) bishops should give more attention to women alone: divorced, widowed, single, and religious; (6) the heritage of women as well as men in the Church should be taught; and (7) "the women of the Lincoln Diocese should have the same rights of ministry and service to the Church as men do, and all laity should have the same rights as lay people in other dioceses as allowed by Canon Law."⁴²

In the late 1980s, CALL became increasingly active, repeatedly pointing out Lincoln's pre–Vatican II stance. For example, Lincoln's diocesan lay ministry training was restricted to men who would be formally installed as lectors or acolytes, but the diocese had no diaconate program. (Generally speaking, only those men destined for ordination as deacons or as priests are formally installed as lectors or acolytes). In Lincoln, even installed acolytes could not take communion to the sick. Only priests visited the sick, and on a restricted basis. The diocese had a moribund liturgy committee, no diocesan pastoral council, no diocesan school board, very few parish councils, and had never held a diocesan synod. The atmosphere in Lincoln attracted conservative priest-candidates from outside the diocese—in 1988 seven of ten were not from Lincoln.[43]

CALL kept up its newsletter—a simple attempt at breathing a bit of the spirit of Vatican II into the Lincoln diocese—for ten years, until late 1991, when it seemed a new bishop would soon appear on the horizon. CALL's newsletter reported in October 1991 that women religious, who had been permitted to read scripture during Mass at chapels in a hospital and a nursing home, were now forbidden to do so, thereby ending any liturgical participation by women anywhere in the diocese.[44]

The critical mass of neuralgic issues boiled down to one: women. Ten years after CALL was founded, the bishop still refused to allow women to perform liturgical functions proper to laity at Mass, serve as parish trustees, serve on the lay committee for vocations, or serve on the diocesan development committee. Nor were women consulted on the bishops' pastoral on women or even replied to when they wrote to ask about it.[45]

In 1991, the CALL newsletter included a few "women's" cartoons—including a three-part confessional cartoon from the Davenport *Catholic Messenger*: (1) "I confess father, I'd like to be a priest"; (2) "Nonsense child . . . a woman could never hold a position of importance in the church"; (3) ". . . that'll be three Hail Marys." CALL reprinted similarly mild cartoons from *Punch*, the *Women's Journal Advocate*, and the *Dayton Daily News*.

Overall, the individuals who comprised CALL do not seem to be other than educated Catholics asking for what Vatican II promised and canon law allowed. But Bishop Flavin kept an iron grip on the diocese he had headed since 1967 and never explained his anti-woman stance.[46]

Bishop Flavin retired in March 1992 and was quickly succeeded by Bishop Bruskewitz. With the new bishop in town, CALL's members thought they could enter into dialogue. They suspended their newsletters and essentially disbanded, rejoicing in the change of episcopal leadership. The new bishop seemed more in tune with the times—he was even allowing women to serve as lectors in some circumstances.[47] Soon, the most active members of CALL asked to meet with the new bishop, not as representatives of a now-defunct organization, but rather as individuals wishing to enter into dialogue with their diocesan bishop. Bishop Bruskewitz first met with Diana McCown, CALL's former president, but their meeting was not particularly substantial. They did agree, however, to meet together again, along with others.

But the bishop had some requirements. Bruskewitz stipulated that the persons with whom he would meet read three then-recent books published by the conservative Ignatius Press: Donna Steichen's *Ungodly Rage: The Hidden Face of Catholic Feminism*, a ranting stream-of-consciousness report of a few radical feminist conferences from the late 1970s to 1990; Helen Hull Hitchcock's *The Politics of Prayer: Feminist Language and the Worship of God*, a collection of essays against inclusive language; and "Women in the Priesthood: A Systematic Analysis in the Light of the Order of Creation and Redemption," the PhD thesis of German priest and theology professor Manfred Hauke.[48]

The last requirement brought them up short. While there were passing references here and there in CALL newsletter reporting one or another speech or symposium, particularly on the Women in Theology group at the University of Nebraska, the ordination of women as priests had never been a CALL agenda item, nor was it an issue for the individuals who wished to meet with the bishop: James A. McShane, Gordon Peterson, Jerry Johnson, Donna McCown, and Elizabeth A. "Betty" Peterson. They were professors and professionals interested in opening dialogue. They read the works, talked about them, and wrote for an appointment to meet with the bishop. He never responded.

In retrospect, it appears the CALL leadership was tarred by the rage let loose in Bishop Bruskewitz by the books he read and asked them to read. There is no connection between CALL's leadership and the real and imagined abuses reported by Steichen, who wrote, "The goddess movement is best understood as one serving the broader, more politically revolutionary Gnosticism represented by the coalition of which groups like Call to Action are the base."[49]

Even so, Bishop Bruskewitz refused to speak with the former CALL members about their concerns. These five, and others who had been involved in the CALL movement, quickly realized there would be no changes with the new bishop. They also believed that as a local group they would not be able to bring about any changes. They were headed in the direction of Vatican II, which had closed nearly thirty years earlier without any noticeable impact on the Diocese of Lincoln, and their efforts at bringing their church into the present, if not the future, were now stymied by a new bishop whose own agenda, and evident

attitude toward women, would not permit dialogue. In short, Bruskewitz appears to have imagined covens of Wiccan radicals meeting in
Nebraska kitchens plotting the overthrow of Catholicism.

The CALL leaders were patient, believing the bishop would get
around to their requests for dialogue. As they waited and watched,
there was no movement toward contemporary church realities or
practices in the Lincoln diocese, which seemed disconnected from the
rest of the United States.

Soon, glimpses of Bishop Bruskewitz's barricading against the
imagined onslaught of raving feminists promised by Steichen began to
appear. In June 1993, Bruskewitz threatened loss of priestly faculties—
the ability to celebrate sacraments—to any priest who allowed women
or girls as altar servers at a Mass celebrated within the diocese. He was
within his rights as diocesan bishop to ignore the provisions of Canon
230, which allow any lay person to perform the duties of lector or
acolyte. But he was in direct opposition to the typical practice in the
United States, a year earlier ratified by the Pontifical Commission for
the Interpretation of Legislative Texts and more fully defined a year
later by the US Bishops Committee on the Liturgy.[50]

Perhaps predictably, in the face of Bishop Bruskewitz's attitude
and tight control, CALL's remnants reorganized and affiliated with
the Chicago-based national Call to Action, which identifies itself as a
Catholic movement working for equality and justice in the church and
society. In 1992, equality and justice in the church and society were
precisely what the CALL core members were seeking. Their issues
were lay oversight of finances and greater lay participation in decision
making and liturgical ministry, in accord with Vatican II and the 1983
Code of Canon Law, which replaced the 1917 Code in which both
Bishops Flavin and Bruskewitz were trained while in seminary.[51]

So the membership remnants of CALL decided to affiliate with the
national Call to Action and developed a local affiliate Call to Action–
Nebraska (CTA-N) in 1995–1996. The initial open meeting of CTA-N,
on February 24, 1996, at Mahoney State Park (on the main road
between Lincoln and Omaha just inside the Diocese of Lincoln),
included approximately seventy Catholics. The major speaker that day
was Dr. Maryanne Stevens, a Sister of Mercy then chair of the theology department at Creighton University, invited to speak about the
ethics of dissent.[52]

The events were perhaps predictable. A woman religious from another
diocese would be addressing assembled Nebraskans within the Lincoln
diocese about legitimate dissent. Three or four days prior to this initial

CTA-N event, Stevens received a telephone call from Creighton's Vice President for Academic Affairs, asking if her talk would be about abortion. It was not, she said, but rather would focus on internal practices of the Catholic Church. Within thirty minutes Stevens received a similar telephone call from an assistant to Creighton's president saying they had received a letter from the Lincoln chancery demanding she be forbidden from speaking. Stevens then learned that a similar letter was sent to the president of her religious congregation. She also learned from the Omaha chancery that copies of the letters had been sent there as well and that the Archdiocese of Omaha was ignoring them.

Stevens did speak that day—she asked that she not be taped—about the role of conscience and Catholic social teaching as distinct from moral teachings, about the role of the bishop as a point of unity in a church where individuals were treated as adults, and about the distinction between doctrine and practice. From all accounts, her talk was standard post–Vatican II fare.[53]

But this was an event created by the old CALL crew, held within the territorial limits of the Lincoln diocese. The bishop was already suspicious of their intent and beliefs—how much did they uphold of Catholic doctrine?

The opening meeting also included a Mass celebrated by a priest of the Archdiocese of Omaha, Father Jack McCaslin, who may or may not have realized that the state park sat within the Diocese of Lincoln. On careful reflection, Nebraska priests might recall the diocesan line of demarcation is the Platte River, which creates the northern boundary of the park. Even so, it is easy to be mistaken because the park is much closer to the city of Omaha than to the city of Lincoln. The park was chosen as a central location for interested parties from Lincoln and from Omaha and others the third Nebraska diocese, Grand Island. But they were meeting in the Lincoln diocese and to celebrate a public Mass such as this in another diocese a priest should obtain the permission of (or at least notify) the diocesan bishop, in this case Bishop Bruskewitz. McCaslin did not do so.[54]

The Mass was the centerpiece of the half-day open organizational meeting, which followed three prior organizational meetings. In retrospect and from the outside, it appears to be the line drawn in the sand between pre– and post–Vatican II Catholics in the middle of Nebraska. The seventy or so attendees in 1996 were mostly individuals who were of age or nearly so during Vatican II. They remembered the pre–Vatican II Catholic Church of the 1950s, even of the 1940s, in the United States. They were in large part its products—educated

Catholics who took their faith and their church seriously and who wanted to gain access to what Pope John XXIII's "open windows" had promised: transparency in church administration, more participation by laity (especially women) in the liturgy, and the ever-unstated but ever-present desire for simple respect from the clergy, who in parts of Nebraska still appeared to regard laity as sheep to be shepherded, and rather stupid sheep at that.

The organizers and attendees were not obvious dissidents. But what, exactly, did they believe? Father McCaslin says he arrived a little late. A planner of the Mass, former Grand Island priest Richard Maciejewski,[55] provided an "Affirmation of Faith" that clearly skirts the basic tenets of the Nicene Creed, and Father McCaslin objected. Whether the group actually recited the "Affirmation of Faith" (instead of the Nicene or Apostle's Creed) is a central point in the debate between and among the parties to the later events. It was a Saturday, so no Creed was required for the Mass. The "Affirmation of Faith" handed out that day begins "I believe in people, and in a world in which it is good to live for all humankind," affirms belief in Jesus of Nazareth, and ends, "I believe in the resurrection—whatever it may mean."[56] In later correspondence founding CTA-N member James A. McShane defended the "Affirmation of Faith," arguing that it did not replace, but enhanced, the Creed. There is no evidence that the former CALL, now CTA-N leadership recognized any of the liturgical, and thereby fundamental theological, errors they incurred. To recite the "Affirmation of Faith" without the Nicene or Apostles' Creed is tantamount to heresy, as Father McCaslin surely recognized. Similarly, another prayer on the typescript, a "Penitential Prayer," can fairly be judged as an attempt at "relevance" that falls short of what the Catholic Church intends at the Penitential Rite of the Mass.

The event planners also provided a Eucharistic prayer obtained from the national Call to Action, which had apparently been used previously in Chicago.[57] In later correspondence, Professor McShane admits to the errors in the Eucharistic prayer and evidences his regret. As printed on the sheets distributed at the Mass, the CTA-N Eucharistic prayer is not among the ten approved Eucharistic prayers ordinarily celebrated and is considered sacramentally invalid since the word "commemorate" rather than "remember" is used after the consecration. Father McCaslin recalls digressing from the printed Eucharistic prayer, or even not using it at all, because of its obvious invalidity. McCaslin also says he told the organizers there was no need for Call to Action–Nebraska to create more trouble than it needed.[58] According to Rich Maciejewski, McCaslin did not use the printed Eucharistic prayer.

There were also 12 pages of music typical of the 1970s and 1980s—by Carrey Landry, John Foley, Dan Schutte and others—provided by Maciejewski, who played the guitar for the Mass.[59]

The meeting did not intend to be a gathering of heretics, but rather a meeting for those who thought Vatican II might have something to say to Nebraskans, particularly to those in the diocese of Lincoln. The abilities of the laity, and particularly of women, to participate in liturgy and in church were uppermost in their minds. They who gathered that day on the banks of the Platte River believed that Nebraska Catholics needed an organization that would allow them to speak freely about any and all issues of Catholic renewal and social justice and were filled with the exuberance of the moment. They wanted dialogue; they wanted reform. They thought they had a legitimate right to each.

Bishop Bruskewitz did not agree. He seems to have been advised of earlier organizational meetings, and he (or his chancellor, Monsignor Timothy Thorburn), sent two college students to the February 24 meeting at Mahoney State Park. According to a CTA-N member present that day, the two took a Mass booklet and departed before the ceremonies began.[60] They therefore were only able to report what might have been.

The organizers of CTA-N were in contact with the chancery, but the exchange of letters was less than friendly. Monsignor Thorburn, who had begun seminary studies for the Archdiocese of Omaha, but transferred to the Diocese of Lincoln before ordination, seems to have been CTA-N's chief nemesis and point of contact. Writing for the organizers, Professor McShane wrote a few days after the meeting to Thorburn complaining about the interlopers: "Given your intemperate response to the previous NCTA [Nebraska Call to Action] meeting, I had misgivings about admitting persons to our deliberations who were there not for their own benefit, nor concerned about open discussion . . . I pass over in silence the judgments appropriate to your unwillingness to do your own dirty work."[61]

Two days later, two other organizers, Lori Darby and John Krejci, a Nebraska Wesleyan sociology professor and married former priest, threw down the gauntlet: "We are in the process of forming CALL TO ACTION, NEBRASKA, and an affiliate of the national CALL TO ACTION organization. As we go through the organizing process, we are trying to bear in mind the words of Pope John XXIII, 'In essentials, unity; in other things, diversity; in all things, charity.'"[62] The next day, March 7, Monsignor Thorburn replied to James McShane's letter:

> The first meeting they [the students] attended was announced in various public *fora*. There was no indication, at least on the announcement that I saw, that it was in anyway a closed meeting. The second meeting was announced to me by Dr. John Krejci. I presumed that the information he provided was an invitation, rather than a taunt or a "dare". Apparently I was mistaken.
>
> Because your group has presented itself as a Catholic organization which addresses Catholic issues, the Catholic Church has every right to make an assessment, through highly educated lay representatives, of your organization. In fact, Call to Action, Nebraska has been found to be inimical to the Catholic Faith and a serious impediment to evangelization. As such, be assured that observers from the Catholic Church will attend any open meetings (if any more open meetings are held) of Call-to-Action that take place in the Diocese of Lincoln. While I may attend myself some time, I am surprised that you would object to having lay representatives attend. We are in, after all, the post Vatican II Church.[63]

Meanwhile, Bishop Bruskewitz replied to the Darby-Krejci letter in a less-than-pastoral tone:

> A priest-friend of mine, who had formerly been a Protestant minister, said that the difference between a dissenting Catholic and a Protestant is that the Protestant has integrity. . . .
>
> Your organization is intrinsically incoherent and fundamentally divisive. It is inimical to the Catholic Faith, subversive of Church order, destructive of the Catholic Church discipline, contradictory to the teaching of the Second Vatican Council, and an impediment to evangelization . . .
>
> Please advise any Catholics from the Diocese of Lincoln, who are members of your group, that such membership constitutes a grave act of disrespect and disobedience to their lawful bishop. This letter is to be considered a formal canonical warning to them about this matter. After April 15, 1996 appropriate ecclesiastical censures will be imposed on those Catholics from or of the Diocese of Lincoln who attain or retain membership in your organization.[64]

Just days later, on March 22, 1996, Monsignor Thorburn published a formal canonical warning in the diocesan newspaper, *Southern Nebraska Register* and announced Bishop Bruskewitz's "Extra Synodal Legislation" decreeing that Catholics of the Lincoln Diocese who belonged to any of 12 organizations, including the national Call to Action and Call to Action-Nebraska, would be automatically placed under interdict on April 15, 1996, and if their membership persisted, automatically excommunicated one month later. (An interdict is a warning that carries the effective penalty of excommunication.) The forbidden list of organizations included Call to Action and Call to Action–Nebraska, five Masonic organizations, two groups that promote abortion, two groups connected with the right-wing break-away Archbishop Lefebvre, and the Hemlock Society, which promotes assisted suicide.[65] The Masons had been named in the 1917 Code of Canon Law, now replaced by the 1983 Code of Canon Law.

But the notice, as published in the *Southern Nebraska Register*, was not signed by the bishop, who in fact and in law is the only person who can legislate for his diocese. Hence a question arises about the canonical basis for Bruskewitz's unilateral determinations regarding the organizations. There is little argument to be raised against including some of the societies, especially those that are clearly antithetical to Catholic teaching, such as the pro-abortion Catholics for a Free Choice and the Hemlock Society, which advocates assisted suicide. The Lefebvre organization, the Society of St. Pius X, is a more difficult call, for their errors are primarily juridical in nature. In fact, a prior attempt to excommunicate members of the Society of Saint Pius X by the Bishop of Honolulu ultimately failed.[66] (These events in Nebraska took place well before the much-publicized papal rescinding of excommunication of the four illicitly ordained bishops of the Society of Saint Pius X, particularly of Holocaust-denier Richard Williamson.)

As for Call to Action–Nebraska and Call to Action, each is presumably an association of the Christian faithful seeking church reform. At the time, the issues of CTA-N, and perhaps of the national CTA, were within the realm of permitted dialogue. The main national issues were not those of today, which include acceptance of homosexual activity and women's ordination as priests, but neuralgic issues of episcopal oversight and leadership that grated against Vatican II's call to update. CTA-N leaders were genuinely perplexed, both at their being banned and at the swift violence of the bishop and his minions.

When CTA-N organizer Professor McShane, wrote the diocesan chancellor, Monsignor Thornburn, to ask the basis for the bishop's actions, the chancellor replied with a laundry list of canons.[67] He cited numerous canons from the sections in Book II of the Code of Canon Law, The People of God, regarding the obligations and rights of the Christian faithful, it would seem implying that at least some of the named organizations were organizations of the Christian faithful. Many were not.

In fact, Monsignor Thorburn had already asserted the diocese's right to investigate Call to Action specifically because it was a Catholic organization. He had dispatched the two students to observe the Mahoney State Park meeting. Strangely, the chancellor does not cite

Canon 305, which asserts the duty of vigilance over associations of the Christian faithful by competent authority. That is, by citing earlier canons that specifically mention associations of the Christian faithful, the bishop (or his chancellor) again by implication named Call to Action–Nebraska at least (if not the national Call to Action) as an association of the Christian faithful. But Thorburn does not cite the proper canon, Canon 305, to justify his assertion that he is thereby taking care that "the integrity of faith and morals is preserved in them," that is, within associations of the Christian faithful.[68] Canon 305 further allows that organizations are subject to his vigilance whether or not they are headquartered within his diocese, provided they are active within its boundaries. That would—in theory at least—give Bishop Bruskewitz authority to investigate the national group as well, but not to penalize its members nationally.

Even given the canonical cloudiness of the situation and the relative rancor between and among the parties, there remains the fact of the Mahoney State Park Mass, within the Diocese of Lincoln, that apparently included a non-Catholic (even non-Christian) creed and attempted, at least, to use an invalid Eucharistic prayer. Declaring other than an acknowledged Creed would place a person outside Catholicism anyway. That is, declaring a non-Catholic, non-Christian creed is tantamount to heresy.

CALL TO ACTION AND CALL TO ACTION–NEBRASKA

It is important to distinguish between Call to Action–Nebraska and the national Call to Action at the time. The Nebraskan Call to Action members, who felt defeated in their efforts to bring the Diocese of Lincoln up to speed with other US dioceses regarding the changes allowed and encouraged by Vatican II, thought that affiliating with a national group would help their cause. Perhaps one or another had attended a national convention—like those caricatured by Steichen in *Ungodly Rage*—but like any other conventioneers they could not have seen and heard everything, nor did they need to accept the opinions of disparate speakers brought in for the events.[69] Besides, with whom else would they affiliate? The other prominent national lay group—Voice of the Faithful (VOTF)—was not founded until 2002, and VOTF's initial focus at least was on the clergy sex abuse scandal spreading outward from their founding locale, the Archdiocese of Boston.[70] (Voice of the Faithful has steadfastly kept its distance from Call to Action issues, especially the ordination of women priests, even while numbering among its members individuals who personally—or even publicly—might not adhere to one or another church discipline.)

Yet it seems the issues of sex and gender as embraced at least by Call to Action on the national level, if not by every member of Call to Action–Nebraska, are what most riled Bishop Bruskewitz.

CALL TO ACTION

The national organization Call to Action is one of a number of organizations that grew as an outgrowth of the immense reaction to what came to be called "the spirit of Vatican II." When the aging Cardinal Angelo Roncalli, Patriarch of Venice, became Pope John XXIII, many thought his would be a caretaker papacy.[71] Rather, on January 25, 1959, the 77-year-old pontiff called the Second Vatican Council intending, as the saying goes, to "open the windows" to allow fresh air—and thinking—into the church. That spirit of renewal, still contentious and contested in many parts, included the initial impetus for a new form of lay action in the church.

The council ran in four fall sessions: 1962, 1963, 1964, and 1965. Pope John XXIII died before the council's second session and was succeeded in June 1963 by 65-year-old Giovanni Battista Montini, Cardinal Archbishop of Milan, who took the name Paul VI. The council closed in 1965, and its decrees were subsequently published, studied, discussed, and, in many quarters, implemented.

The oft-used analogy of opening the windows to let fresh air into the church indicated a nod to more involvement by the laity, the non-ordained secular and religious people who had (and have) no place in church hierarchy.

In his encyclical letter *Octogesima Adveniens* (May 14, 1971) Paul VI issued, literally, a "call to action" to the laity:

> It is to all Christians that we address a fresh and insistent call to action. In our encyclical on the Development of Peoples we urged that all should set themselves to the task: "Laymen should take up as their own proper task the renewal of the temporal order. If the role of the hierarchy is to teach and to interpret authentically the norms of morality to be followed in this matter, it belongs to the laity, without waiting passively for orders and directives, to take the initiatives freely and to infuse a Christian spirit into the mentality, customs, laws and structures of the community in which they live". Let each one examine himself, to see what he has done up to now, and what he ought to do. It is not enough to recall principles, state intentions, point to crying injustice and utter prophetic denunciations; these words will lack real weight unless they are accompanied for each individual by a livelier awareness of personal responsibility and by effective action.[72]

What Paul VI was asking for was a new way of thinking—a *"novis habitus mentis"*—that would encourage the lay involvement envisioned by Leo XIII in his call for social justice in his encyclical letter On Capital and Labor (*Rerum Novarum*).[73]

When the Second Synod of Bishops opened on September 30, 1971, Pope Paul VI told the assembled bishops that it was the laity who must respond to the "call to action" to create a just world.[74] This Second Synod of Bishops had two topics for consideration: the ministerial priesthood (in 1970 the Dutch bishops had called for a married priesthood and for women priests) and justice in the world. The final synod document, noted for its brevity, reaffirmed the Western tradition of priestly celibacy and that "action on behalf of justice and participation in the transformation of the world appears to us as a constitutive dimension of the preaching of the gospel."[75] The synod further wrote, "While the Church is bound to give witness to justice, she recognizes that anyone who ventures to speak to people about justice must first be just in their eyes. Hence we must undertake an examination of the modes of acting and of the possessions and lifestyle found within the Church itself. Within the Church, rights must be preserved."[76] That Second Synod of Bishops also called for an end to unjust social structures:

> Listening to the cry of those who suffer violence and are oppressed by unjust systems and structures, and hearing the appeal of a world that by its perversity contradicts the plan of its Creator, we have shared our awareness of the Church's vocation to be present in the heart of the world by proclaiming the Good News to the poor, freedom to the oppressed, and joy to the afflicted. The hopes and forces which are moving the world in its very foundations are not foreign to the dynamism of the Gospel, which through the power of the Holy Spirit frees people from personal sin and from its consequences in social life.[77]

The Second Synod of Bishops' call for justice is repeated on the national Call to Action website, which mistakenly claims the documents of Vatican II in general, and specifically the words of Paul VI, as *legislation* for their agenda.[78] The words of the synod, and of Pope Paul VI, echo the sentiments of the CALL newsletter writers and the apparent intent of the Call to Action–Nebraska founders; that is, to create a more transparent and just society within the church.

However, the Call to Action agenda as promoted both nationally and locally was arguably a more liberal Catholic agenda, one that included the line-drawing buzzwords that tend to stop all conversation in deeply conservative pockets of the church, particularly in the United States. In a retrospective, "Spirituality Justice Reprint," at the time of its twenty-fifth anniversary, Call to Action reviewed its accomplishments, including hosting German theologian Hans Küng before an audience of 1,800 persons, and wrote: "After Küng, CTA over the years has made it a point to provide a platform for theologians and pastoral leaders persecuted by the Vatican and the hierarchy. The list includes Charles Curran, Bill Callahan, Theresa Kane, Matthew Fox, Edwina Gateley, Carmel McEnroy, Barbara Fiand, Paul Collins, Michael Morwood, Lavinia Byrne, Jeannine Gramick, Robert Nugent and Bishop Jacques Gaillot. Publicity for Sri Lankan Fr. Tissa Balasuriya's appearance at CTA in 1997, combined with massive international outcry organized via the Internet, was unusually effective: the Vatican rescinded Balasuriya's yearlong excommunication two months later."[79] While Charles Curran is best known for arguments about Paul VI's encyclical letter On Human Life (*Humanae Vitae*) (July 25, 1968), which banned artificial means of birth control, and Jeannine Gramick and Robert Nugent are best known for ministry to and advocacy for homosexuals, a constant thread in the work of the persons CTA lists is the ordination of women as priests.

Both nationally and through its 53 regional affiliates as of 2009, Call to Action then as now argued for married clergy, women priests, and contraception. Increasingly, over the years Call to Action has broadened its interests in human sexuality to include questions surrounding public church recognition of active homosexuals.

The wider inclusion of married priests in the Latin Rite remains a legitimate area for discussion. Indeed, the 2005 Synod of Bishops on the Eucharist raised significant discussion on married clergy.[80] The possibility of women priests is argued to have been definitively settled with John Paul II's apostolic letter On Reserving Priestly Ordination to Men Alone (*Ordinatio Sacerdotalis*) (May 22, 1994), but scholarly and popular discussion continues.[81] The contraception debate has all but ended—Catholics widely ignore Catholic Church teaching on the matter.

The clearer strain of discussion and dissent around the world focuses on the first two, perhaps related issues—married priests and women priests. While married priests are officially tolerated, little raises more ire than the concept of women priests.

The notion of ordaining women is the focus of puerile, even locker room, comments by some. The standard comment is that ordaining a woman is the same as ordaining a lamppost or a dog. Worldwide headshaking followed the Congregation for the Doctrine of the Faith's updating John Paul II's apostolic letter On Safeguarding the

Sanctity of the Sacraments (*Sacramentorum Sanctitatis Tutela*) (April 30, 2001), reinforces (and extends) the ban on women's ordination:

> The more grave delict of the attempted sacred ordination of a woman is also reserved to the Congregation for the Doctrine of the Faith:
>
>   1. With due regard for can. 1378 of the Code of Canon Law, both the one who attempts to confer sacred ordination on a woman, and she who attempts to receive sacred ordination, incurs a *latae sententiae* excommunication reserved to the Apostolic See.
>   2. If the one attempting to confer sacred ordination, or the woman who attempts to receive sacred ordination, is a member of the Christian faithful subject to the Code of Canons of the Eastern Churches, with due regard for can. 1443 of that Code, he or she is to be punished by major excommunication reserved to the Apostolic See.
>   3. If the guilty party is a cleric he may be punished by dismissal or deposition.[82]

Except for the prior notification of the Congregation for the Doctrine of the Faith announcing an automatic excommunication for "the attempted ordination of a woman," and Canon 1024, which declares "Only a baptized male validly receives sacred ordination" no modern Magisterial determination has been made regarding ordination of women to the diaconate. That is, the preponderance of historical evidence supports women as deacons, whereas the evidence for women priests and bishops is sketchier. This newest assertion of authority by CDF throws another blanket over the burgeoning understandings of the distinctions between and among grades of order. Later sections of this work go into the question in deeper detail.

Another major issue for Call to Action is the historical fact, present reality, and future expansion of a married priesthood within the Roman Catholic Church. Even so, the matter of married priests is somewhat more tenuous, since so many cultures (and bishops) accept the fact that many of their priests are in committed relationships with women. Additionally, the majority of Eastern Catholic Churches have retained their historical married priesthood. From time to time one or another priest publicly leaves the priesthood to marry, as in the 2007 case of Bishop Tamás Szabó, military ordinary of Hungary who quit soon after he turned fifty, married, and refused to speak publicly about it.[83]

While married priests and women priests are controversial issues in some quarters, discussion regarding human sexuality is the most contentious and most confusing. Following the 1968 publication of *Humanae Vitae*, all manner of discourse and dissent was let loose. The Canadian Conference of Catholic Bishops issued its "Winnipeg Statement," which called the teaching of *Humane Vitae* a difficult

standard to which Catholics should aspire, but that their failing would
not excommunicate them. Contraception remains a convoluted question, which of necessity branches to methods of population control
that incur abortion and those that do not. Official Catholic teaching on contraception also has implications regarding homosexuality.[84] Official church teaching considers homosexual acts and all other
sexual acts not directed at (or open to) reproduction as objectively
disordered.[85] That is, the Catholic Church has made a moral (not psychological) determination about homosexual activity equivalent to its
determinations about other sexual activity not directed at procreation
with marriage. Needless to say, popular culture in developed Western
countries rails against these determinations.

In 2007, the USCCB took the rather extraordinary step of announcing that two pamphlets by Marquette University Professor Daniel C.
Maguire, one regarding abortion and contraception and another on
same-sex marriage are "false teaching." Maguire sent the pamphlets to
270 Catholic bishops and the one on same-sex marriage to members
of Congress and to Wisconsin state legislators (Marquette University
is in Milwaukee, Wisconsin).[86] A few months earlier, Call to Action
objected to then-Milwaukee Archbishop Timothy Dolan's announcement that the pamphlets are against church teaching.[87]

These three issues—married priests, women priests, and human
sexuality—remain at the core of the Call to Action national agenda,
which today advocates married priests, women priests, and a broad-
ening of Catholic teaching on contraception and homosexuality. In
1991, Call to Action published a manifesto in *The New York Times*,
handed out at a CTA-N organizational meeting in early February
1996, which detailed its "Call for Reform in the Catholic Church,"
including a variety of social action issues, a call to incorporate women
into all levels of ministry and decision making, an end to mandatory priestly celibacy, consultation with the people to "develop a just
teaching on sexuality," more financial accountability, more emphasis
on ecumenism, more emphasis and attention to bishops' conferences,
and openness regarding diocesan decisions on school and parish clos-
ings.[88] The full plate it presented was carefully worded but expandable
to accept further policy developments.

The Call to Action agenda in 1996 may not have been quite
as obviously out-of-bounds as it later was to become—its 2008
convention included a presentation by Marek Bozek, a renegade
priest of the Diocese of Springfield-Cape Girardeau, Missouri,
who moved to the Archdiocese of St. Louis without his bishop's

permission to head a downtown Polish parish whose property and funds were about to be confiscated by then Archbishop Raymond L. Burke.[89] Call to Action's prospective major speakers for 2010 included Joan Chittister, OSB, and retired Episcopal Bishop John Shelby Spong, along with various individuals whose positions skirt, and in some cases directly oppose, Catholic teaching. Emily Jendze-jec, chair of its "CTA 20/30" younger members group, echoes the general thrust of Call to Action issues, stating they are working for "the full inclusion of lesbian, gay, bisexual and transgender people in our church . . . equal rights of women in church leadership . . . an end to structural racism in our church communities . . . transparency and honesty . . . [and] justice."[90]

In the mid-1990s, when Call to Action–Nebraska was getting underway, lines were not clearly drawn. Even Joseph Cardinal Bernar-din, at the time Archbishop of Chicago, within whose diocese Call to Action was and is headquartered, spoke in conciliatory terms in March 1996 when the Lincoln fracas arose. Cardinal Bernardin's statement says that Call to Action "has taken certain positions which are con-trary to church teaching and discipline. It has also taken positions, especially in the social sphere, which are compatible with that teach-ing." Bernardin continued that he did not think "cutting off Call to Action's members completely from the Catholic community would serve any good purpose."[91]

As Bishop Bruskewitz was attacking the fledgling Call to Action—Nebraska in the winter of 1996, there was significant scholarly and national public debate at various levels of each of the CTA-N stated goals, which did not include questions related to priestly celibacy or the ordination of women as priests or any hidden or overt pro-homosexual agenda. The CTA-N founders told the *Lincoln Journal-Star* that "The group is made up of many faithful Catholics who wish to discuss issues such as ecclesiastical authority and infallibility, the role of the laity, whether priests should marry, the ordination of women, and birth control."[92] The key word, "discuss," apparently was over-looked by the Lincoln chancery, which arguably lost the opportunity to engage in the very evangelization it said CTA-N disrupted.

By now Call to Action—at least on the national level—seems to have gone beyond advocacy within the realm of legitimate discussion (even prescinding from married priests and women priests) to advocacy for abortion and active homosexuality as acceptable choices for Catholics, presumably following logic akin to that published by Professor Maguire through pamphlets and on the website of the organization he heads,

The Religious Consultation on Population, Reproductive Health, and Ethics.[93] The Call to Action website links to numerous reform organizations on the matters of women's ordination and married priests, as well as to several organizations with at least non-Catholic, if not anti-Catholic, agendas, including various organizations that seem to promote homosexuality and the pro-abortion group Catholics for a Free Choice (now called Catholics for Choice).[94]

By the time of its 2006 national conference in Milwaukee, Call to Action clearly leapt over the bar even on "discussable" matters, moving from advocacy of women priests to acceptance of unsanctioned women priests. The 2006 meeting included Sunday morning Mass celebrated by members of Roman Catholic Womenpriests, who had been ordained by other women members of the movement on a riverboat in Pittsburgh the previous July. (Subsequent Call to Action national meetings held similar Masses.)

Further, among the contemporary official statements of Call to Action is the advocacy of homosexual rights within the church. For example, its former director wrote Archbishop Harry Flynn of St. Paul, Minnesota, to complain about his forbidding the celebration of Mass for a gathering of New Ways Ministry, which describes its mission as "a gay-positive ministry of advocacy and justice for lesbian and gay Catholics and reconciliation within the larger Christian and civil communities."[95] Its leaders are regular presenters at Call to Action conferences.

While its more recent website statements are carefully worded, the organization continues to encompass a radical view in its annual meetings, an inclusivity reflected in its 2008 call for nominations to its board of directors, which specifically asked for persons "from the GLBT community."[96]

According to the CTA-N online newsletter, the Diocese of Lincoln was among the major "action" issues at the 2006 national Call to Action conference, along with the closing of an historically black parish in New Orleans and several parishes in the Boston Archdiocese and the impasse over Father Marek Bozek and St. Stanislaus church in St. Louis.[97]

Call to Action also seems to consider the birth control debate of the 1960s as closed—in its favor—and is linked to the pro-abortion Catholics for Choice, founded in 1973 as Catholics for a Free Choice. While the CTA-N leaders clearly wanted discussion, perhaps even catechesis to official thinking, on the issue of birth control, it is not clear that all its members (if any) were invested in the abortion debate. That one member joked to a chancery official he was "in a mixed marriage" (his wife favored legalized abortion while he did not) hardly constitutes a policy statement on behalf of the group.[98]

The question of married clergy, also an agenda item for Call to Action, remains a legitimate point of debate in the church as a whole, but it would make sense that the bishop would want to control any discussion of it in his diocese if he could. Following the twenty-first synod of bishops, Pope Benedict XVI's post-synodal apostolic exhortation The Sacrament of Charity (*Sacramentum Caritatis*) (February 22, 2007) restates the norm of a celibate priesthood for the Latin Church and seems to consider the matter closed, even though significant calls for restoration of the tradition of married clergy in the Latin Church came from the assembled bishops—particularly from the English-language groups—during the fall 2005 synod. The "Pastoral Provision" to receive married, former Anglican clergy and ordain them priests has only complicated the debate.

In the years since CTA-N's founding, the national Call to Action continues to draw a mixed group of Catholics. Not all adhere to all its positions, but there seems no other place to gather (other than Voice of the Faithful). Among the speakers at the 2006 national Call to Action Milwaukee meeting was church historian David J. O'Brien, professor of Roman Catholic Studies at the College of the Holy Cross, Worcester, Massachusetts, who in the mid-1970s helped organize the original Call to Action Conference in Detroit "The Spirit of Vatican II" on behalf of what was then called the National Conference of Catholic Bishops. As Steichen breathlessly reports in *Ungodly Rage*, the Call to Action conference was suggested by Sister Marie Augusta Neal, SNDdeN, and Sister Margaret Cafferty, PBVM, was a major player in "that extravagantly progressive venture."[99] In fact, despite its current digressions from official Catholic Church teaching, the roots of Call to Action are in Vatican II.[100]

From 1974 to 1976, Professor O'Brien, then a bishops' conference staffer, led a process that had eight bishop-chaired committees write the reports and draft resolutions from eight hundred thousand survey responses compiled before the meeting. The final resolutions adopted by 1,351 delegates included recommendations that the church should study or consider greater financial accountability, acceptance of legitimate theological pluralism, married priests, and the ordination of women as priests. There were no demands, but the general drift of the resolutions was that the laity should have more say in the church. Then-Bishop Bernard Law attended the meeting and urged one of its chairs to adjourn it immediately, saying there were certain issues that would anger Rome. But the meeting went on, and, according to Margery Frisbie,

> within a decade maybe eighty-five percent of A Call to Action resolutions were implemented by the bishops. They did not ratify the controversial stands on optional celibacy and the ordination of women that upset participants like Cardinal Law. However, there was a positive aftereffect: the use of widespread hearings for the bishops' letters on peace and the economy published within the next decade. Many of the concerns that surfaced at A Call to Action resurfaced in the bishops' pastoral letters on racism, cultural diversity, Hispanic concerns, and nuclear weapons.[101]

Twenty years later, in 1996, as Nebraskan CALL members were looking for a national organization with which to affiliate, Call to Action had moved beyond its post–Vatican II headiness and social advocacy roots to become an organization openly adversarial to some Catholic teachings. Its agenda, and the fact of a local Call to Action group within his diocese, as has been demonstrated, was more than Bruskewitz would stand for. In fact—and in law—since the bishop is charged to govern, sanctify, and teach in his diocese, Bruskewitz exercised his right (and some would say duty) to advise Catholics of groups he considered adversarial to the Catholic Church. He may have overextended his reach, if not technically, at least in the public eye.

While, as noted earlier, the 1917 Code specifically names the Masons, the revised Canon 1374 in the 1983 Code of Canon Law leaves the naming of forbidden societies up to local authorities.[102] Canon 305.1 requires a diocesan bishop to maintain vigilance over associations of the Christian faithful that operate within his diocese.[103] In either case, while Bruskewitz was technically correct in his judgment about Call to Action, it is worth underscoring he should have called to Canon 305 relative to Call to Action and Call to Action–Nebraska.

In addition, Bruskewitz may not have followed proper administrative procedures in his warning about Call to Action and the other groups—his diocesan chancellor signed the initial warning—but Bruskewitz later codified his determinations in what he termed "Extra Synodal Legislation," thereby creating local law for his diocese. (The legislation was not discussed by the synod but simply included in the synod statutes.) Those Catholics over whom he had episcopal jurisdiction were forbidden to belong to Call to Action. If they belonged, he decreed, they were excommunicated. Call to Action–Nebraska appealed to the Apostolic Signatura in Rome, which quickly replied their case had been sent to the Congregation for Bishops.

In 1996, the Diocese of Lincoln produced a 119-page book of "Statutes for the Diocese of Lincoln, Nebraska resulting from the collaborative efforts of the Bishop, Priests, Religious and Laity of the Diocese." Chapter 1, section 7 includes "Forbidden Societies" and lists "the Masons and their auxiliary organizations, Planned Parenthood, Society of Pius X, Call to Action (in its various forms), Catholics for a Free Choice, the Hemlock Society." But section 7 was never discussed at the synod, and the only input apparent is that of Bishop Bruskewitz and Monsignor Thorburn. This section became "Extra-Synodal Legislation."[104]

The hue and cry that arose over Bishop Bruskewitz's actions drew great media interest and became a cause célèbre among the wider circle of liberal Catholic organizations, the one feeding the other. The nationally televised NBC *Today Show* interviewed the two men most obviously at loggerheads: Fabian Bruskewitz and Nebraska Wesleyan sociology professor John Krejci, one of the two CTA-N founders and a married former Catholic priest who attended the Pontifical Gregorian University in Rome with Bishop Bruskewitz.[105] When Call to Action–Nebraska appealed the edict and its members argued their excommunications were lifted during the appeal, Bruskewitz was having none of it.[106] The bishop personally refused communion to Krejci, who then approached the altar and self-administered communion after the bishop put down the ciborium. For whatever reason, Bruskewitz did not ask that Krejci be arrested for disrupting a religious service, although Krejci says the bishop instructed the pastors of three nearby churches to refuse him communion as well.[107]

Meanwhile, CTA-N continued to meet, in small groups and with annual meetings, often featuring speakers whom Bishop Bruskewitz opposed. Sometimes Bruskewitz made his views vehemently public, as the editors of the *National Catholic Reporter* noted:

> there is the intensity of his spleen, the sheer lack of civility and decency, not to mention charity, in the vitriol coming from the Lincoln chancery. In a 1997 column called "Ask the *Register*," written by an anonymous priest, Patty Crowley, 84 at the time, cofounder with her late husband of the Christian Family Movement and, in the 1960s, the first woman ever to serve on a papal commission, was the subject of a question. The *Register* answered: "Crowley is a very old degenerate who roams about promoting sexual immorality. Nobody pays much attention to what she says, except perhaps some depraved members of the Call-to-Action sect. Her views deserve no consideration whatsoever."[108]

As Bishop Bruskewitz continued to rail against CTA-N, and especially against women, a definite pattern emerged. He was most energetic in attempting to have some women religious silenced in or near his diocese.

One speaker he tried to silence was Sister Theresa Kane, RSM, who publicly asked Pope John Paul II to include women in all forms of ministry in the Catholic Church during his 1979 visit to the United States. Shortly before her April 1999 talk to CTA-N (to be held in the Archdiocese of Omaha), Sister Doris Gottemoeller, RSM, president of the recently formed Sisters of Mercy of the Americas, informed her a Vatican official had asked about Sister Theresa's assent to *Ordinatio Sacerdotalis*: "If it is the intention of Sister Theresa to propose a vision of the Church which is not in accord with the faith of the Church as articulated by the Holy Father, this Congregation, with deep concern, asks you to intervene and by your authority to impede her from speaking."[109] The Vice President of the Sisters of Mercy replied on her behalf: "she has assured us that it is not her intention to take issue with papal teaching as expressed in *Ordinatio Sacerdotalis*."[110]

The following year, Sister Jeannine Gramick, then a member of Baltimore Province of the School Sisters of Notre Dame, was called to Rome and given a list of "Obediences" to which she had to assent to retain membership in her religious community. Her April 8, 2000, speech at the YMCA Camp Kitaki in the Lincoln diocese was on the list. She had ignored a March 2000 demand by Bruskewitz that she not speak in the Lincoln diocese: "The Holy See has informed me that as the Ordinary of the Diocese of Lincoln, I have the right to formally prohibit you from speaking in this diocese . . . This is hereby done with this letter."[111]

In the following years, Bishop Bruskewitz repeatedly objected to women speakers, even though he had declared CTA-N "non-Catholic" and its speakers were either not speaking at a Catholic location or not speaking within his diocesan boundaries. Sister Helen Prejean spoke in 2001. Bruskewitz objected to Sister Joan Chittister, OSB speaking in 2002. His main complaint appears to have been the proposal or discussion of the ordination of women as priests.[112]

Meanwhile, members of Call to Action–Nebraska thought the appeal of their excommunications was going forward, although it appears it did not. The organization has never heard directly from the Congregation for Bishops. Various individuals argued that the excommunications were not legal, as the issue and its commentary grew deeply ugly. Over the years, Bishop Bruskewitz would occasionally assert that Rome denied their appeal, but he provided no proof.

Finally, in February 2006, Professor McShane, who prepared the original appeal in 1998, wrote Bishop Bruskewitz again asking about its status. The bishop apparently forwarded his letter, and other materials, to Cardinal Giovanni Battista Re, then Prefect of the Vatican's Congregation for Bishops. In late 2006, Cardinal Re wrote Bruskewitz:

> . . . the Holy See considers that Your Excellency's ruling in the case of "Call to Action Nebraska" was properly taken within your competence as Pastor of that diocese. The judgment of the Holy See is that the activities of "Call to Action" in the course of these years are in contrast with the Catholic Faith due to views and positions held which are unacceptable from a doctrinal and disciplinary standpoint. Thus to be a Member of this Association or to support it, is irreconcilable with a coherent living of the Catholic faith.[113]

Cardinal Re's letter indicates an administrative, not a judicial, decision by a curial department on behalf of the pope, affirming the right of the bishop to act in his own diocese, presumably in accord with Canons 1374 and (had it been cited) 305, as well as within the various constraints of Canons 1313–1320, which qualify the bishop's authority to levy penalties.

However, there is no decree of the Congregation for Bishops on the matter. The liceity of Bruskewitz's excommunication decree, however, could well depend on form rather than on substance since by then the national Call to Action clearly existed as an advocacy group opposed to moral and disciplinary teachings, if not doctrinal teachings, of the Catholic Church.

Cardinal Re's entering the fray further muddied the waters already stirred by the collision between Bishop Bruskewitz and the by then three hundred or so members of Call to Action–Nebraska, sixty of whom lived in the Lincoln diocese. It remains unclear whether Re was communicating an administrative decision on behalf of the Congregation for Bishops or presenting a personal opinion. Re called for authority to the Holy See—a diplomatic term for the Apostolic See—suggesting an administrative decision made by someone else. But there is no known formal decree from the Congregation for Bishops regarding Bruskewitz's de facto excommunication of CTA-N members.

COMMUNION AND AUTHORITY IN LINCOLN, NEBRASKA

Call to Action–Nebraska members who live within the confines of the Diocese of Lincoln remain under penalty of excommunication unless they recant their membership in the local and national Call to Action.

While Bishop Bruskewitz claimed to be operating with the authority of Rome, he clearly acted out of step with his fellow bishops. In an unusual move, *The Pilot*, official newspaper of the Archdiocese of Boston, editorialized against Bruskewitz's 1996 excommunication pronouncement precisely because he made it without consultation with his brother bishops.[114] But Bishop Bruskewitz's actions then and since argue against any consultation or coordination with the other bishops of the United States, on this or apparently on other matters. He continued to attend USCCB annual meetings while ruling his diocese as an independent fiefdom. He clearly did not join with other bishops in post–Vatican II moves to liberalize church practice without changing magisterial teaching, although he eventually allowed women readers at Masses (excepting when qualified men were available, and not at Masses he celebrated) and women Eucharistic ministers for nursing homes. And he remained out of step with other bishops regarding the sex abuse scandal.

Independent of Bishop Bruskewitz's fractious actions within his diocese, diocesan transparency regarding sex abuse statistics and procedures for dealing with accused clergy came to be common practice in the United States following the 2002 "Dallas Charter" of the USCCB.[115] Call to Action–Nebraska (and the USCCB Office of Child Protection) repeatedly points out the Lincoln diocese is alone—or nearly so—in the US in refusing to cooperate in USCCB policy-mandated annual sex abuse audits or reporting.

One of the assumed promises of John XXIII's opened windows was a transparency in church matters and affairs, such apparently not valued by Bruskewitz. The deep history of secrecy about priest abusers and substantial intransigence in widely publicized civil actions against individual dioceses have been met by USCCB attempts to answer the legitimate questions of Catholic laity who, after all, fund the dioceses, which in turn fund the USCCB.

The USCCB National Review Board was headed by former Pace University president Patricia O'Donnell Ewers from 2004 to 2007 and then by Judge Michael R. Merz of Cincinnati. Milwaukee social worker Diane M. Knight was appointed head in 2009.

The National Review Board is served by the paid staff of the Office of Child and Youth Protection. The office was first led by former Special Agent and Executive Assistant Director of the Federal Bureau of Investigation, Kathleen L. McChesney, and, since 2005, by Teresa M. Kettelkamp, a retired colonel of the Illinois State Police.

In late 2003, Monsignor Thorburn, as Bruskewitz's Vicar General, sent a letter—apparently to the John Jay College investigators—stating that Bishop Bruskewitz "does not recognize any jurisdiction claimed over him or his pastoral activity by the 'National Review Board'" and that he "is prepared to take any appropriate and suitable measures necessary, including legal action, were that Board, your institution, or the United States Conference of Catholic Bishops to attempt to coerce him by adverse publicity, the threat of such, or other similar actions."[116] In March 2006, Bruskewitz turned up the heat. He was quoted in conservative blogs: "Some woman named Patricia O'Donnell Ewers, who is the Chair of something called 'A National Review Board for the Protection of Children and Young People', has said that her Board 'calls for strong fraternal correction of the Diocese of Lincoln' . . . Ewers and her Board have no authority in the Catholic Church and the Diocese of Lincoln does not recognize them as having any significance."[117]

Neither has the Diocese of Lincoln participated in the USCCB's annual Survey of Allegations and Costs performed by the Center for Applied Research in the Apostolate at Georgetown University.

While refusing to cooperate with USCCB policy, Bruskewitz was reportedly simultaneously ending a few sex abuse suits with cash and confidentiality agreements. His actions were publicly noted and decried by members of Call to Action–Nebraska. Meanwhile, Bruskewitz, who warned former presidential candidate Senator John Kerry to stay away from the communion rail while campaigning in the Lincoln diocese, effectively barred members of Call to Action–Nebraska from communion, a Catholic burial, last rites, and even confession without publicly recanting their membership.

Their excommunication is *latae sententiae*, or automatic, which some canonists argue it is not liable to appeal. Neither is it lifted when a member moves out of the Lincoln diocese (the new diocesan bishop would have to lift it). While Call to Action members who pass through Lincoln incur no penalty, because Bishop Bruskewitz has no jurisdiction over them, the neighboring Archdiocese of Omaha holds that persons in its church leadership roles—from clergy to parish school teachers to lay ministers—cannot belong to any of the groups named by Bruskewitz.[118] Other bishops ban Call to Action activities from their church properties, much as they ban Voice of the Faithful activities.[119]

Meanwhile, the more usual controversies waned in Lincoln, the only US diocese then remaining without female altar servers, in the

face of the continued highly acrimonious excommunication controversy. Positions harden over time. The bishop's excommunication
announcement and letter-of-the-law response to the USCCB com-
bine to grant sympathy to Call to Action–Nebraska, even in the face of
growing traction among individual US bishops against national Call
to Action.

Despite what could be administrative errors in his legislation,
Bruskewitz is technically in the right. According to Canon 1374 he can
determine that an organization is anti-Catholic, although that canon
might not apply to organizations of the Christian faithful such as Call
to Action, which are covered by Canon 305.[120] Canon 1374 initially
requires a *ferendae sententiae*, or imposed (as opposed to automatic)
penalties: a "just penalty" for simple membership and an "interdict"
for officers. In response to queries, Lincoln chancery staff calls to C.
1315, which allows the diocesan bishop to raise the bar, in this case to
excommunication of all members and officers. But Catholic penal law
requires such be announced by proper decree. The Code of Canon
Law further requires that the diocesan bishop act in concert with his
neighboring bishops.[121] Bruskewitz did not consult the Archdiocese
of Omaha—his Metropolitan See—on his actions.

Assuming Bishop Bruskewitz's law is legitimate—which it administratively may not be—priests are supposed to refuse sacraments to
excommunicated persons to avoid a public scandal. And bishops' conferences have no authority over any individual diocesan bishop, who
reports to the pope through the Congregation for Bishops.

CONCLUSIONS

At the heart of the juridical impasse between Call to Action–Nebraska
and the bishop of Lincoln is a collision of views of "church." Bishop
Bruskewitz, a "strict constructionist," rules above and beyond the
sea change effected by Vatican II regarding the place of the "laity"—
the unordained—in the church. The educated laity in Lincoln whose
views eventually coalesced, for the most part, with those of Call to
Action at first carefully trod the line between magisterial teachings and
Vatican II renewals. They had no need to challenge faith and morals;
they merely wanted updating—recall their earliest requests were for
women readers and Eucharistic ministers, more transparency regarding finances and governance, and a voice in parish and diocesan decision making.

That the Mahoney State Park meeting eventually became the line drawn in the sand between the two camps appears a misreading of the intentions of each. The diocese, for its part, was suspicious of the "unauthorized" gathering of laity within its boundaries. Its emissaries (some would say spies) returned with "proof" of the group's heretical status—an unauthorized version of a creed that seems to doubt the central Christian belief in the resurrection of Jesus.

For their part, the ex-CALL, now CTA-N membership and their growing list of followers were tired of what they saw as a purely hierarchical model of the church, which represented the typical caricature of the role of the laity as "pray-pay-obey." That they disbanded as CALL when the new bishop was soon to be named, however, gives evidence of their willingness to work within the system.

Both sides, Bruskewitz and the CALL-become CTA-N members, may indeed have had hidden agenda items, but the preponderance of initial distrust and suspicion seems to have been inside the chancery. That suspicion (and patent disrespect) hardened the positions of the CTA-N members, especially as communications became increasingly acerbic on both sides. At the heart of their respective views, however, is the place and status of women—all of whom are lay members—in the church.

Views on these issues, ranging from married clergy to women's participation in church (specifically in liturgy) to more transparency in church governance and finance each involved women. Each could have been addressed, and perhaps solved at least in part, by Bruskewitz on his own authority.

Even discussion regarding wider ordination of married men is well within the pale. The Catholic Church has ordained married men to the restored permanent diaconate since 1972 and increasingly admits married men to priesthood. Lincoln has but three married deacons, all of whom moved from another diocese, none with permanent preaching faculties.[122] Women's legitimate participation in liturgy, still somewhat restricted, is clearly something the bishop could have done—or at least discussed—on coming to Lincoln. For Lincoln to participate in the USCCB studies regarding sexual abuse and sexual abuse procedures would not deny the rights of the bishop but, rather, would place him squarely within the particular law for the Catholic Church in the United States as approved by the Vatican.

The pointed end of the problem is that issues were raised by laity to bishops (Flavin and, later, Bruskewitz) who were apparently unwilling to listen. The scenario has played out in other dioceses as well, but not along such clearly drawn lines.

In general, most of the debate over what has come to be called "lay participation" in the church sits in the chasm between the clerical and lay, viewed more or less unevenly depending on who is considering the question and how. The fact of the lay-clerical divide is the result of accruing forces over centuries—the early church held no such distinctions—and some have called its usefulness, even its precise definition, into question.[123]

In the direct wake of Vatican II, the late Jesuit Cardinal Avery Dulles wrote *Models of the Church*, now a classic text and starting point of discussions on ecclesiology. Dulles defined the post-Vatican II church as (1) institution (unified with clearly defined boundaries); (2) mystical communion (union of all people of faith); (3) sacrament (transmitter of grace to the world); (4) herald (transmitter of the Gospel message to the world); and (5) servant (bound together by Christian service to humanity).[124] Depending on the lens, any individual can see one or more facets of this pentagon as having priority. The challenge is to see it rest in tension, allowing each facet to complement, rather than compete, with the others.

Nevertheless, Dulles's five models open doors as well as windows for more participation by lay persons in the church, but not to the degree envisioned by Call to Action and similar societies, which appear to want a democratically governed institution. Their constant references to opinion polls as to what should and should not be allowed in terms of Catholic moral teaching is clear indication of the collision of views, but a collision that probably could have been avoided in Lincoln.

The Lincoln impasse presents apparently irreconcilable positions. Magnifying the distinctions between the two is the ongoing discussion outside Nebraska, before and since, among theologians and others on what has come to be called the "role of the laity." These writers typically do not seek to overturn or circumvent the authority of the diocesan bishop directly, but they routinely call for more participation on the part of and more accountability to the majority of the members of the church—the laity.

The discussion about the role of the laity exploded after Vatican II with writings by such luminaries as French Dominican theologian and Cardinal Yves Congar (1904–1995). Congar's book *Lay People in the Church* drew in stark relief pictures of the passive laity envisioned by the 1917 Code of Canon Law and the laity now asserting themselves, as he said they ought, in the mid-twentieth century[125] and continues with Paul Lakeland (*Liberation of the Laity* and *Catholicism at the Crossroads: How the Laity Can Save the Church*)[126] and others who give voice to a model that includes more lay participation—even authority—than Dulles could have envisioned.

Specifically, the questions of communion and authority raised by the dual intransigencies of Fabian Bruskewitz come from his perceptions of three areas of his concern: (1) his rights as bishop of his diocese, (2) his understanding of the non-authoritative role of bishops' conferences, and (3) his understanding of the consequent irrelevant status of USCCB staff and committees.

To him, it would seem the larger questions present themselves thus: in the case of the national sex scandal, individual diocesan bishops abrogated their responsibility and then acted as a group, which then sought to impose its determinations of how to act on an individual diocesan bishop. Bishop Bruskewitz's nonresponsiveness, rooted in his understanding that he reports only to Rome, would be correct except that the USCCB policy was vetted by the Vatican, which apparently accepts the way the policy is being executed. That is, the USCCB policy as vetted by Rome is, in certain parts, particular law for the Catholic Church in the United States. Hence Bishop Bruskewitz may be defying not only legitimate policy but also law that truly binds him. The assembled bishops are assuredly executing requirements of the Church without him.

In his insistence on the vested authority of the diocesan bishop, Bishop Bruskewitz disrupted the effective collegiality assumed within bishops' conferences. He acted independently in defining forbidden societies and raising the penalties attendant to membership, neither in concert with the bishops of his province nor with his national episcopal conference, and he embarrassed other diocesan bishops—including his metropolitan archbishop (the Archbishop of Omaha)—into acting regarding Call to Action and the other groups. Even so, the USCCB has no official policy on Call to Action (or Voice of the Faithful). Some local ordinaries treat Call to Action and Voice of the Faithful in similar fashions: refusing membership meetings on church-owned or church-controlled property, but none has levied or announced a penalty of excommunication for membership.[127]

Bishop Bruskewitz's actions paint him as a "juridical" (collaborative, political) bishop, rather than a "communal" (collegial, ecclesial) bishop, and the reactions of Call to Action–Nebraska and of the USCCB to him crystallize the tensions between these two styles of governance.

PART II

SACRAMENTAL AUTHORITY

ARCHBISHOP MILINGO, THE VATICAN, AND MARRIED PRIESTS NOW!

The exercise of authority in the Church is to be recognised and accepted as an instrument of the Spirit of God for the healing of humanity. The exercise of authority must always respect conscience, because the divine work of salvation affirms human freedom. In freely accepting the way of salvation offered through baptism, the Christian disciple also freely takes on the discipline of being a member of the Body of Christ. Because the Church of God is recognised as the community where the divine means of salvation are at work, the demands of discipleship for the well-being of the entire Christian community cannot be refused. There is also a discipline required in the exercise of authority. Those called to such a ministry must themselves submit to the discipline of Christ, observe the requirements of collegiality and the common good, and duly respect the consciences of those they are called to serve.

—Anglican-Roman Catholic International Commission
joint statement, "The Gift of Authority"[1]

The case of Bishop Bruskewitz shows how a Catholic bishop can act independent of the other bishops of his province, and in his case, independent of the Catholic bishops of the United States. Yet his authority within his diocese can remain unchallenged. The technical question of juridical authority, with him or with anyone else, rests in the question of jurisdiction and office. Bishop Bruskewitz, without question, had proper episcopal jurisdiction as the bishop of the Catholic diocese of Lincoln, Nebraska. But he effectively became a church law unto himself.

In Bishop Bruskewitz's case, one can question whether he, as diocesan bishop chose to "observe the requirements of collegiality and the common good, and duly respect the consciences of those [he is] called to serve," as described in the Anglican-Roman Catholic joint statement "The Gift of Authority." Were the needs of the church of Lincoln, Nebraska served? Without doubt, Bruskewitz and his staff would say yes. But were the needs of the larger church served? He evidenced little, if any, collegiality with the other bishops of the United States. Further, he did not address many neuralgic issues, most clearly legitimate questions regarding women's participation in liturgy and ministry and more married men as deacons.[2] Bruskewitz eventually allowed women to fulfill allowed liturgical roles only late in his term.

Emmanuel Milingo, the married and now excommunicated archbishop emeritus of Lusaka, Zambia, is similarly a law unto himself. When he first broke from Rome in 2001, Milingo claimed the entire world as his territory and began a worldwide movement for married Catholic priests called Married Priests Now! Despite his lack of territorial jurisdiction, as a validly ordained priest and bishop Milingo had the power of order and therefore could validly, although not licitly, confer sacraments.

The Catholic Church laicized ("defrocked") Milingo in December 2009, and in August 2010 he was installed by breakaway African groups as patriarch of Africa for the southern African region.[3] As in the case of the groups with which he affiliated, Milingo's chief complaint against church discipline for priests is the law that Latin Rite priests remain celibate. He appeared traditional in all other matters regarding women.

Up until his laicization, one could liken Milingo's situation to that of the late Archbishop Marcel-François Lefebvre (1905–1991), the first Catholic archbishop of Dakar, Senegal, and later bishop of Tulle, France. At first glance, Lefebvre is as conservative as Milingo is liberal. Lefebvre founded the traditionalist Society of Saint Pius X (SSPX) in November, 1970, establishing a seminary in Ecône, Switzerland the following year.[4]

Rome quickly granted Lefebvre's group official approbation as a religious order, granting permission to incardinate (or "enroll") clerics—to have priests and deacons as members of the order.[5] By 1976, however, Pope Paul VI denounced Lefebvre as "disobedient to the new liturgy." On July 23, 1976, Lefebvre received a *suspensio a divinis*, suspending him from all priestly (and episcopal) acts, to which he replied six days later, asserting his right as priest and bishop to celebrate sacraments. Despite the suspension, Lefebvre continued to ordain priests, but simultaneously appeared headed toward reconciliation with Rome. Then, on June 30, 1988, despite explicit warnings from Rome, Lefebvre ordained four members of his society as bishops, incurring automatic, or *latae senentiae*, excommunication for him and for them.[6] Within a few days, John Paul II established the Pontifical Commission "Ecclessia Dei," charged with overseeing the situation.

Lefebvre's traditionalist views included a rejection of ecumenism—he would have bridled at the joint Anglican-Roman Catholic statement at the head of this chapter—and he did not entertain questions about religious tolerance. He rejected the 1970 Latin Mass for celebration of Mass in favor of what is popularly called the 1570 Tridentine Mass (of the Council of Trent) as published in the Roman Missal by Pope John XXIII.[7] His followers contend they are the true members of the Roman Catholic Church, but they tend to pick and choose the documents and decrees of Vatican II that they consider "authentic."[8] Neither the Catholic Church nor most commentators will recognize members of the Society of Saint Pius X as Roman Catholic.[9]

The development and fact of Milingo's Married Priests Now! could be seen as a break from Rome's discipline somewhat similar to that of the Society of Saint Pius X. While Married Priests Now! never had even the short-lived Vatican approval that the Society of Saint Pius X enjoyed, Milingo also considers himself Roman Catholic and argues that his differences are disciplinary, not doctrinal.

However, Milingo's disciplinary digressions regarding ordinations mirror those of Lefebvre. In the United States, Milingo has ordained at least four men as bishops and two as priests. He holds to the Vatican's ban on women priests, but may not hold so strictly against the restoration of the ancient tradition of ordained women deacons.[10] Even so, Milingo's clear focus is on a married priesthood, through both the restoration of resigned married priests to active ministry and the ordination of married men as priests.

WHO IS EMANUEL MILINGO?

Emmanuel Milingo was forcibly retired as Archbishop of Lusaka, Zambia (formerly Northern Rhodesia) by Pope John Paul II in 1983, apparently because he melded African faith healing and Catholic liturgy. Milingo never intended to disconnect from the Catholic Church, for which he was ordained priest at the age of 28 and bishop at 39, but his incorporation of African spiritualism into Catholic practices gained increasing criticism in Africa and in Rome. He maintained throughout his tenure in Lusaka, however, that his only faith was Roman Catholic.

Ethnically an Nguni, Milingo was born on June 13, 1930, in the small farm village of Mnukwa in the eastern province of Zambia and raised in the Zulu warrior tradition.[11] After working as a cattle herder from the ages of eight to twelve, he ran away to enter St. Mary's Presbyterial school, a mission school operated by the White Fathers (Society of Our Lady of Africa) in the Zambian border town of Chipata, about a ninety-minute drive west of Malawi (formerly Nyasaland). Milingo had never been outside his village, was illiterate, and spoke only Nguni. However, he quickly progressed, learning to read and write both English and Chewa (also known as Chinyanja), the language of the Malawi.

As Milingo advanced in his education, he asked that his given name, Lotte, be changed to Emmanuel, apparently in reaction to his learning the Old Testament story of Lot and his wife. He prepared for ordination to work in what was then the Vicariate Apostolic of Lusaka, Zambia.[12] He attended two seminaries in Malawi, the Kasina minor seminary and the Kachebere major seminary, and was ordained priest in 1958. He served as a parish priest for seven or eight years, excepting two years during which he obtained diplomas in sociology in Rome and in education in Dublin.[13] From 1963 to 1966 he was parish priest in Chipata, Zambia, and there founded the volunteer Zambia Helpers Society to bring health care to poor villages. The society now operates a hospital near the capital city of Lusaka.[14] From 1966 to 1969 Milingo was secretary of mass media at the Zambia Episcopal Conference, during which time he developed an impressive radio ministry. Also during that time, in December 1969, he founded the first of three religious orders, the Daughters of the Redeemer, which he insisted would maintain distinctly Zambian traditions and culture.[15]

LUSAKA

In 1969, Pope Paul VI consecrated Milingo as Archbishop of Lusaka. He was the first African archbishop of Lusaka, following two Polish Jesuits who had successively led the territory since 1927.[16] The co-consecrators were Cardinal Sergio Pignedoli (1910–1980), then Secretary of the Congregation for the Evangelization of Peoples, and Cardinal Emmanuel Kiwanuka Nsubuga (1914–1991), then archbishop of Kampala, Uganda.

At 39, Milingo was also one of Africa's youngest bishops, a member of a new generation of African leaders influenced (if not formally) by the ways of Vatican II. Inculturation was a mainstay of his ministry. Gradually, he brought his native traditions into Catholic ceremonies in Lusaka, eventually drawing so much attention to his particular way of inculturating African beliefs into Christianity that he could no longer escape notice. He became known as a healer—he says he discovered his healing power in 1973[17]—and that he was reclaiming the healing powers of all the ordained. However, he brought his native rituals to bear in both discussion and practice so much that detractors said he incorporated pagan rituals—practices of African spiritualism—into Catholic sacraments.

It must be understood at the outset that Milingo was a fairly conservative Catholic, the sort of cleric sometimes called "orthodox." However, as he became increasingly isolated in his own archdiocese and concurrently found common ground with the Catholic charismatic movement in the mid-1970s, following his attendance at a training session in Ann Arbor, Michigan, where he found a warm reception and assistance. He wrote sometime later of how deeply that experience touched him: "In 1976, when I was in Ann Arbor, Michigan, with the Word of God Ecumenical Charismatic Community, God spoke through the community's prophet. His message was 'You will still have to suffer. However, you will come out of it.' . . . I for my part pondered over the message, but failed to guess the nature of the suffering in store for me."[18]

At about this time, Milingo also began to preach widely on behalf of the poor of Africa, especially as they were exploited by the rich, making no friends among the powerful. The preponderance of priests in Lusaka—and in all of Africa at the time—were non-African missionaries, mostly Europeans unable or unwilling to understand Milingo's adaptations in the service of inculturation of Catholicism in Africa. According to political scientist Norbert Brockman: "The issue that Milingo brought to crisis was inculturation: the development of an authentic African Christianity growing out of African values, including spiritual ones. Inculturation challenged Western control of African Christianity and its Western cultural roots . . . [specifically]: the African Christian's mentality had to be liberated from colonialism."[19] What was the colonialization Milingo denied? Milingo's actions are well documented, although he repeatedly disclaimed any intent to form a separate religion or sect. He attempted at least to operate within the confines of Catholicism, although Mona Macmillan points out in her Introduction to Milingo's collected writings, *The World in Between: Christian Healing and the Struggle for Spiritual Survival*, that "orthodox Christians would be afraid of his being seen as just another *sing'anga* or traditional healer, perhaps more powerful and certainly cheaper than the rest."[20]

Milingo's faith healing drew the most attention. He served as best he could as archbishop, but his healing ministry continued and expanded exponentially. By the end of 1978, his popularity and reputation created a situation well beyond his control. Over 1,300 persons came to his fixed monthly healing sessions, and, on average, two hundred additional people besieged him weekly. He was inundated with requests for his healing ministrations no matter where he was.

Matters were out of hand. In a closed session of the Zambia Episcopal Conference, he asked the advice of the other bishops, who most strongly suggested he give up his healing ministry.

Abandoning healing ministry was not what Milingo wanted. He twice convened his archdiocesan staff to seek their advice. Their recommendation was that the healing ministry should continue, but not in its present form. The situation he found himself in was truly dire. Persons within his archdiocese, apparently not a few, had gotten involved in various forms of spirit worship, allegedly even going so far as making pacts with the devil. Milingo's task, as he saw it, was to free these persons from their pacts and heal their psychic and physical ills resultant from their error. He says he was not in league with spiritualists, but rather was attempting to help his flock recover from consorting with them. He wrote:

> When people come to tell me their stories they cannot believe that the devil will ever leave them alone. As they say themselves "We went too far, we spoke with the dead. We sat on the graves and saw human beings in the form of white ghosts. Do you really say that God can reverse the coin and consider me once more his beloved child?" I assure them that they will be accepted by God and that we shall offer them special divine protection. It is true that they went too far. There is no objection to having an ambition to become rich, but one must work for it using normal means. The consequences of using the help of the underworld are indeed terrible.[21]

Milingo eventually decided to bend to the will and recommendation of the bishops' conference. He warned of protest from the people, but accepted the assembled bishops' decision that he should cease his healing ministry.

Archbishop Milingo sent a circular letter to his diocese announcing his decision.[22]

That it was never my intention to work outside the Church of Rome, nor the local Church in Zambia. It has never been my intention to look extraordinary, nor to call for admiration. I came into the healing ministry by a pure love from Jesus Christ, who gave the gift of healing, not of right, but by favor and privilege. Hence since I want to remain a faithful servant of the Catholic Church Universal and local, may you all know that I have decided to follow the advice of the Bishops. My last public healing session therefore will be 25th February 1979.[23]

While he may have thought that would be the end of the matter, Milingo's situation only worsened. He did discontinue healing services but was besieged by letters, visits, and telephone calls from those wishing to be healed.

As archbishop, Milingo also maintained his connection with the charismatic movement as well as his high profile in Zambian political affairs, which did not sit well with powerful European missionaries and with government officials.

Unlike Bishop Bruskewitz in Nebraska, Archbishop Milingo appeared, at least, to be attempting to act in concert with the bishops of his province. He complained about the people who still came to him for healing. He wrote to then Secretary of the Congregation for the Evangelization of Peoples Archbishop Duraisamy Simon Lourdusamy (b. 1924), who appears to have held the portfolio on Milingo and his troubles: "They have never learned to obey. The Bishops must speak openly to them and bind them under obedience not to come to me."[24] Like Milingo, Lourdusamy, a native of India, became a bishop in his late thirties and was named Archbishop of Bangalore at 43. Their common bond of early promotion may have tempered Lourdusamy's early responses to Milingo's situation.

Archbishop Milingo's stated willingness to accede to the determinations of the Zambia Episcopal Conference, which no doubt met with approval from Rome, evidences his sincerity in his efforts at collegiality. That is, there is no hint of duplicity in his statement. He seems to be willing to accede to the will of the local bishops' conference.

While Milingo may have incorporated some questionable practices into his services, he readily agreed to stop all healing services. But the public—his flock—would not hear of it. His complaint and plea was that the people should submit to authority: if not his, then to that of the assembled bishops of Zambia. But what authority did they have in his diocese? The mark of his willingness to cooperate with his national bishops' conference—unlike Bruskewitz—was his wish not to act outside their usual norms. That is, while there seems nothing specifically wrong—at least at the beginning—with Milingo's actions, they are not in keeping with the practices in neighboring Zambian dioceses.

The situation was further complicated by the fact that the white European missionary priests who predominated in the Lusaka archdiocese were increasingly aligned against Milingo, despite his being the archbishop. They resented Milingo's charismatic renewal, which uncharacteristically (for Europeans) highlighted the presence of evil spirits, and they (and others) complained that Milingo's emphasis on spiritual healing ignored the remedies of modern medicine, particularly psychology.[25] It appears that Archbishop Milingo's attempt at reconciling Christianity with African beliefs was misunderstood most deeply by the non-African missionaries who believed their work was to free Africans from those very beliefs.

A clear cultural divide opened in Lusaka and elsewhere in Zambia. Clerics from two distinct cultures, European missionaries and native Africans, disagreed as to how African people might be freed from "evil spirits." The crux of the issue is clear: the Europeans wanted to free the Africans from belief in evil spirits; Milingo wanted to free the Africans from any hold evil spirits might have over them, including their very belief. The nuanced distinction between the European point of view and that of Milingo is at the root of the problem.

Witchcraft, where it attempts to bring evil on others, was and is outlawed in Africa, and is certainly opposed to Catholic teaching. Milingo believed the non-African missionaries did not understand or distinguish various African beliefs in the spirit world. Milingo believed he understood how to bring the freedom of Christ to those Africans inhibited by what was clearly a negative spirituality, particularly how to bring Christian freedom from the fear of witchcraft.[26] Milingo wrote:

> All these would dare ask me: "On whose authority do you write about witches and spirits with certitude?" I boldly say in Latin *"Expertus potest credere."* Having passed through the experience I can dare to write with authority and certitude. I have talked with the witches, and I have dealt with the dead. I have gone beyond theory. I too have been forced to know this by the privilege of the Lord to prove to the people that Jesus is truly one Lord and Savior, and that He is Lord of the dead and the living.[27]

Milingo's Christian faith, as evidenced earlier, did not "translate" the possible legitimacy of his activities to the non-African Catholics who questioned his practices.

Not only did Milingo incur the ire of European missionaries and other members of the Zambia Episcopal Conference, he also increasingly annoyed those in political power by his insistent preaching on behalf of the poor. Concurrent with his troubles with missionary clerics in his diocese and with the Zambia Episcopal Conference, as archbishop Milingo's preaching on behalf of the poor eventually caused him to lose supporters in government. He had political support at first, but increasingly lost it through his own actions. When Zambian President Kenneth Kaunda used the occasion of Milingo's fiftieth birthday celebration to chide all sides in the internal church dispute, Milingo took umbrage at Kaunda's publicizing internal discord. Further, Milingo did not abandon his charismatic beliefs.

Some time later, when presiding at a confirmation, Archbishop Milingo told the assembly that their calling on the Holy Spirit would be very effective, and they had best sit down. The result was much charismatic mayhem, with people shaking, falling down, and screaming. Milingo was soon accused of having returned to his healing ministry.[28]

Was he performing exorcisms—the full Catholic ceremony of expelling evil spirits? Soon the Apostolic Nuncio—the Pope's representative in Zambia—released a letter to all the Zambian bishops specifying the church regulations regarding exorcisms. In one sense, Milingo had continued his healing practices all along, focusing on spirit possession and exorcisms. While the Catholic Church doctrinally accepts the possibility of spirit possession, it also believes exorcism should be used sparingly and as a means of last resort.

The Catholic Church strictly limits exorcisms and exorcists. Each exorcism must be approved by the diocesan bishop, and each exorcist must be specifically appointed for the specific exorcism of a specific person (or, sometimes, place). Exorcism is not a Catholic sacrament, but a specified rite that may be used with some leeway as to specific prayers or scripture readings chosen at the discretion of the exorcist, usually a priest, always selected by the bishop. Since Milingo was the diocesan bishop, in theory, at least, he could judge an exorcism necessary and appoint himself as exorcist. Milingo more readily saw the need for exorcism and performed many on his own authority.[29]

Archbishop Milingo's attitude was in keeping with the practices of the larger African community and African Traditional Religion. According to A. O. Igenoza, the essential components of African Traditional Religion are belief in a Supreme God, in divinities, in spirits and shadows, in the abilities of ancestors to influence the present, and the practices of magic, divination, and medicine.[30] Christian missionaries did not seem to take traditional spiritualities into account. Therefore, Igenoza writes, the Christianity that came to Africa was—at that time at least—largely a failure because it "was not allowed to touch the innermost being and the emotions of converts."[31] Igenoza, writing in 1985, argues for "a Christian (and not a Western) *Weltanschauung* to meet the religious aspirations of African Christians,"[32] and that would include exorcism:

> A Christian *Weltanschhauung* which duly recognizes the existence of evil spirits but which Jesus has conquered through his resurrection and endless life is in urgent need of reiteration and demonstration . . . The popularity which such a ministry could enjoy even in the mainline churches in Africa may be evidenced by the thousands of people who trooped out to the open-air rallies of the controversial Catholic Bishop, Emanuel Milingo, who hopes that the use of the power of Jesus "with ease and authority would be realized so that the Christian life would be truly meaningful to my fellow Africans."[33]

Milingo defended his readily performing Catholic exorcisms by likening its action to that of the sacraments of reconciliation (confession) and baptism. He reportedly said,

> Though the formula used in the sacrament of Confession does not directly expel the evil one, the mention of deliverance from sins is genuinely an exercise of exorcism. In the old formula there were two most important elements of exorcism. One was *"Dominus noster Jesus Christus te absolvat."* (May the Lord Jesus Christ deliver you) . . . The second element makes a priest recognize his role as a minister of Christ, and so he relies on the authority of Jesus Christ and concludes by delivering a penitent in the name of the Trinity: *"Et ego autoritate sua te absolvo a peccatis tuis in nomine Patris et Filii et Spiritus Sancti, Amen."*[34]

But the Apostolic Nuncio—the pope's representative to Zambia—had ordered Milingo to stop performing exorcisms, effectively nullifying (or attempting to nullify) Milingo's episcopal authority over the matter. Milingo replied indirectly to the nuncio's letter, eventually producing a 23-page booklet, *Open Letter to My Brother Bishops* (1981), detailing his beliefs, actions, and recommendations regarding spirit healing and Catholic exorcisms in Africa. That, of course, only made things worse.[35]

The Vatican then commissioned Cardinal Maurice Cardinal Otunga (1923–2003) of Nairobi and Bishop Nicodemus Kirima (1936–2007) then of Mombassa to conduct an investigation, which they did to a limited extent. They took testimony from neither the laity who sought Milingo's healing nor the archdiocesan group of women who supported him. Nor was Milingo's secretary, Father Hugo Hinfelaar, interviewed.[36]

Without question, the Vatican had become convinced that Milingo was a problem and needed to be removed. His enemies in Africa—from Jesuit missionaries to Zambian President Kenneth Kaunda—coalesced for various reasons around that solution. In 1982, Milingo was ordered to Rome for a "rest" by letter from the Apostolic Nuncio.[37]

ROME

As it turned out, physicians in Rome found Archbishop Milingo neither unbalanced nor otherwise ill, but his controversial activities and the deep traction gained by his detractors in Africa were sufficient for the Vatican to disallow his return. He asked for—but did not immediately receive—an audience with Pope John Paul II to discuss his situation,[38] and he wrote a long appeal to the pope asking for permission to "go home" to Zambia.[39] Concurrently, Milingo's situation—and notoriety—were not lost on Western media, which characterized the difficulties with his healing ministry as problems of inculturation.[40]

Archbishop Milingo's entire situation must be viewed in context. As a bishop in communion with Rome, he—like Bruskewitz—"reported" directly to the pope. Yet he had no immediate access to John Paul II even though he was in Rome. A year or so after requesting an audience, Milingo finally met with the pope, on July 6, 1983, who explained that Milingo's fellow bishops felt it best he not return to Africa. Here the efforts of collegiality worked against a single bishop and effectively removed him from jurisdiction and authority.

By now, however, Milingo had taken up his healing ministry in Rome. "Your bent," the pope reportedly said, "is to the healing ministry. Let us then discuss together what you can do in Rome."[41]

Milingo's forced resignation as archbishop of Lusaka—at age 53—soon followed. One month later he was appointed Special Delegate to the Pontifical Commission for Migration and Tourism (later called the Pontifical Council for the Pastoral Care of Migrants and Itinerant People),[42] where he was given office space but no real portfolio. He had a post that legitimized him and a place to receive visitors, but no jurisdiction and no juridical authority beyond the sacramental. Technically, he did not have authority of his own accord for exorcisms, although he might have imputed that the bishop of Rome—the pope—gave him the necessary permission. Archbishop Milingo—he retained his title—spent much of his time building a healing ministry from the commission's headquarters in the Trastevere quarter of Rome.

Meanwhile, the African bishops did everything they could to erase all traces of Milingo's by now deep-rooted influence in Africa. They made sure the people of Zambia knew Milingo would not return, publishing in *AFER* (*African Ecclesial Review*) "A Letter from Members of Zambia Episcopal Conference to the Catholics of Zambia on

Recent Events in the Archdiocese of Lusaka" both to announce and to underscore their point.[43]

In short order, Mona MacMillan edited and published a slim book of Milingo's pamphlets and speeches that sought to defend and explain his healing ministry. Cited earlier, *The World In Between: Christian Healing and the Struggle for Spiritual Survival* was well reviewed around the world.[44] One reviewer, Stephen Chan of the University of Zambia, accurately interprets the book's attempt to exonerate Milingo and present his ministry as one of African inculturation of Catholicism. Chan calls the work a memoir "full of compassion for a flock persecuted in several spiritual senses, by a spirit realm and by an unregarding church with custody over what is or is not spiritually admissible—even if it is real; or at least real to those who suffer from it."[45]

Public discussion continued and then waned. Milingo maintained his healing ministry while holding a Vatican office. At some point in the mid-1990s he returned to Zambia and briefly reconciled with his successor archbishop of Lusaka. But once his faith-healing practices again stepped beyond the Roman pale as understood by the Zambian bishops, Milingo was again banished to Rome.

Milingo lived in Zagarolo, outside Rome, with three religious sisters of the Daughters of the Redeemer as cooks and housekeepers, continued his faith healing just under the Vatican's radar and developed a wide following. At first he held services in Santa Maria Addolorata, the Argentinean national church in Rome, until 1986 or 1987. He then moved due to overcrowding to the Ergife Palace Hotel in Rome, five kilometers (slightly over three miles) east of Vatican City. The hotel is 56 kilometers (nearly 35 miles) northeast of Zagarolo, about a 45-minute drive in the best of traffic conditions. It is rumored at least that at some point he also performed his healing services aboard cruise ships off the Italian coast, arguing that he was beyond any jurisdiction on the open seas.

Milingo's rituals must be understood specifically within the context of questionable jurisdiction: did he have permission, that is, was he stably assigned as an exorcist for the diocese, and was he using the approved ritual in the approved manner? That is, did the diocesan bishop, the pope, appoint him exorcist for the Diocese of Rome? And did he use approved texts? An eyewitness report of Milingo's faith healing and exorcisms seems to present Milingo as using the approved Roman Rite of Exorcism, with some use of English. This could be in keeping with the ritual. There is leeway for the exorcist to use preferred readings and prayers, even in the vernacular, although the Rite's instructions to the exorcist state that "the Latin text has some special unction and disruptive values for Evil Spirit."[46]

Vittorino Lanternari's 1998 account of Milingo's exorcisms seems to indicate Milingo followed the Rite, although Lanternari insinuates Milingo's intent is to stir up mass hysteria among the crowd: "It is important to insist here on the preemptory and threatening tones that Milingo adopts when hurling attacks against witchcraft, evil spirits, black and white magic, curses, in summary, Satan . . . In the climate of emotion and terror thus generated, reactions are spontaneous and a contagious fear spreads through the people and contrition, remorse and even panic ensue."[47] Little in Lanternari's description of Milingo's actions is at variance with the ordinary performance of exorcism according to the Roman Ritual, except for the public nature of the exorcisms and the ensuing public reactions. Milingo is described as following the ritual's instructions, although Lanternari apparently misunderstands Catholic belief regarding possession and the Roman Ritual itself. In fact, his description of Milingo appears critical of the ritual itself. Even so, his presentation of Milingo's activities (one of the few "outsider" accounts) is understanding of, if not sympathetic to, the confluence of circumstances that generated Milingo's large following in Rome.

In the late 1990s, Milingo seemed to be well in control of what he believed, and his belief did not seem at odds with Catholic teaching. He later got involved with the Unification Church. In an interview published on the Moon True Parents Organization website, Milingo discusses exorcism and possession:

> I have had people who came to me saying they had evil spirits, and I had to say to them "If you were possessed, you wouldn't approach me." In these cases there are no demons. I can't send away devils where there are none. In most of these cases we speak of psychological obsessions or fixations. Part of my apostolate is to pray for such people for whom it is not clear whether the problem is of psychological or spiritual nature. For me it is therefore very important to be able to discern which problems are obsessions, which are fixations and which are actually possessions.[48]

Coincidentally, throughout Milingo's Roman exile, the Roman Catholic Rite of Exorcism was being revised. Other liturgies of the Roman Ritual had been revised and translated to the vernacular in the years following the Second Vatican Council, but the Rite of Exorcism was left, unrevised, in Latin. By 1999, the Rite had been revised and in a January press conference, Cardinal Jorge Arturo Medina Estévez,

Prefect of the Congregation for Divine Worship and the Discipline of the Sacraments, announced,

> We should stress that the diocesan bishop's authorisation is required to perform an exorcism; this authorisation can be granted for a specific case or in a general, permanent way to the priest who exercises the ministry of exorcist in the diocese. The Roman Ritual contained the instructions and liturgical text for exorcisms in a special chapter. This was the last chapter and had not been revised after the Second Vatican Council. The revision has taken ten years, resulting in the current text approved by the Supreme Pontiff, which is made public today and is available to the pastors and faithful of the Church. One more task still remains within the competence of the respective Bishops' Conference: the translation of this ritual into the languages spoken in the various regions; these translations must be precise and faithful to the Latin original, and must be submitted, in accordance with canon law, for the *recognitio* of the Congregation for Divine Worship.
>
> The ritual we are presenting today contains, first of all, the rite of exorcism properly so-called, to be performed on a possessed person. This is followed by the prayers to be publicly recited by a priest, with the bishop's permission, when it has been carefully determined that there is a satanic influence over places, objects or persons, but which has not reached the point of a true and proper possession.[49]

Given John Paul II's reported comment to Milingo when they met following his removal from Lusaka—that Milingo's real talent was in healing—Milingo at least could think he had authorization to perform exorcisms. However, healing and exorcism are not the same. Milingo continued his healing ministry, which often included exorcisms and was essentially ignored by the Vatican. Concurrently, with the continued slow decline of John Paul II, Milingo was increasingly marginalized. Eventually he lost his only appointment—that to Migration and Tourism, which had provided him with office space and a title of sorts—when he reached the Vatican's mandatory retirement age of seventy in 2000.[50]

MARRIAGE, MOON, AND MARRIED PRIESTS NOW!

Archbishop Milingo burst onto the world stage slightly over a year after his Vatican retirement when, on May 27, 2001, he married Maria Sung, a Korean acupuncturist in a mass "blessing ceremony"[51] at the New York Hilton celebrated by Unification Church founder Rev. Sun Myung Moon. The act, which includes the husband and wife sharing the Holy Wine of Ecumenical Blessing, as it is termed, effectively separated Milingo from the Catholic Church. Needless to say, the Vatican denounced his act, not the least because it was in concert with

Moon, who believed he has a Messianic role in world salvation, had been implicated in various questionable events, and was once a major defense contractor.

At the time, Moon's Unification Church controlled several related and unrelated highly profitable enterprises, including True World Foods, Inc., which provided frozen fish and sea foods as well as most of the raw fish served in US restaurants. Tax evasion charges regarding Moon's international network of corporations and holding companies landed him in US Federal prison for 18 months in the early 1980s, and he was banned from entering some countries, even while he managed a 120-city speaking tour in 2005. Moon's enterprises control the ultraconservative *Washington Times* newspaper and its foundation, which has donated over one million dollars to various conservative political causes in the United States. At the time, Moon's net worth was variously estimated at $10 billion, and he could afford to support a wayward archbishop, especially if such support advanced his cause to reform religion worldwide. In 1993, Moon said in a public lecture: "My enemies are America and Christianity. How am I going to win over those enemies . . . Jesus was supposed to be married and then go to Rome. He should have converted Rome and if that had happened there would not have been a Pope, Catholicism, Protestantism and Churches etc."[52] Moon, clearly no friend of Catholicism, had gained sway over Milingo, who was married in a mass wedding ceremony over which Moon presided. Moon's ceremony is a religious ceremony of blessing, effectively giving couples permission to marry. But canon law forbids clerics to contract marriage—to marry woman—and states the prior bond of ordination nullifies any attempt at such.[53]

At the time of the ceremony, because Milingo publicly participated in a non-Catholic (and, it would argue, non-Christian) marriage ceremony, the Vatican published a formal canonical warning, by which the Congregation for the Doctrine of the Faith warned Milingo he would be excommunicated if he did not renounce the marriage and separate from Maria Sung.[54] Further conditions of the document were that he must sever all links with the Family Federation for World Peace and Unification (the newer name for Moon's Unification Church) by August 20, 2001, and declare his acceptance of priestly celibacy. The Congregation summed up its view of his errors in its first paragraph: "noting the grave public conduct and statements whereby the Archbishop has attempted an asserted 'matrimonial union' with the Korean Maria Sung, has adhered to the sect of the Reverend Sun Myung Moon called the Family Federation for World Peace and Unification, and has failed in communion with the Successor of Peter and the College of Bishops"[55] and demanded several actions for his reunification with Rome, that is, to avoid formal excommunication: "a) to separate from Maria Sung; b) to sever all links with the sect, Family Federation for World Peace and Unification; c) to declare publicly his fidelity to the doctrine and ecclesiastical discipline of celibacy, and to manifest his obedience to the Supreme Pontiff by a clear and unequivocal act."[56] The document, dated July 16, 2001, was signed by then Prefect of the Congregation for the Doctrine of the Faith, Cardinal Joseph Ratzinger, now Pope Benedict XVI, and by the Secretary of the Congregation, Archbishop Tarcisio Bertone, SDB, later a Cardinal and Benedict XVI's Secretary of State.

After meeting with Pope John Paul II on August 7, 2001, Milingo recanted his actions and returned to the fold, abandoning the woman with whom he presumably had a consummated marriage. The attitude of the church regarding married clerics, embedded in canon law, is painted here in bold colors. The general law, for both Eastern and Western Catholic Churches, is that a married man may be ordained but an ordained man may not marry. In practice, the majority of the 22 Eastern Catholic Churches ordained married men as deacons and priests; only unmarried men, either monks, widowers, or lifelong celibates, may be ordained bishops. In the Latin Rite, or Roman Catholic Church, married men may be ordained deacons and, by exception (typically, former Protestant or Anglican clergy) as priests. As in the Eastern Churches, only unmarried men may be ordained bishops.

The law was apparently not lost on Milingo, who left his wife. A week later his erstwhile wife, Maria Sung, began a hunger strike in Rome, gaining media notoriety for her cause. She was joined in her fast by 12 other Unification women on August 26. Within a few days, on August 29, she was able to meet with her husband, after which she said she accepted his renunciation of their marriage.[57] The consequences of Milingo's abandoning a woman to whom he had promised fidelity was never successfully defended to the public mind. Church officials consistently took the position that his prior "marriage" to the church, through his ordination promise of celibacy, cannot be overridden nor dismissed. To the general public, his abandonment of his wife made him a scoundrel and the Vatican complicit in his behavior.

The public relations consequences of Milingo's abandoning his wife were not lost on the Vatican. About a year later, journalist Michele Zanzucchi conducted a one-hundred-question interview with Milingo at the Argentinean headquarters of Focolare (Mariápolis Andrea) at a meeting directly approved and arranged for by Archbishop Bertone. The titles of the book resultant of the interview, published in Spanish as *El pez rescatado del pantano*[58] (*The Fish Rescued from the Swamp*) and in Italian as *Il pesce ripescato dal sludge* (*The Fish Rescued from the Mud*) gives comment on how the Vatican views Moon's Federation, women, or both. In the interview, Milingo—at the time "unmarried"—steadfastly refuses to discuss the question of priestly marriage or his own marriage to Maria Sung.

There is little public record of Milingo's activities following the Zanzucchi interview, which does not seem to have been translated into English and is therefore less available to both Milingo's African flock and American media. Milingo's now dual problems of faith healing and priestly marriage—the latter a point of deep interest in Africa—made Milingo even more of a threat to the African bishops and of greater interest in the United States.

During the ensuing five years, for all practical purposes Milingo remained under house arrest in Rome, refused permission to travel except with a bodyguard. He did manage to visit Zambia twice, each time under armed guard.[59]

Milingo lived for five years under these conditions until, in June 2006, he simply walked out of his residence to a waiting car when everyone was expecting him to be napping. For a time his whereabouts were unknown—one wag remarked he might turn up in Ecône[60] (location of the headquarters of the Society of Saint Pius X), but he soon surfaced in Washington DC, beside former Catholic priest George Augustus Stallings, Jr., an African American and patriarch of his own Imani Temple African-American Catholic Congregation.[61] Stallings and Okinawa native Soyami Kamimoto, 29, received a marriage blessing at the same 2001 Unification ceremony Milingo and Sung, and sixty other couples, participated in.

Now the agenda appeared to be a married Roman Catholic priesthood. During the ensuing summer of 2006, Milingo was busy organizing his Married Priests Now! movement, reaching out to the national organization of former Catholic priests in the United States, CORPUS (the name comes from Corps of Retired Priests United for Service),[62] and otherwise connecting with American friends and supporters. It would appear that both he and those whom he contacted wanted to create a means of canonical jurisdiction for each other—in effect, a schismatic church; he needed clerics and members and some married priests in CORPUS needed and wanted a bishop to legitimize them.

As it happened, Milingo and Sung had never formally married, and so Stallings performed a Catholic marriage ceremony—legal in the District of Columbia—shortly before they all attended a public news conference announcing Married Priests Now![63]

In a July interview in an Arlington, Virginia hotel room, Milingo told *National Catholic Reporter* journalist John L. Allen, Jr., that he broke from the Catholic Church a second time after five years of "doubts and difficulties." All along, he said, he thought of himself as married to Maria Sung and progressively found official Catholic non-acceptance of his healing ministry intolerable. "People knew my gift was beyond doubt," he told Allen. "But the dioceses didn't want me." He questioned the structure of the church that, he said, "separates itself from humanity."[64]

By this time, for Milingo, a married priesthood and faith healing appear intertwined to one cause, and Milingo was well on his way to complete schism and excommunication.

Then, on September 24, 2006, Milingo ordained four married men—including George Stallings—as bishops, effectively creating at least a schismatic group within the Catholic Church if not a separate church of its own and incurring automatic, or *latae sententiae*, excommunication, much like Lefebvre.[65] (Stallings had been previously ordained bishop by Richard Bridges of the Independent Old Catholic Church, although they severed relations within a year.)[66]

Precisely because he ordained bishops, the Vatican announced Milingo was *latae sententiae* excommunicated, much as it had declared Lefebvre excommunicated. As with Lefebvre, there is no question that Milingo was sacramentally empowered to ordain bishops—he had already been co-consecrator of five African bishops—but he did not have the legal authority to do so. In a further complication, his newly ordained bishops ought to have been in communion with Rome; some of these four already had broken with Rome through prior acts, including receiving ordination from non-Catholic bishops.

Milingo's acts were not in keeping with custom. Legitimate candidates had to be "in communion with Rome," but they were not. In the Roman Catholic Church, "in communion with Rome" is typically understood to mean a candidate for episcopal orders has been chosen by the pope from among three candidates submitted by the territory's Apostolic Nuncio or Delegate, who presumably has made secret inquiries within their respective dioceses. At episcopal ordinations, the diocesan chancellor or the papal nuncio reads the papal document authorizing the ordination prior to the ceremony. Milingo ignored these requirements. Beyond, although Milingo was well aware the Catholic Church typically requires three, or at least two, bishops to ordain a new bishop licitly, he was the sole consecrator.[67]

Undeterred, Milingo subsequently ordained two married men as priests—including an ordained deacon of the Archdiocese of Newark—on December 10, 2006, in West New York, New Jersey.[68] These actions were clearly illegitimate but possibly valid.

Liceity—legitimacy—requires that the ordaining bishop, if he is not the diocesan bishop of the person to be ordained, receive a dimissorial (permission) letter from the ordinand's bishop or religious superior.

That is, the sacramentality of the ordination is not questioned because Milingo is—or at least at the time was—a Catholic bishop, and Catholic teaching is that a bishop (and only a bishop) is empowered to ordain individuals as priests. However, the legitimacy, or liceity, of their ordinations is open to question: Milingo was not their diocesan bishop and the bishops of the territories where the men resided did not provide the dimissorial letters that would have given Milingo permission to perform the ordinations. These technicalities are in addition to the fact that the men were married.

The fact that these men were married does not automatically forbid their ordinations; the canonical impediment of marriage is not invalidating. Under other circumstances, the ordaining bishop would request a derogation, or waiver, from the law, assuming such was possible. The norm in the Latin Church is that those ordained as priest be unmarried, but married men can be ordained, while the ordained cannot get married. The Pastoral Provision for married former Episcopalian clergy in the United States was presaged by Pope Paul VI and finalized by Pope John Paul II.[69]

In any case, the men Milingo ordained as priests and bishops believe they are valid Roman Catholic priests and bishops, even though they are not juridically in communion with Rome. Here their situations might mirror those of other validly ordained priests; for example, those of the Polish National Church, whose ordinations are considered valid but whose juridical authorities—their bishops—are not in communion with Rome.

With such churches and communions, the Vatican maintains various levels of recognition. Throughout history, there have been many legitimate Catholic bishops who, for various reasons, have departed from communion with Rome and dependence on Vatican authority. Some of these departed with large followings and established churches, usually territorial and at first considered according to national boundaries. These at their inception maintained the same teachings and practices of the Catholic Church. Over time, some have drifted further afield, although several have not. Those the Catholic Church recognizes as having valid sacraments by definition have recognition of valid priestly orders. Milingo's problems were—at first—solely juridical: he wanted to ordain married men as priests and bishops. So the question arises: was Milingo's group becoming a separate church?

In a November 4, 2006, open letter to the USCCB, Milingo and his four new bishops argued their case, pointing out that there are perhaps twenty-five thousand former Catholic priests who have resigned for various reasons, most of them in order to marry. The letter, signed by Emmanuel Milingo and the four men he ordained as bishops, Peter Paul Brennan, Joseph J. Gouthro, Patrick E. Trujillo, and George Augustus Stallings states: "The Married Priests Now! Prelature with its archbishops, bishops and priests considers itself to be a Roman Catholic Personal Prelature in Communion with Benedict XVI and is part of the Roman Catholic Church. We are Roman Catholic bishops and do not want to fracture the Communion of the Church. Our cause is great because it is for the survival of the Church."[70]

To be clear, within the specific context of the question of ordaining married men as priests (although not as bishops) Milingo does not seem to be a juridical or sacramental radical, even though his own marriage and cooperation with Moon cannot be overlooked. Even though CORPUS and other, similar groups are accepting of active homosexuality and of other issues supported by more liberal groups, such as Call to Action, Milingo was at first in no way interested in changing anything other than current church law regarding priestly celibacy, either by ordaining married men (beyond the limits of current restrictions) or by official recognition of the concubinage arrangements of so many priests, particularly among those in Africa and Latin America. As he stated on his website, "You have heard that one priest from Rome, who had confessed that he was homosexual, but had no remorse for it. We have applications of homosexual priests to join our Movement of Married Priests Now! But we are actually married priests, married to women. We have wives, not our fellow masculine husbands, who by agreement one plays the woman."[71] One clear distinction between

Milingo and CORPUS is Milingo's objection to actively homosexual clergy, and his solution is a married priesthood. Milingo believes the predominance of deviant sexual behaviors in the Catholic Church (and he clearly includes homosexual activity as a deviant behavior) are resultant of the law of celibacy.

Milingo's objections to active homosexual clergy resonate in the most traditional halls of the Anglican Communion, especially within the Episcopal Church in the United States, splintered as it has been by the consecration of partnered homosexual priest, V. Gene Robinson, as Bishop of New Hampshire in 2004 and subsequent consecration of Mary Douglas Glasspool as a suffragan bishop for the Episcopal Diocese of Los Angeles in 2010.

Milingo is constant in his argument for a married priesthood, one that would legitimize the many barely hidden illicit relationships of priests around the world. Milingo complained widely about what he called open disregard for the discipline of priestly celibacy in the Catholic Church. In 2001, he told a Zambian newspaper, "Secret affairs and marriages, illegitimate children, rampant homosexuality, pedophilia and illicit sex have riddled the priesthood to the extent that the UN Commission on Human Rights has investigated the church for sexual abuse, and the western media is filled with stories of lawsuits and scandals surrounding the Church."[72] Throughout, Milingo considered himself Roman Catholic. He attended daily Mass at Sacred Heart Church in Washington, near the condominium he shared with his wife until leaving the United States in early 2007. He then lived in Korea, Brazil, Italy, and Africa, variously promoting his Married Priests Now! movement, ordaining married men, performing faith healing services, and publicly celebrating Mass.

The United States has not allowed him to return since he overstayed his visa on his last visit, and the Vatican withdrew his diplomatic passport in 2007, shortly after married priests in Zambia announced their public ministry.[73] The Vatican also cut off Milingo's retirement salary for a short time, then reinstated it with back payments, perhaps in recognition that denying him his earned pension forced his further dependence on Moon.[74]

In September 2007, the Catholic bishops of South Korea warned their faithful against Milingo.[75] When in South Korea, Milingo resided in the Moon-owned Cheongshim Villa, a retirement community near the Moon-sponsored Cheongshim Graduate School of Theology in Seolak-MyunGapyung-Gun, Kyunggi (also spelled Gyeonggi) Province.[76]

At one point it seemed Milingo would center his movement in São Paulo, Brazil. Brazil is home to the largest national grouping of married priests, the breakaway Brazilian Catholic Apostolic Church (Igreja Católica Apostólica Brasileira, ICAB), founded in 1945 by Brazilian bishop Dom Carlos Duarte Costa, a former Roman Catholic Bishop of Botucatu who resigned his office in 1937. ICAB now has 58 dioceses and claims it has five million members in 17 countries. It is the founding church of the Worldwide Communion of Catholic Apostolic National Churches (Igrejas Católicas Apostólicas Nacionais), a federation of 14 national independent Catholic churches that essentially accepts Catholic doctrine but dispenses from priestly celibacy.[77]

Milingo did not remain long in Brazil and did not appear aligned with the Brazilian Catholic Apostolic Church, although his own organization, Married Priests Now! at one time claimed 18,600 priests in Brazil alone.[78] On April 14, 2007, Milingo celebrated a public Mass in São Paulo for one thousand followers of Sun Myung Moon's Unification Church, and, as the *Irish Times* wrote, then as now Milingo's cause remained married priests: "The Virgin Mary sent me a message saying, 'The situation of the priests in the Catholic Church is disastrous and if you do not do something the consequences will be terrible,'" the *Irish Times* quotes him saying. "At first I wept and felt helpless but then I undertook this mission."[79]

Despite his connections with Moon, Milingo continued to insist he was still Catholic: "A real Christian is one who knows how to love without distinction," he told the *Irish Times*, "There are many shared points on which Rev. Moon and I can build in order to work together. If we go on with exclusion against Moonies or Muslims or whoever, then we contradict what we call ecumenism."[80] Milingo exercised his own style of ecumenism in Africa in mid-2008, when he held meetings that led to the formation of a "prelature" attached to his movement. He wrote in a September 2008 email to his followers, "we formed a Christian unified front. We ended up by calling our union and unity: 'The Zambian Catholic Apostolic Prelature.' We felt that 'a diocese' would sound too close to the Roman Catholic Structure. We have Methodists, Presbyterians, Theosophists, Pentecostals and Evangelicals. We look forward to have soon with us the Anglicans, the Lutherans and the Seventh Day Adventists."[81] (An apostolic prelature is the Catholic Church's term for a missionary diocese—Zambia itself was once an apostolic prelature.) The questions arise: is there in Zambia Married Priests Now! as a movement and "The Zambian Catholic Apostolic Prelature" as a new sect? It is patently impossible for Catholic theology to square with the beliefs of Seventh Day Adventists and Theosophists.

Milingo had initially planned to base his movement in the United States at Stallings' Imani Temple but then transferred his US headquarters to Belvedere, Moon's 35-acre Tarrytown, New York, where he overstayed his visa. He could not attend a December 2007 meeting of his Married Priests Now! group in Rome—in mid-October, 2007, the Vatican had withdrawn his diplomatic—and so his travels depended on his obtaining visas with his Zambian passport. He did get to Rome in January 2008, ostensibly to attend medical appointments and to promote a new book. While in Rome he was publicly denied communion at a Catholic Mass, and his Vatican pension was once again suspended.[82]

The Vatican's actions underscored the fact of Milingo's excommunication and its own willingness to play hardball. Under the papacy of Polish John Paul II, the African archbishop who gained his See through the resignation of a Polish Jesuit had been accorded the respect and privileges of a dotty old uncle, and he was talked back to communion with Rome after his 2001 marriage.

That had all changed in 2005, with the election of Cardinal Joseph Ratzinger, head of the Congregation for the Doctrine of the Faith. The new pope, Benedict XVI, would not accord Milingo the respect or courtesies either Paul VI or John Paul II did. In fact, despite Benedict's overtures to married Anglican priests, particularly Episcopalians in the United States presumably disaffected by partnered homosexual bishops, the papacy of Benedict XVI was not taking kindly to Milingo's efforts to rally resigned and married priests in the world, along with the many active presumed celibate priests currently in concubine relationships with women.

Milingo's passion was to return to Africa, where the movement for married priests continues to solidify. The Zambia Episcopal Conference warned Catholics of Zambia against him, with a statement posted on the Conference website:

ZEC's Statement on the status of Emmanuel Milingo

The Zambia Episcopal Conference wishes to once again clarify the status of the former Archbishop of Lusaka, Emmanuel Milingo, in the light of media reports that he is planning to come back to Zambia in the near future. We reiterate that the former Archbishop has been excommunicated. Excommunication means that he is no longer part of the Catholic Church. By his own actions, he has knowingly and willingly cut himself off from the Catholic Church. He therefore cannot preside over any religious function in the name of the Catholic

Church. If indeed he wants to come back to Zambia, it is within his rights to return to his homeland. However, we urge our Catholic faithful to be aware that if he holds religious functions, then those ceremonies will be done outside the Catholic Church. Therefore they are not Catholic services.

Signed: Most Rev. Telesphore G. Mpundu, Archbishop of Lusaka
President—Zambia Episcopal Conference[83]

The attitude of the Zambian Bishops' statement strangely echoes Milingo's own request to the Vatican while he was still bishop of Lusaka and when he was barred from his healing ministry by order of Rome at the request of the Zambian bishops. He wanted to obey, he wrote, because the people would not stop coming. "I am terribly harassed by people, at home, at my office, through letters and telephones. They have never learnt to obey. The Bishops must speak openly to them and bind them under obedience not to come to me . . . I shall appreciate your advice. What a mental torture to learn to be hard and harsh to the sick by your orders, and this is what I am trying to learn. But in spite of this they are coming, coming, coming."[84]

Milingo's connection with both Catholic priests and people is his conviction that the power structure of the Catholic Church is uneven and unfair and that celibacy is an unnecessary means of controlling clergy (and, indirectly, laity). No matter whether in the United States, South Korea, Brazil or Africa, these last parts of Milingo's message resonate deeply with many Catholics, for whom priestly celibacy seems to promise an unending decline in vocations and an unending saga of pederasty scandals. When viewed against the international meltdown resultant of the expanding clergy sex abuse scandal, a married priesthood seems, to many, to make ultimate sense.

MARRIED PRIESTS, FAITH HEALING— AFRICA, ROME, AND AROUND THE WORLD

It is important to recall that Emmanuel Milingo did not begin his exile out of Africa on the question of a married priesthood. In Zambia and elsewhere in Africa, the question of celibacy is conflicted, for a number of priests live relatively openly with wives (canonically termed "concubines"). The church in Africa has been plagued as well with problems of sexual abuse of women religious by bishops, priests, and seminarians, problems improperly addressed or covered up by African bishops. The horrific stories of abuse in Africa have been told and covered up, and told, and covered up again, although they really only became widely known in the late 1990s, well after

Milingo left Africa. Even so, they are the backdrop against which Milingo's detractors worked.[85]

Milingo's troubles were centered on his healing ministry. Milingo seems to have been bewildered at first by his powers. One account by him is typical: "I was in Kabwe on 8 July 1973, and was healing the sick after Mass. I used my right hand to communicate what people call healing radiations. Those who have *mashawe* [illness believed to have been caused by witchcraft] began to shake and cry. We prayed for them. One of them had been carried to the church on a bicycle but she walked home after the healing. I began to believe that the Lord Jesus approved of what I was doing. But I still did not understand the source of this power."[86] That he "did not understand the source of this power" speaks to Milingo's simplicity. He does not claim it for himself; nor does he claim he is a special agent of God.

Milingo's healing ministry, which encompassed both physical and spiritual ills, drew many to him and was the basis and cause of his celebrity in Africa. One case demonstrates his notoriety. Mother Theresa Gacambi, superior general of the Assumption Sisters of Nairobi, Kenya,[87] had been injured in a car accident in 1970. By 1973, several operations left her with a maimed hand and one leg shorter than the other. Milingo's friend, Malawian Bishop Patrick A. Kalilombe, M.Afr. (b. 1933), asked Milingo to help her. Milingo reports he asked God for a vision of her illness and that he envisioned a clay pot—shattered and put together imperfectly. He had drawn a picture to represent what he saw—and when he eventually met her she said that it correctly represented her condition. Following two sessions of prayer with Milingo, Mother Gacambi reported she was healed—and she never returned to doctors' care.[88]

Milingo's healing of Mother Gacambi only made things worse, as unfounded rumors about the nature of their relationship arose. Further, those who believed Milingo actually healed Mother Theresa Gacambi were more drawn to his ministry, with the resulting events discussed previously. Milingo attempted to defend and explain his ministry through various pamphlets and circular letters, later collected and published by Mona Macmillan in London in 1984 and one year later in the United States.[89]

THE EXCOMMUNICATIONS OF ARCHBISHOP MILINGO

Canonically, Milingo's actions resemble those of the late Archbishop Lefebvre. Shortly before he died, Lefebvre ordained four Society of Saint Pius X priest-members as bishops. Almost immediately, the Vatican initiated measures to heal the rupture, even establishing a commission within the Congregation for the Doctrine of the Faith to deal with the Society. [90] A major sticking point has been the episcopal orders of the four, particularly their intransigence on points of doctrine. International complaints arose when, in early 2009, Benedict XVI lifted the decree of excommunication on the four Lefebvre bishops in an attempt to recall them and the society to communion with Rome. One of those four, Richard Williamson (b. 1940), is a Holocaust denier.

Milingo's four bishops believe they are validly ordained, as with the four Society of Saint Pius X members. They argue they are on a "secret list" kept by the Vatican of those groups with valid apostolic succession, such as the Orthodox Churches, the Union of Utrecht Old Catholic Churches, and, in a separate category, the Society of St. Pius X and Married Priests Now![91]

Married Priests Now! bishops also pointed to the prior, canonically illegal ordination of bishops of the Chinese Patriotic Association for justification of their own validity. The Chinese bishops, however, were elected by the priests and lay people of their dioceses to replace aging bishops. The Vatican recanted its threats of excommunication in the Chinese cases and has since made it appear at least that the bishops were somehow joint appointments of the Vatican and the Chinese Patriotic Association. It has further moved to legitimize bishops of the Chinese Patriotic Association. These, and in fact all cases of what are termed "vagan" bishops, revolve around questions of authority and jurisdiction. The question revolves around whether the Holy See authorized the creation of one or another bishop or if a valid bishop left the church. If neither applies, then he is a vagan bishop.

For all his acceptance of women as wives and mothers, Milingo seems to retain his opposition to women priests. Objections to women priests may have helped separate him from George Stallings nearly immediately after he ordained Stallings as bishop.[92] Neither does Milingo agree with Stallings' acceptance of homosexual activity or birth control. While Milingo might accede to the possibility of ordaining women deacons, he is not likely to do so himself. His reluctance may not be credited to total acceptance of Catholic practice but rather reflects his age and cultural conditioning.[93] Milingo's response to the possibility of women in ministry was to found religious orders.

Regarding Milingo's ordinations of priests and bishops, the technical question raised is the relationship between "liceity" and "validity." Does an action need to be legitimate in order for it to be valid? Specifically, must an ordination be within the confines of legitimate authority in order for it to be a valid ordination? Are the Milingo bishops and priests sacramentally bishops and priests? Recall that ordinations can be considered sacramentally valid even when canonically illegal. The legal restrictions Milingo ignored are many. He ordained married men as bishops and priests. His ordinations of priests were not sanctioned by the diocesan bishop. His ordinations of bishops were not sanctioned by Rome, lacked the proper paperwork from the papal nuncio or delegate to the given country (certifying papal approval) and were irregular in that Milingo acted alone, without two other validly ordained bishops.

The concept of absolute ordination—that only the bishop's laying on of hands and the prayer of consecration are the matter and form of valid ordination[94]—has spawned any number of "independent" Catholic communities, which have a more or less valid claim to orders.[95] Typically, however, when clergy of these "independent Catholic" communities request to be received into the Catholic Church they are received as lay persons. These communities, however, are historically and administratively far removed from the Catholic Church and from Union of Utrecht Old Catholic Churches that the Catholic Church officially recognizes. In the case of Milingo, as with Lefebvre, the Vatican is watching the actions of a validly ordained territorial archbishop who was "retired" from his archdiocese.

No matter, it can be argued that Milingo's actions do not create Catholic priests or bishops. The operative question is whether—and where—Milingo is beginning a new church that could eventually be recognized by the Catholic Church as having valid sacraments due to their clergy having received valid ordinations within lines of apostolic succession as other breakaway groups of modern times. These others include the Polish National Church and those Union of Utrecht Churches recognized by Rome,[96] specifically, the Old Catholic Church of the Netherlands, Catholic Diocese of the Old Catholics in Germany, Old Catholic Church of Austria, Christian Catholic Church of Switzerland, Old Catholic Church of the Czech Republic, and the Polish-Catholic Church of Poland. These, along with the Orthodox Churches and certain Churches of the East (the Armenian Apostolic Church, for example), are recognized as having valid sacraments and orders, and Catholics are advised they can receive sacraments from their priests when "necessity requires it or true spiritual advantage suggests it."[97]

The histories of the Old Catholic groups are intertwined and varied, and their beliefs and practices often digress from Catholic doctrine, but in some respects they partly echo Milingo's cause. All ordain married men to all ranks of order: deacon, priest, bishop.[98]

For example, the Catholic Apostolic National Church, Province of Zambia, headed by its Archbishop Luciano Mbewe, seems to be such a church. It has created parallel structures to the Catholic Church in Zambia, but the Zambia Episcopal Conference (ZEC) in Lusaka says Mbewe's group is not part of the Catholic Church.[99] While the ZEC declared its intention to sue the organization over the use of the word "Catholic,"[100] the group maintained both the name and its claim to Catholicity.

The Catholic Apostolic National Church shares a name similar to the International Catholic Apostolic Church network of churches discussed earlier, but it is not connected to them except that it traces its apostolic succession through them via Carlos Duarte Costa (1888–1967), the Rome-educated former diocesan bishop of Botucatu, Brazil. The founding church of the Worldwide Communion of Catholic Apostolic National Churches (Igrejas Católicas Apostólicas Nacionais) is the Brazilian Catholic Apostolic Church (Igreja Católica Apostólica Brasileira), founded by Costa.

Duarte Costa, born to rank and prominence and named bishop at the age of 36, was an outspoken critic of the Vatican's practice of awarding Vatican passports to high-ranking German former Nazis (including Adolf Eichmann and Dr. Josef Mengele) and of the Brazilian government's acceptance of the practice. His twenty-year reign as diocesan bishop (1924–1945) ended with his forced resignation. Duarte Costa had convinced a battalion of Brazilian soldiers to join the struggle against the Brazilian government, and then-president Getulio Vargas asked the Vatican to remove him. Duarte Costa continued alone, implementing the reforms he had sought from Rome: liturgical use of the vernacular, institution of a permanent diaconate, communion for all under both species, and, particularly, a married priesthood. Since a great part of Rome's consternation with Duarte Costa concerned his administration of the diocese, especially his placing large resources at the disposal of the poor, he had a ready-made following among large numbers of Brazilians. Duarte Costa had been consecrated bishop by Rio De Janeiro's Archbishop, Cardinal Sebastiao Leme da Silveira Cintra (1882–1942), and operated under his protection until da Silveira Cintra's death, when Bishop Jayme de Barros Câmara (1894–1971) replaced him in 1943 (de Barros Câmara was elevated to Cardinal in 1946).

In June 1944, Duarte Costa was imprisoned in Belo Horizonte for three months, charged with being a communist sympathizer. He was freed following intervention by the government of Mexico and the United Nations. About a month after he was imprisoned, his faculties were suspended, and a year later the Vatican excommunicated him. In response, he formed the breakaway Brazilian Apostolic Catholic Church.[101] In 1948, the separatist church was briefly closed by Brazilian courts until it instituted different rites and insignia (gray cassocks) from the Catholic Church. At his death in 1961, Duarte Costa had 50 priests and 37 bishops in his church, which in 1970 began to refer to him as "San Carlos of Brazil." He was succeeded by Luis Fernando Castillo Mendez, whom he had consecrated bishop, and who now heads the international federation of National Catholic Apostolic Churches, which estimates its combined membership at approximately four million persons.

To this confusing list of churches is added the Ecumenical Catholic Church of Peace, for which Milingo was enthroned by a gathering in Cameroon of thirty Old Catholic bishops and priests as patriarch in 2010.[102] In order "to stem the vices of prostitution, fornication, adultery, homosexuality and pedophilia" the church requires its leaders to be married.

QUESTIONS OF COMMUNION AND AUTHORITY

Milingo may not have planned to found a breakaway church at first. When he again burst onto the world stage during the summer of 2006, he adamantly denied any intent to form a separate sect funded by Rev. Sun Myung Moon, in Africa or anywhere else. In a July 2006 interview with journalist John Allen, following the press conference announcing formation of Married Priests Now!, Milingo said he wanted to reconcile married priests with the church and promote better understanding between Catholicism and Moon's Family Federation for World Peace and Unification.[103] But subsequent pronouncements in Italy and Korea, his activity in Brazil and in Africa, and the activities of his followers in Africa and the United States led him farther and farther away from the Catholic Church.

Milingo did appear in New Jersey with Duarte Costa's successor, Worldwide Communion of Catholic Apostolic National Churches head Luis Fernando Castillo Mendez. Garbed in gray cassock and red bishop's biretta, Castillo Mendez blessed the assembly, comprised largely of married resigned Catholic priests, members of CORPUS.[104] CORPUS members, for the most part, are men both licitly and validly ordained who have left active ministry for a variety of reasons. Its earliest members were priests who simply left to get married and who expected to be returned to active ministry, but newer members comprise a larger variety of individuals. What CORPUS members were (and presumably still are) missing was episcopal legitimization of their priesthood—a bishop or bishops to be "attached" to. Milingo could provide this. But CORPUS quickly distanced itself from Milingo and Married Priests Now! because of his objections to openly homosexual priests, women priests, and his ties to Moon.[105] (Peter E. Hickman of the Ecumenical Catholic Communion,[106] who claims to be a vagan Old Catholic bishop,[107] has been friendly to CORPUS and to other rebel Catholic communities. Hickman ordained Mary Ramerman of the Spiritus Christi community in Rochester, New York, in 2001.)[108]

While the Worldwide Communion of Catholic Apostolic National Churches is fairly distant from the Catholic Church, the actions of its founding bishop, Duarte Costa in Brazil, form an interesting canonical background to the current state of affairs regarding Milingo. In 1945, following his excommunication, Duarte Costa ordained a 65-year-old married man, Salomão Barbosa Ferraz (1880–1969), who had been ordained in 1917 as an Anglican priest, as a Catholic priest, and bishop. Still married to Emília C. Ferraz and father of Esther Ferraz (b. 1916),[109] Barbosa Ferraz reconciled with the Catholic Church in 1958, and in 1963 Pope John XXIII named him titular bishop of Eleutherna.[110] Barbosa Ferraz served on a working commission for the Second Vatican Council and made an intervention at one of the sessions.

Since the close of Vatican II, numerous other bishops have been ordained or consecrated by bishops who claim the provenance, or apostolic lineage of orders, created by Duarte Costa. However, Rome only officially notes Salomão Barbosa Ferraz, once a member of the breakaway Brazilian Apostolic Catholic Church, as a validly consecrated bishop.[111] Even so, numerous church groupings claim apostolic succession via the "Costa Line," including the following in the United States: The National Catholic Church of America (part of the Worldwide Communion of Catholic Apostolic National Churches) and the Charismatic Catholic Church of Belém (Brazil), not part of the Worldwide Communion of Catholic Apostolic National Churches. Milingo once seemed to be affiliated with this latter church and preached and held services there.

Milingo's continued travels and activities evidenced large financial backing and his serious intent to organize validly ordained married and resigned Catholic priests as well as validly ordained Catholic priests in active ministry who have contracted civil marriages or who wish to marry. His quest challenges the canonical concept that prior ordination makes subsequent valid marriage impossible. Even so, Vatican permission is sometimes given for an ordained person (usually deacons) to validly marry. Married Catholic deacons whose wives die are sometimes given permission to remarry, although the legitimate reasons that must be presented to Rome are quite limited. Current regulations expect the widower deacon to "need" a wife only to free him from familial responsibilities where he is performing "significant ministry."[112]

Milingo traveled to Italy, Brazil, and Africa from Korea, seeking a permanent following and home. He appears to have been cut off from Moon-related funding as well as from his $5,000 per month Vatican pension. On the one hand, it would seem the Vatican recognizes not only the injustice of eliminating the pension—he did, after all, work in Migration and Tourism for a number of years—but also that their response to his creating Married Priests Now! and reuniting with Maria Sung both gave him international publicity and drove him more into the debt of Moon. Their stopping his pension made him increasingly—if not wholly—in Moon's debt. But now Moon has told Milingo he is on his own. His funding must come from elsewhere.

The cover of Milingo's 2007 autobiography, *Confessioni di uno Scomunicato*, depicts Moon in the upper left hand corner looking bemused. Moon looks neither at the façade of St. Peter's Basilica (to his right) nor at Archbishop Milingo in mitre with crosier (beneath him). The publisher's blurb is telling: "A mystic, like Padre Pio, or a revolutionary like Martin Luther? What is the true mission of Archbishop Milingo? Is it to fight for the end of priestly celibacy?"[113]

Milingo is not the only Catholic bishop to marry or get into Roman hot water because of his relationship with women. The bishop of Hungary's Military Ordinariate, Tamás Szabó, resigned in 2007 reportedly to marry a woman staffer at the Hungarian Defense Ministry, possibly a member of their armed forces. Szabó said only that his private life was no one's business, and he has remained out of the news. Throughout history other bishops have resigned—or been forced to resign—and a few have begun the churches mentioned earlier. Most live quiet lives; a few have later reconciled.

The thick line between cleric and lay is never fully erased for a bishop who resigns and leaves active ministry in the Catholic Church. He is typically required to remain celibate and often required to maintain other requirements of the clerical states, including recitation of the Liturgy of Hours (Divine Office). One notable recent exception is

Fernando Armindo Lugo Méndez, former Roman Catholic Bishop of San Pedro, laicized on June 30, 2008, and sworn in as president of Paraguay on August 15, 2008. Lugo Méndez, named bishop at the age of 44, resigned as bishop and requested laicization in order to run for office, for which permission was denied. The decision was reversed after he won the presidency.[114] Since then, three women have come forward claiming he fathered their children while he served as bishop, one claiming that other Paraguayan bishops knew of his duality as early as 2004.

While Lugo Méndez's intent seems to have been political reform, he (or at least one of his concubines) may benefit from his laicization. Milingo never sought an exception from the rule of celibacy to allow political involvement; he steadfastly argued against what he saw as a sexually corrupt church. He and his movement flatly argue for married clergy, upending terms agreed to by Catholicism and Orthodoxy regarding deacons and priests: a married man may be ordained but an ordained man may not get married, and wholly opposing the common Orthodox-Catholic rule that bishops must be celibate (either monks, widowers, or lifelong celibates). Milingo does not distinguish the before and after conditions of the married priesthood but repeatedly and forcefully argues that priests should be married.

Milingo repeatedly connects priestly celibacy to the multiple tragedies of alcoholism, sex abuse, and loneliness among celibate priests, and in a 2006 press conference, publicly asked if the Vatican "is in such a state of denial that it cannot see the need for a married priesthood?"[115] Milingo's press conference came on the heels of a rare meeting of the members of the Roman Curia, apparently called to discuss the Milingo situation. No report was ever issued from the secret November 16, 2006, meeting, and Milingo asked in his press conference if that might be because the Curia actually discussed the possibility of a married priesthood. "We can hardly believe that a meeting of the Cardinals who head the Dicasteries was called to simply reaffirm celibacy. The report that was not released is the important one. What did the Cardinals say about a married priesthood? Is the Vatican in such a state of denial that it cannot see the need for a married priesthood?"[116]

In fact, despite a number of interventions regarding a married priesthood during the Twenty-first Synod of Bishops on the Eucharist, held in Rome, synod documents give ample evidence of Rome's overall resistance to a wider married priesthood. Multiple interventions decried the lack of priests for faithful starving for Eucharist, but there were few interventions on possibilities for married priests. Cardinal

Angelo Scola (b. 1941), Patriarch of Venice, suggested ordaining *viri probati* (tested married men, leaders in their faith communities) as "Mass priests"; Bishop Denis G. Browne (b. 1937) of Hamilton, New Zealand, wondered about the return of married former priests to active ministry, saying: "We as church need to be continually open to finding ways in which the Eucharist can become easily available to all of our faithful people. We need to be sensitive to the questions that the faithful often ask us, e.g., 'Why does it seem to be possible for former married priests of the Anglican Communion to be ordained and function as Catholic priests, while former Catholic priests who have been dispensed from the vow of celibacy are unable to function in any pastoral way?'"[117] These interventions regard only the Latin or Roman Catholic Church, which is in full communion with the Eastern Catholic Churches that never abandoned the ancient tradition of ordaining married men within their patriarchal territories.[118] However, the elderly Cardinal Nasrallah Pierre Sfeir (b. 1920), Patriarch of Antioch (for the Maronite Church in Lebanon), said the married priesthood is problematic in Eastern Churches because a married priest's obligations to his family sometimes compete with his parish commitments or the bishop's ability to move him to another parish.[119] Sfeir's comment bespeaks an intractable clerical attitude toward marriage and, by extension, toward women. It presents no understanding that priests—or at least some priests—could manage priestly ministry and a family quite well and negates the current practice of allowing Catholic ministry by married former Anglican priests. The practice of moving priests from parish to parish every so often is disruptive of family life but not an impossible obstacle to it. (Consider careers as with organizations divergent as the military and IBM.)

Celibacy, rather, can operate as a control mechanism. On the one hand, the ability of a bishop to move a priest at will ensures—to some extent—his control over parish finances and perhaps safeguards against long-term embezzlement. On the other hand, it can infantilize the priest, often causing the development of a fatuous clericalism that is involved only with the clerical "system", and that in the long run does not serve the church.

Other Eastern Catholic hierarchs disagreed with Cardinal Sfeir. Catholic Melkite Patriarch Grégoire III (Loutifi) Laham, BS, head of the Synod of the Greek-Melkite Catholic Church, had already plainly stated that "celibacy has no theological foundation" early in the proceedings, earning a rebuttal from the synod's general relator Cardinal Angelo Scola, Patriarch of Venice. Laham said, "In the Eastern Church married priests are admitted . . . marriage is a symbol of union between Christ and the church," while, Scola asserted that "in the Latin Church theological reasons exist" for celibacy,[120] although he did not detail them.

The most serious point, however, is the one Milingo raised indirectly in his comments about the meeting regarding the Curia's meeting about his situation with Benedict XVI. In these discussions about the ordination of married men to priesthood, each discussant is a celibate male—including and especially those from the Eastern Churches. It is also important to note that, at least among the interventions noted earlier, the more liberal interpretation of the need for a married priesthood came from the younger bishops in attendance.

PERSONAL PRELATURES AND FUTURE POSSIBILITIES

One wonders if the Vatican would ever make concessions that would allow Milingo's group—even though it could now appear to be made up mainly of priests without laity—to become a personal prelature, a non-territorial diocese along the lines of the international Opus Dei.[121]

Or could Milingo's following be considered along the lines of the Society of Saint Pius X? In 1988, Pope John Paul II established the Pontifical Commission Ecclesia Dei to deal specifically and directly with Archbishop Lefebvre's followers, especially in light of his ordination of four of the society's priests as bishops. The pope minced no words in declaring those clerics excommunicated:

> In itself, this act was one of *disobedience* to the Roman Pontiff in a very grave matter and of supreme importance for the unity of the church, such as is the ordination of bishops whereby the apostolic succession is sacramentally perpetuated. Hence such disobedience—which implies in practice the rejection of the Roman primacy—constitutes a *schismatic* act.(3) In performing such an act, notwithstanding the formal *canonical warning* sent to them by the Cardinal Prefect of the Congregation for Bishops on 17 June last, Mons. Lefebvre and the priests Bernard Fellay, Bernard Tissier de Mallerais, Richard Williamson and Alfonso de Galarreta, have incurred the grave penalty of excommunication envisaged by ecclesiastical law.[122]

However, the Commission also ensured that the Latin Mass was available to Roman Catholics who wanted it, within the limitations: "respect must everywhere be shown for the feelings of all those who are attached to the Latin liturgical tradition, by a wide and generous application of the directives already issued some time ago by the

Apostolic See for the use of the Roman Missal according to the typical edition of 1962."[123] In 2008, Commission Prefect, Cardinal Darío Castrillón Hoyos, offered personal prelature status to the Society of Saint Pius X provided it would accede to four points before the end of the month.[124] According to the Society of Saint Pius X:

> Cardinal Castrillon Hoyos' document expressed five demands: besides a posi-
> tive answer requested before the end of June [2008], the Society of St. Pius X,
> in the person of its General Superior, had to commit itself (1) "*to give a response
> proportionate to the pope's generosity*"; (2) "*to avoid any public comment which
> would not respect the person of the Holy Father and would have a negative impact
> upon ecclesial charity,*" (3) "*to avoid claiming a magisterium superior to the Holy
> Father's and not to set the Society in opposition to the Church,*" (4) "*to demonstrate
> its will to act in all honesty and ecclesial charity, and in the respect of the authority
> of the Vicar of Christ.*"[125]

At issue with the society, as with Married Priests Now! and so many other breakaway formerly Catholic groups, is papal authority. In the case of Milingo, it is the discipline of married priests; in the case of the Society of Saint Pius X some issues are theological. At their root, the problems regarding the society are disciplinary: it rejects certain docu-ments of the Second Vatican Council.

By accepting personal prelature status, the Society, which says it is active in at least 31 countries, could return this rapidly growing move-ment to union with Rome. The Tridentine Mass is already permitted where local diocesan bishops find it welcome and needed.[126] Society sacraments and orders are valid—at least their priestly and episcopal orders are valid, and their celebration of Eucharist is valid. Catholics who receive absolution after confession to society priests are validly absolved, assuming they do not know the difference or are in dire need. In fact, any validly ordained priest—schismatic, laicized, or oth-erwise without faculties—can absolve in an emergency.

The existing papal permission for the 1570 Tridentine Mass may not be enough for the Society of Saint Pius X to accept Rome's offer of personal prelature status, even though it could create a canonical home for those who prefer the older liturgy. Until that occurs, how-ever, the Society is in schism from the Catholic Church, which defines schism as "the withdrawal of submission to the Supreme Pontiff or from communion with the members of the Church subject to him" (Can. 751).

By analogy, the followers of Massachusetts former Jesuit Leonard Feeney, who was excommunicated in 1953 for refusing to accede to ecclesiastical authority, were similarly schismatic. Feeney, who refused to stop preaching "outside the church there is no salvation," established a religious order of men and of women, the Slaves of the Immaculate Heart of Mary (*Mancipia Immaculati Cordis Mariae*, or MICM). He was formally reconciled with the church in 1972 and chose to profess the Athanasian Creed, one of the three creeds accepted by the church, the others being the Nicene and Apostles' Creeds. The Athanasian Creed begins, "Whoever wishes to be saved needs above all else to hold the Catholic Faith; unless each one preserves this whole and entire, he will without a doubt perish in eternity." And ends, "This is the Catholic Faith; unless everyone believes this faithfully and firmly, he cannot be saved."[127] Other Creeds cannot be so easily interpreted to say "outside the Church there is no salvation." Followers of Feeney, members of the Slaves of the Immaculate Heart of Mary split in 1971. One group became an autonomous (Roman Catholic) Benedictine monastery of men in Still River, Massachusetts, which now celebrates Mass in English. Others in Still River, where they were founded, have been regularized.

However, there are groups in Richmond, New Hampshire; Ohio; and California that are not regularized. Like the Society of Saint Pius X, they can be called "traditionalists," and probably "schismatic."

These groups—the Society of Saint Pius X and the followers of Leonard Feeney—are like the followers of Milingo with one major distinction: married clergy. All three argue they are maintaining tradition, but only one seeks to legitimize the wives of priests.

THE UNDERGROUND CHURCH IN CZECHOSLOVAKIA

The questions of communion and authority that plague groups that break away from the Catholic Church are not easily overcome. Typically, the longer the split endures, provided the split-off group prospers, the harder it is for its leadership to accept the juridical authority of Rome, even where there are no real doctrinal distinctions.

The cases of the Society of Saint Pius X and of the followers of Leonard Feeney are distinct in that they believe they are adhering to an older tradition of Catholicism, one that was dismantled by the reforms and changes of Vatican II.

The followers of Archbishop Milingo, on the other hand, believe Vatican II did not go far enough, in that it did not reinstitute the tradition of a married priesthood in the Western Church. While there have been a few instances of married men becoming Latin Rite Catholic priests, these are typically in the context of men already serving as ministers of other Christian denominations (usually Anglican). One interesting exception is the regularization of married men ordained as priests and bishops in the Czech underground church by Felix M. Davídek (1921–1988).

Davídek, a priest of Brno, in Moravia, the Czech Republic, was ordained bishop in 1967 by Bishop Jan Blaha (b. 1938), one day after Blaha was ordained bishop by Bishop Peter Dubovský, SJ (1921–2008), Auxiliary Bishop of Banská Bystrica, Slovakia. Today the Catholic Church recognizes two bishops ordained by Davídek: Oskar Formánek, SJ (1915–91), and Dusan Spiridion Spiner (b. 1950). Spiner agreed in 1992 not to act as a bishop and currently lives in Olomouc in Moravia, Czech Republic.

Davídek also ordained a number of married men as priests in the underground Czech church, called *Koinótés*, which existed in hiding from approximately 1964 to 1989. After the fall of communism in Czechoslovakia, the Catholic Church absorbed the underground church. Fifty celibate male priests became Latin Rite priests; 18 married male priests became Eastern Catholic priests.[128] Four married male priests refused to be conditionally reordained on the grounds that they did not need a second, conditional ordination or that they refused to become Eastern Rite priests.[129] One of these married priests, Jan Kofroň, was re-ordained conditionally (*sub conditione*) in June 2008 by Václav Maly (b. 1950), Catholic auxiliary bishop of Prague, and serves as a married Catholic priest.

There are others ordained in *Koinótés* who prefer to be married Latin Rite, Roman Catholic priests. One solution proposed during the papacy of Benedict XVI is to incorporate these men into Eastern Catholic Churches by exception and grant them bi-ritual status, meaning they would technically belong to an Eastern Catholic Church that allows married priests but would function "bi-ritually" as Roman Catholic priests.

SOME CONCLUSIONS

The difficulties of married priests are clearly juridical and can have juridical resolutions. As with Davídek's priests and bishops, one can barely mount an argument against the sacramental validity of Milingo's priestly and episcopal ordinations. However, Rome has stated it does not recognize Milingo's ordinations or consecrations and does not intend to do so. Therefore, unlike the priests and bishops of *Koinótés*, Rome does not seem willing to gather Milingo and his followers into the fold.

Meanwhile, the four men Milingo ordained as bishops in the United States—Peter Paul Brennan, Joseph J. Gouthro, Patrick E. Trujillo, and

George Augustus Stallings—have distanced themselves from Milingo, who does not appear to have a significant structure or following outside Africa. Married Priests USA, the successor group in the United States to Married Priests Now! counts Peter Paul Brennan as president. George Stallings has left the group and no longer makes mention of his episcopal consecration by Milingo[130]

Milingo seems to be mostly attracting men who have left Catholic priesthood for marriage. That is, his priest-followers in Africa appear to be former Roman Catholic priests, ordained validly and licitly within their former dioceses. While Milingo did not at first have much of a ministerial structure or a coherent hierarchy in a restricted territory (such as Davídek had with *Koinótés*), he may have addressed these lacks by his enthronement as Patriarch of Southern Africa in what appears to be a church of his own making.

The clandestine ordinations of married men in a church suffering the ravages of communism were well accepted by the Czech Church in part because of tradition and in part because of necessity. Two-thirds of the *Koinótés* priests were celibate; one-third were married.[131] Rome absorbed the celibate priests to the Latin Rite, requiring conditional re-ordination. Married priests were required to accept both conditional re-ordination and the transfer of Rite to a Byzantine-Slavic Rite despite a surfeit of married Eastern Catholic priests.

As for Milingo, the Vatican appears at this point to doubt his sanity, which would cause it to deny validity to his ordinations. The fact that his follower-bishops have broken away from him and that CORPUS as an organization has distanced itself from him seem to be in line with what may be the Vatican's reasoning. While Milingo's ordinations are clearly illicit, they also could be invalid due to defective form if Milingo was judged to be (or suspected of being) mentally unstable.

The distinctions in these situations are interesting and important. Davídek and Lefebvre ordained priests and consecrated bishops irregularly. Rome has granted liceity to some of Davídek's ordinations and consecrations, but not all. That is, the ordinations and consecrations were performed by a validly consecrated bishop, Davídek; some have been accepted, some were accepted conditionally, and some were not accepted at all. Again, among Davídek's episcopal consecrations, Rome recognizes those of Bishop Oskar Formánek, SJ (1915–91), and Bishop Dusan Spiridion Spiner (b. 1950).

A major distinction between Davídek and Lefebvre is that Lefebvre had prior warning, and refusal of permission, to consecrate (and ordain) and was considered to have left the Catholic Church at the time he ordained and consecrated. For example, with Bishop Emeritus Antônio de Castro Mayer (1904–1991) of Campos, Brazil, as co-consecrator, Lefebvre consecrated four SSPX priests as bishops: Bernard Tissier de Mallerais, Richard Williamson, Alfonso de Galarreta, and Bernard Fellay. None of the four—despite the provenance of their orders and their penalties of excommunication having been lifted—is considered a Roman Catholic bishop.

Nevertheless, Davídek, operating under the cloak of secrecy, fully intended to do as the Catholic Church does and—so far as is known—ordained and consecrated with the proper matter and form. Likewise, it can be argued that Lefebvre intended to do as the church does, at least in his ordination of his four original bishops, despite his renouncing of certain documents of the Second Vatican Council, but he had in effect left the Catholic Church, and so could not act in concert with it.

Catholic theology of ordination—at least in the West—most clearly renders the ordinations performed by Davídek as at least possibly valid. Those who returned to non-clandestine ministry were conditionally (not unconditionally) re-ordained, and two of the several men consecrated bishops in the underground church—Formánek and Spiner—are recognized as validly ordained bishops.

So at least in this retrospective view, those ordained before any definitive break with Rome (such as Milingo's marriage to Maria Sung and Lefebvre's refusal to adhere to Roman directives) would be considered validly, even licitly, ordained and/or consecrated, whereas those ordained or consecrated after Milingo or Lefebvre's break with Rome are neither.

Here Rome's logic seems to follow more closely that of the Eastern Churches. While in the Eastern Churches (Catholic and Orthodox) absolute ordination is theoretically impossible because ordination depends on being ordained to serve a specific community, Western notions of ordination hold more strictly to the validity or invalidity of the action of the ordaining prelate. Questions of liceity do not in and of themselves render ordinations valid or invalid. But questions of communion with Rome do.

So if a bishop (for example, Bishop Davídek) within his purview as leader of *Koinótés* intended to do as the church does in ordaining priests and consecrating bishops for a specific community in need, these are more easily recognized and regularized. But if a bishop (for example, Milingo or Lefebvre) has definitively broken from the church, by his actions or stated beliefs or both, his ordinations and/ or consecrations cannot be considered validly Roman Catholic.

Of course, the latter battery of individual cases resulting from the actions of Milingo and Lefebvre presents a canonical noodle soup, should Rome ever attempt to regularize them. But the first test of validity, it would seem, is whether the ordaining prelate intended to do as the Catholic Church does and in communion with it. For both Milingo and Lefebvre, this appears to be an insurmountable obstacle.

ORDAINED WOMEN IN THE UNDERGROUND CHURCH

The juridical complications presented by Emmanuel Milingo, Marcel-François Lefebvre, and Felix Maria Davídek result from their sacramental power as bishops. None had clear juridical authority to ordain bishops. Lefebvre argued necessity, which is more easily recognized and argued in the case of the Czech underground church.

Lefebvre cites Canon 1323 of the Code of Canon Law, which exempts persons who break the law from penalty, but only in cases of true necessity and where there seems no alternative. However, as commentators point out, "if the legal violations . . . will cause significant pastoral damage, an offender is not exempt from all imputability."[1]

Davídek argued genuine need for pastoral care and sacraments, with the approval of *Koinótés* members. Even so, the Disciplinary Document issued by the Congregation for the Doctrine of the Faith regarding *Koinótés* priests calls their ordinations illicit and attempts to cast doubt on their validity. The document intimates that the ordaining prelate, Davídek, did not following proper "form," which includes intent, perhaps insinuating that Davídek's purported defective intent was due to mental instability.

After all, Rome could reason, who in his right mind would ordain a woman? After discussion that nearly split *Koinótés*, Davídek ordained women as deacons and as priests. Were they sacramentally ordained? Once the Catholic Church could again operate openly, Czech church spokesmen routinely ducked questions regarding the women, admitting only: "We are dealing with these cases," (Rev. Dominik Duka said), "the women in the meantime have agreed not to exercise these functions."[2]

One of the women ordained was Ludmila Javorová (b. 1932), who affirmed both her priesthood and her accession to authority in interviews with Hartford Seminary professor Miriam Therese Winter. Winter published a full-length version of Javorová's story in 2001 as *Out of the Depths: The Story of Ludmila Javorova, Ordained Roman Catholic Priest*:

> Winter continued, "Ludmila says, 'If the bishop says I do not have faculties,'"— the right to perform priestly functions—"'then I don't' I pushed her on that. 'Do you really think they took the priesthood away from you?' 'Absolutely not,' she replied, 'I am a priest forever.'
>
> "There's a difference, you see," said Winter, "between faculties and priest-hood. Ludmila has distinguished between the sacramental—the gift from God, the call, the vocation—and the canonical, the authoritative. She says the bish-ops and Rome have the right to rescind her faculties, but they can never take away her priesthood."[3]

Davídek ordained Javorová in 1970 for *Koinótés*. Winter reports that *Koinótés* had two initial bishops—Davídek and Jan Blaha, and, eventu-ally 18 others—17 of whom were consecrated by Davídek, who also ordained approximately 68 priests.[4] It seems as many as six women were ordained as deacons and Javorová at least also as priest. None functions publicly.[5]

Interesting conditions led to the ordinations of women in *Koinótés*. Davídek was the accepted head of the underground church, which he initiated following the August 1968 Soviet invasion of Czechoslova-kia. The church spread, especially through Moravia, and by late 1970 Davídek was determined to ordain women. His argument was that women had been excluded from ordination for only the past thou-sand years and there was no dogmatic foundation for their exclusion. In his view, "neolithic thinking" about women solidified objections to their ordination. Convinced his local church had the right, he called a pastoral synod to discuss the church's needs. Uppermost on the agenda was the ordination of women (married men had already been ordained and were part of the synod proceedings.)

The story of the synod is told by Masaryk University professors Petr Fiala and Jiří Hanuš, who had access to the private archives of Lud-mila Javorová, who remains the most publicly known of the women ordained. Javorová served as Vicar General of *Koinótés*. In the now-defunct British periodical *The Month*, Fiala and Hanuš present the five major points Davídek submitted to the synod in support of the ordination of women for *Koinótés*:

1) The Church all over the world should feel obliged to respect the *kairos*; 2) The ordination of women under certain circumstances can be defended on pastoral-sociological grounds; 3) The cultural-anthropological aspect of the ordination of women should also be regarded as important; 4) The ordination of women is supported by the tradition of the Church; 5) Consequently, necessary alterations should be made to Canon Law.[6]

The synod proceeded to meet secretly in the small village of Kobeřice. Davídek pressed his point: "Today we recognize that, indeed, under the influence of gnosis and also under the influence of paganism, something in the Church has been brought to a halt if women could hold the office of deacon in early Christianity but not in the twentieth century. If we want to return to the invigorating sources of the early Christians in everything else, then we must also embrace this part of their practice. The Church should refrain from preventing it."[7] There was significant opposition to ordaining women on the part of three of the four bishops who ended up leaving *Koinótés* within a year.[8] The vote on ordaining women, taken at 5:00 a.m. on December 26, 1970, resulted in a tie.

Ludmila Javorová's private archives included sound recordings of the synod proceedings. Fiala and Hanuš translated and published large portions of Davídek's synod remarks, including the following:

I believe that this Pastoral Synod deals with a concrete and necessary practice in a given region. Different regions have different problems—it has been so since the beginning of the Church. Now, we have the basic guiding principle: what to do for salvation, and how to do it best in a particular place. The synod covers all Czecho-Slovak Churches, plus 72 Czech parishes from Romania and settled in this country. The pastoral realm of our synod consists of the sectors of Bohemia, Moravia and Slovakia and concerns three (possibly four) rites. Furthermore, we must bear in mind that the Synod is not territorial (not related to any diocese). In ecclesiology, the basic emphasis is laid on calling (the mission of the Church). Nowadays, each parish community represents a perfect Church because Christ is present in it and the connection with the Pope is maintained. Two conditions are necessary for a schism: a deliberate break from Rome, and an agreement by both sides. This is the aspect of *votum ecclesiae*, which I consider very important. The Pope is not the whole Church just as you and I are not the whole Church. Therefore, canonical excommunication only concerns individuals in the state of *contra dogmatum*, not the extending of orthodox practices. Everything related to the salvation of souls belongs to the orthodox practice . . . Magisterium is also characteristic of the whole Church, though it legally extends only to the bishops. The vocation to teach is ascribed to the whole Church. The entire Church is infallible. Therefore, I consider the dogmatic aspect to be the fundamental premise.[9]

Soon after the synod closed, Davídek ordained Ludmila Javorová as priest.[10] The question perdured: in doing so was "the connection with the pope" maintained? If so, was Ludmilla, already a deacon, a validly ordained Catholic priest?

PART III

JURIDICAL AUTHORITY,
SACRAMENTAL AUTHORITY, AND
WOMEN'S ORDINATION

Canon 749.1. The Supreme Pontiff, in virtue of his office, possesses infallible teaching authority when, as supreme pastor and teacher of all the faithful, whose task is to confirm his fellow believers in the faith, he proclaims with a definitive act that a doctrine of faith or morals is to be held as such.

2. The college of bishops also possesses infallible teaching authority when the bishops exercise their teaching office gathered together in an ecumenical council, when, as teachers and judges of faith and morals, they declare that for the universal Church a doctrine of faith or morals must be definitively held; they also exercise it scattered throughout the world but united in a communion among themselves and with the successor of Peter when together with that same Roman Pontiff in their capacity as authentic teachers of faith and morals they agree on an opinion to be held as definitive.

3. No doctrine is understood to be infallibly defined unless it is clearly established as such.

—Code of Canon Law

While Bishop Bruskewitz can levy his juridical authority without challenge within the confines of his diocese, and Archbishop Milingo (like the late Bishops Lefebvre and Davídek) can attempt to confer valid sacraments worldwide, each conforms in his own way to the teachings of the Catholic Church.

Bishop Bruskewitz insists he is in union with the Catholic Church via his direct relationship with the Pope. Others find his communion flawed, in that he refuses to act in concert with the other bishops of his province. Still, he remains in doctrinal accord with the magisterium.

Archbishop Milingo, on the other hand, directly challenges what he believes is an unnecessary administrative requirement—priestly celibacy—and perhaps validly confers priestly and episcopal orders on married men. He does not act according to current law, is considered as having left the Catholic Church, and has actually been excommunicated. Until his affiliation with Moon, however, he was in doctrinal accord with the magisterium.

Bishop Lefebvre was perhaps more like Bishop Bruskewitz in his insistence on communion and authority dependent on the letter of the law as its exercise is reserved to the bishop, although he did not act in accordance with the directives of Rome. Lefebvre considered himself in doctrinal accord with the magisterium even though he disagreed with pertinent teachings, especially those emanating from Vatican II.

Bishop Davídek is perhaps more like Archbishop Milingo in his dismissal of church requirements in order to supply for a church in need, specifically in the matter of married priests, and more like Bishop Bruskewitz in his asserting juridical authority over his defined underground church. Some of Davídek's actions have been retroactively ratified, in whole or in part. Some of his episcopal ordinations have been deemed valid. Some of the priests he ordained have been conditionally re-ordained, as opposed to unconditionally ordained, allowing for the possibility that an unrepeatable sacrament of holy orders had already been imparted. Such is particularly important in considering the cases of the women Davídek ordained. Davídek believed he was in doctrinal accord with the magisterium, arguing that the matter of women's ordination revolved around liceity, not validity.

The distinctions and similarities between and among these bishops are echoed in Canon 749, quoted earlier, on the teaching authority of the pope and the bishops. Bishop Bruskewitz depends on his direct juridical relationship to the pope; Archbishop Milingo and Bishop Lefebvre depend on their direct sacramental relationship to the apostles. Bishop Davídek sought to provide bishops, priests, and deacons to serve a clandestine community in need. Each bishop believed himself in union with Rome and in accord with church doctrine, arguing that any deviation from practice he might make was not critical to his being in communion with Rome.[1]

But Bishop Davídek ordained women. The most recent statements from the Congregation for the Doctrine of the Faith stipulate that anyone who participates in the ordination of a woman is *latae sententiae* excommunicated. No retroactive excommunication has been announced or levied on Davídek, nor on the women he ordained, although the Congregation for the Doctrine of the Faith did retroactively call his ordinations into question.[2]

From the official Vatican viewpoint, the matter of women priests touches on teachings that mention, if not mandate, an automatic rupture of communion with the Catholic Church. One must carefully distinguish, however, whether pronouncements on the subject are irreformably doctrinal and comprise infallible teaching that would compromise sacramental authority or whether they are "orthodox practices" (as Davídek claimed) that create juridical mandates, which make ordinations of women illicit, while not necessarily invalid.

Two modern documents frame the discussion on women priests in the Catholic Church: (1) the Congregation for the Doctrine of the Faith's Declaration on the Question of Admission of Women to the Ministerial Priesthood (*Inter Insigniores*) (October 15, 1976), and (2) John Paul II's apostolic letter On Reserving Priestly Ordination to Men Alone (*Ordinatio Sacerdotalis*) (May 22, 1994). Each argues that the ban on women priests is an unchangeable part of Catholic tradition.[3]

Inter Insigniores makes two major points: (1) the priest must physically resemble Christ (the "iconic argument"); and (2) Jesus chose male apostles and the Catholic Church is bound by his choice (the "argument from authority"). *Ordinatio Sacerdotalis* drops the iconic argument but retains the argument from authority. Following the publication of *Ordinatio Sacerdotalis*, the Congregation for the Doctrine of the Faith published its "*Responsum ad Propositum Dubium* Concerning the Teaching Contained in '*Ordinatio Sacerdotalis*'" (October 28, 1995).

The latter of the three documents sets forth an opinion of a curial office: that the Catholic Church does not have the authority to confer priestly ordination on women is to be held definitively.[4] It cannot be overlooked that the signers of this opinion, Joseph Ratzinger and Tarcisco Bertone, are now pope and Secretary of State of the Vatican. However, while the opinion of infallibility rendered by the Congregation for the Doctrine of the Faith might seem to have more weight given the election of Benedict XVI, it must be again underscored there is neither a *de jure divino* assertion of infallibility nor any clear papal statement relative to the infallibility of *Ordinatio Sacerdotalis*, which solely deals with priesthood and is based on the "argument from authority." As in the canon at the head of this section, nothing is infallible unless it is clearly defined as such.[5]

Pope Benedict XVI's involvement with the question of women priests can probably be traced to the 1976 document. In 1969, then-Father Ratzinger was named among the first theologians comprising the International Theological Commission, which was established as an advisory board to the Congregation for the Doctrine of the Faith.[6] His five-year term was renewed, it appears, until he became prefect of the Congregation in 1981. At that time, he concurrently became president of both the International Theological Commission and the Papal Biblical Commission, each of which previously had addressed the question of women priests.

When the Pontifical Biblical Commission examined the question, it did not find for or against women priests. The Vatican website posts thirty-six documents of the Pontifical Biblical Commission (from 1905 to 2008), but not the 1976 Report that found no evidence in Scripture to decide the question of women priests. The Commission report concludes,

> It does not seem that the New Testament by itself alone will permit us to settle in a clear way and once and for all the problem of the possible accession of women to the presbyterate.
>
> However, some think that in the scriptures there are sufficient indications to exclude this possibility, considering that the sacraments of eucharist and reconciliation have a special link with the person of Christ and therefore with the male hierarchy, as borne out by the New Testament.
>
> Others, on the contrary, wonder if the church hierarchy, entrusted with the sacramental economy, would be able to entrust the ministries of eucharist and reconciliation to women in light of circumstances, without going against Christ's original intentions.[7]

So there are really three documents to consider: one each from the Pontifical Biblical Commission, the International Theological Commission, and the apostolic letter of Pope John Paul II, as well as the International Theological Commission's *Responsum ad Dubium* opinion on the latter of the three. The perduring question is whether (and how) current legislation regarding women priests is to be held, particularly since it appears juridically rooted. Is the teaching infallible?

INFALLIBILITY

Catholic Church teaching on infallibility is roundly misunderstood by the general public. The doctrine of infallibility codified in Canon 749 was formally defined by the First Vatican Council in 1870: the pope, speaking *ex cathedra* on a matter of faith or morals, is "infallible."[8] The *ex cathedra* pronouncement is rare.

Within the context of hierarchical teaching, the principal mark of infallibility, the rare clear and unequivocal pronouncement by a pope on a matter of faith and morals, is joined by other ways doctrine may be infallibly defined and taught. A second means by which a teaching can be deemed infallible is where the teaching is evidenced in the exercise of the collective teaching authority of the larger body of bishops. This second means can be understood where the bishops are either gathered in an ecumenical council or when, together with the "Roman Pontiff in their capacity as authentic teachers of faith and morals, they agree on an opinion to be held as definitive" (Canon 749, para. 2).

These two principal means of defining areas requiring necessary ascent on matters of faith and morals reflect the principals of collegiality and ultimate decision making described earlier. When the pope makes a formal and clearly defined infallible pronouncement on faith or morals, it is considered part of dogma. When an entire ecumenical council of the world's bishops agrees on a point of doctrine, that determination also is said to be infallible. The question here revolves around whether the scattered bishops of the world are in union with the Roman pontiff on a teaching that a curial office has opined to be infallible. That is, the curial office calls the teaching infallible and says is to be definitively held. But do the world's bishops agree to the status of the teaching and its content, or both, or neither?

Pre–Vatican II textbook theology presents the determinations of ecumenical councils and final pronouncements by the pope as infallible and adds a third means of "infallibity", arguing that doctrinal decrees of Vatican curial offices express the intent of the pope and therefore require "religious assent of the mind" (the usual term is "*obsequium religiosum*").[9] Such seems to be a back formation: papal staff members propose a doctrine and then require the entire church (including bishops) to hold it definitively, rather than the other way around. The notion of expanded power and authority of the Curia, independent of ecumenical councils of bishops, has come to be termed "creeping infallibility."[10]

Whether the third means of "infallibility" is agreed to or not, those who accept ordination and/or office in the church must affirm its possibility in respect to magisterial teaching. In 1989, the Congregation for the Doctrine of the Faith added three paragraphs to the profession of faith required of every person who is to be ordained or receive a sacred office.[11] The new profession of faith comprises the Nicene-Constantinopolitan Creed, plus affirmations that the individual (1) believes all divine revelation, even if not included in the Creed; (2) holds all the Catholic Church has definitively taught; and (3) adheres with *obsequium* to all official proclamations, even those not defined as definitive.[12] Such would rule out women's ordination, since women to be ordained apparently would have to affirm they could not be ordained.

So, then, what about women's ordination? While a bishop has episcopal powers, and real (or presumed jurisdiction) he cannot override definitive teachings, particularly if he has sworn the new profession of faith.[13] A bishop acts either in communion with Rome or not. As Davídek said: "In ecclesiology, the basic emphasis is laid on calling (the mission of the Church). Nowadays, each parish community represents a perfect Church because Christ is present in it and the connection with the Pope is maintained. Two conditions are necessary for a schism: a deliberate break from Rome, and an agreement by both sides."[14] Davídek presents a basic ecclesiology. The presence of Christ within the parish community and that community's connection with Rome are sufficient for "church." He argues that it is not sufficient for one "church" or the other to sever ties unilaterally. There must be a two-sided agreement on the matter. While Milingo did not (and does not) appear to have a "church," both Davídek and Lefebvre arguably did, Davídek more so than Lefebvre. Did either deliberately break from Rome? Was any break two-sided?

The Catholic Church does not ordain women, and has presented theological argumentation that it cannot ordain women as priests. Hence it would follow that a bishop who ordains a woman breaks with Rome. But those who argue women are capable of being ordained (including Davídek) see the question of the ordination of women as disciplinary (therefore, juridical) and not doctrinal. Further, with Davídek those who argue women are capable of being ordained accept the ordination of women where it is the will of the community.

Independent of a formal declaration of infallibility (by a pope or ecumenical council), others argue that the disciplinary reflects the doctrinal and the constant teaching of the church, agreed to by the world's bishops, forbids women priests. Still others argue the teaching that women may not be ordained is infallible because it has been defined by the Curia acting on behalf of the pope, and the ban on women priests therefore falls into the third method of infallible statement.

On the latter point, that the ban on women priests is infallible because of the opinion levied by the Curia, many canonists offer an opposing view. In 2000, the editors of the Paulist Press *New Commentary on the Code of Canon Law* argued,

> The statement by the CDF of October 28, 1995 (Origins 25 [November 30, 1995] 401, 403), that the teaching to the effect that the church has no authority to confer priestly ordination on women requires the definitive

assent of the faithful since "it has been set forth infallibly by the ordinary and universal Magisterium" is an exaggeration. The teaching (restated in the applet *Ordinatio sacerdotalis*, May 22, 1994, Origins 24 [June 9, 1994] 50–52) does not meet the test of explicitness; neither the pope nor the college of bishops declared that they were making of an infallible definition, nor has it been demonstrated that the whole body of Catholic bishops has taught the doctrine in such as way as to oblige the faithful to give definitive assent. Consequently its infallibility can hardly be considered "manifestly evident."[15]

The operative question, then, becomes: is the teaching regarding women's ordination infallible? As described earlier, there are conflicting views, both about the means to assert infallibility and whether the teaching itself is infallible. Papal pronouncements *ex cathedra* and conciliar teachings by the bishops are "infallible." It is the third means, curial pronouncements, which has engendered the term "creeping infallibility" and contributed to the controversy.

Hence two questions arise: (1) is the teaching on the ordination of women as priests (and bishops) infallible? and (2) if that teaching is infallible, is there anything in Catholic history, doctrine, theology, or law that could overturn the determination of infallibility?

Canonist Ladislas M. Orsy, in *Receiving the Council: Theological and Canonical Insights and Debates*,[16] reviews the question in light of Vatican II. Part of Orsy's book reproduces a "conversation" of sorts carried out between him and then-Cardinal Ratzinger on the specific point of definitive teaching. The central question, Orsy states, is "*Has there been an extension of the doctrine of papal infallibility by the introduction of the category of 'definitive teaching?'*" Orsy writes if the answer is yes, there is an extension of papal infallibility to the category of "definitive teaching," then this event, this extension, is as momentous as Vatican I's initial definition of infallibility. If the answer is no, papal infallibility does not extend to "definitive teaching," then the church has a duty to examine the category's relative weight.[17]

In examining the question, Orsy quotes Louvain theologian Gérard Philips (1899–1972), who was prominent in the development of Vatican II's Dogmatic Constitution on the Church *(Lumen Gentium)*. Philips states the concerns of the First Vatican Council regarding papal infallibility concerned revelation, and the concerns of the Second Vatican Council specified that infallibility extends to the conservation of the deposit of the faith. Philips writes that the Council left the technical explication of other matters, including dogmatic facts, to the realm of technical treatises of professional theologians.[18]

Orsy continues, "the Council Fathers understood but did not define that—if the need ever arose—the pope could exercise his infallibility with a solemn *ex cathedra* act to affirm a truth that is not explicitly in the revelation but is absolutely necessary to safeguard it."[19]

During 1998–1999 Orsy exchanged opinions with Cardinal Ratzinger, all published in the German theological periodical *Stimmen der Zeit*. Orsy detailed what he saw as a new category of infallible statements. Ratzinger essentially responded that "the second level of knowledge" is not a novelty. He also defended the expansion of the term "infallible" as well as the 1989 new and expanded Profession of Faith and Oath of Fidelity,[20] which was even then under revision.[21] When sending his essays to the journal, Ratzinger never used official letterhead of the Congregation for the Doctrine of the Faith.[22]

The published "debate" comprised four essays, an initial essay by Orsy, a response by Ratzinger, another essay by Orsy, another response by Ratzinger, and final comments by Orsy and revolved around the specific authority of two ecclesiastical documents regarding the Profession of Faith and Oath of Fidelity: John Paul II's *motu proprio Ad Tuendam Fidem* (May 18, 1998) and the accompanying commentary by the Congregation for the Doctrine of the Faith under the presidency of then Cardinal Ratzinger.[23]

Central to the *motu proprio* was the addition to Canon 750 of the Code of Canon Law, as follows:

> § 2. Furthermore, each and everything set forth definitively by the Magisterium of the Church regarding teaching on faith and morals must be firmly accepted and held; namely, those things required for the holy keeping and faithful exposition of the deposit of faith; therefore, anyone who rejects propositions which are to be held definitively sets himself against the teaching of the Catholic Church.[24]

The explicit purpose of the *motu proprio* was to codify the Congregation for the Doctrine of the Faith's 1989 Profession of Faith and Oath of Fidelity, a description of which begins the *motu proprio*:

> 1. From the first centuries to the present day, the Church has professed the truths of her faith in Christ and the mystery of his redemption. These truths were subsequently gathered into the Symbols of the faith, today known and proclaimed in common by the faithful in the solemn and festive celebration of Mass as *the Apostles' Creed* or *the Nicene-Constantinopolitan Creed*.
>
> This same *Nicene-Constantinopolitan Creed* is contained in the *Profession of faith* developed by the Congregation for the Doctrine of the Faith, (1) which must be made by specific members of the faithful when they receive an office, that is directly or indirectly related to deeper investigation into the truths of faith and morals, or is united to a particular power in the governance of the Church. (2)[25]

The accompanying commentary, signed by Cardinals Ratzinger and Tarcisco Bertone, states,

9. The Magisterium of the Church, however, teaches a doctrine to be *believed as divinely revealed* (first paragraph) or to be *held definitively* (second paragraph) with an act which is either *defining* or *non-defining*. In the case of a *defining* act, a truth is solemnly defined by an 'ex cathedra' pronouncement by the Roman Pontiff or by the action of an ecumenical council. In the case of a *non-defining* act, a doctrine is taught *infallibly* by the ordinary and universal Magisterium of the Bishops dispersed throughout the world who are in communion with the Successor of Peter. *Such a doctrine can be confirmed or reaffirmed by the Roman Pontiff, even without recourse to a solemn definition*, by declaring explicitly that it belongs to the teaching of the ordinary and universal Magisterium as a truth that is divinely revealed (first paragraph) or as a truth of Catholic doctrine (second paragraph). Consequently, when there has not been a judgment on a doctrine in the solemn form of a definition, but this doctrine, belonging to the inheritance of the *depositum fidei*, is taught by the ordinary and universal Magisterium, which necessarily includes the Pope, such a doctrine is to be understood as having been set forth infallibly. The declaration of *confirmation or reaffirmation* by the Roman Pontiff in this case is not a new dogmatic definition, but a formal attestation of a truth already possessed and infallibly transmitted by the Church.[26]

The contretemps between Ratzinger and Orsy is, in some respects, an exercise in contrasts: Ratzinger, a theologian then on the Curia, and Orsy, a canonist and canon law professor, appear to have been approaching the same topic from different directions. Orsy was interested in whether pronouncements by their very nature or type created law, while Ratzinger was interested in whether pronouncements by their very substance or subject created or required the creation of law. The distinctions are not lost on the topic at hand because once something has been defined as infallible, it cannot be overturned. Hence the application of the term "creeping infallibility" by they who seek further discussion, analysis, even movement on the matter of women priests, as well as the closing remark of Orsy, that the very fact of their debate: "established that the nature of 'definitive doctrine' as it is proposed in the *motu proprio* and explained in its official Commentary can be the object of a legitimate public debate. At the center of an exchange is the question of whether the contents of definitive doctrine, as the examples in the Commentary illustrate them, are or are not identical with the (so-named) 'secondary objects of infallibility' envisaged by Vatican Council I (cf., e.g., DS 3069) that the faithful must accept and hold."[27] At issue is whether in order to be in union with the Catholic Church one must hold that the teaching that the church does not have the authority to ordain women as priests is defined doctrine. That doctrine, however, is that the church does not have the authority to ordain women as priests, not that women are incapable of being ordained.

Independent of the question of infallibility regarding the authority of the church to ordain women, canon law states women cannot be validly ordained. Whether law is attempting to legislate sacramental validity or is merely restating determined theology, Canon 1024 of the 1983 Code of Canon Law plainly states, "A baptized male alone receives sacred ordination validly."[28]

Even so, the vexed question of the ordination of women—as deacons, as priests, as bishops—has ceaselessly spun around in church history. There are genuine examples of women acting as deacons, priests, and bishops. There is historical record of women performing the ministry of each rank of order as well as being ordained.[29] The focus of modern debate has most clearly centered on priesthood and its concomitant sacramental authorities regarding celebration of the sacraments of Eucharist and reconciliation (confession). Curiously, few have noticed that not until the First Lateran Council in 1215 authority to celebrate Eucharist was restricted to priests and bishops.[30]

Despite prior and current legislation, it would seem what the church has done before the church can do again. While discussion continues regarding various statements of curial offices, there has been no plainly infallible statement rendered by a pope or ecumenical council on the question. Even so, no Catholic bishop in communion with Rome has juridical authority to ordain a woman, as deacon, priest, or bishop. So women have, in effect, taken matters into their own hands.

ROMAN CATHOLIC WOMENPRIESTS

Active in the United States, Canada, and Europe, the organization Roman Catholic Womenpriests appears to have at least eight women bishops, including five Americans, and numerous priests and deacons. If the barrier of gender could be overcome, the status of their women bishops—the first two claim to have been ordained by one or possibly two recognized Roman Catholic bishops—can be seen as similar to those bishops ordained by Archbishop Emmanuel Milingo: clearly illicit, but possibly valid, episcopal ordination, but *latae sententiae* (automatic) excommunication. The claim of Roman Catholic Womenpriests that their ordinations are necessary to their own communities echoes the views of Lefebvre and Davídek. It cannot be forgotten, however, that contemporary Catholic Church teaching is that female gender is a diriment (insurmountable) impediment to orders, unable to be dispensed from.[31]

The first seven women priests of the movement, ordained as priests on a riverboat on the Danube on June 29, 2002, were formally excommunicated by the Congregation for the Doctrine of the Faith. The ordinations were performed by Argentine Independent Catholic Bishop Rómulo Antonio Braschi (b. 1941) and Ferdinand (Raphael) Regelsberger, a former Benedictine monk of Kremsmünster Abbey in Upper Austria whom Braschi had ordained bishop.[32] Braschi, himself a former Catholic priest, established an independent Catholic Church in Buenos Aires in 1975 and was ordained bishop in 1998 by Free Catholic Bishop Hilarios Karl-Heinz Ungerer and Bishop Roberto Garrido Padin (b. 1945) of the Independent Catholic Apostolic Church of Brazil. Braschi was ordained again in 1999 by Jerónimo José Podestá (1920–2000), an Argentine Roman Catholic bishop who left the church in 1971. Braschi is not recognized by the Vatican as having received valid episcopal orders, and there is speculation as to whether Podestá actually performed the *sub conditione* second episcopal consecration, which would have taken place well after he left the Catholic Church anyway.[33]

The London-based Catholic periodical *The Tablet* reported that Dusan Spiner, a Catholic priest and bishop whose episcopal ordination by Davídek is recognized by the Vatican, was scheduled to participate in the priestly ordinations but did not. *The Tablet* further reported that prior to the Danube ordinations Spiner ordained six of those first seven women as deacons in Austria.[34]

In 2003, two of the "Danube Seven," as they came to be called, Christine Mayr-Lumetzberger (b. 1956) and Gisela Forster (b. 1946), were ordained as bishops for the movement. They in turn have ordained other women as deacons, priests, and bishops.

One unknown is whether Spiner re-ordained any or all the first seven women as priests and who ordained them bishops. At the 2002 Danube ordinations, Mayr-Lumetzberger told *National Catholic Reporter* writer John Allen, Jr., they planned to ask a third bishop (apparently Spiner) for *sub conditione* re-ordinations.[35] While Braschi's claims to validity are tenuous at best, if the first women priests and bishops can trace the provenance of their orders through Spiner to Davídek, they would have at least a partial claim to validity. Also, theoretically at least, they could argue liceity due to necessity in the same manner as by Lefebvre and Davídek.

While the first seven women ordained in the Roman Catholic Womenpriests movement received formal excommunication papers, from the Vatican's point of view other members ordained as deacons, priests, or bishops are considered as having left the Catholic Church, even lacking formal notification or announcement. In the United States, the numbers of Roman Catholic Womenpriests are increasing steadily and include what the group terms "catacomb," or secret, priests and deacons.[36]

The first US ordination ceremonies for the Roman Catholic Womenpriests movement took place in Pittsburgh on July 31, 2006. A second round of North American ordinations (14 deacons and 9 priests) included 2 men, and took place in 2007 in Quebec, Toronto, New York, Santa Barbara, Portland, and Minneapolis. Two women were ordained as priests in St. Louis in November 2007, and the movement shows no signs of stopping, despite local and Vatican opposition and commentary. There were additional ordinations in each succeeding year, and more are planned.

Official retribution began expanding in 2008. Shortly before St. Louis Archbishop Raymond L. Burke left the United States for his new position as Prefect of the Apostolic Signatura (the equivalent of Chief Justice of the United States), he concluded his canonical investigation into the alleged participation of Cincinnati Sister of Charity Louise Lears in the 2007 St. Louis ordinations. In June 2008, Burke determined Lears had violated canon law with sufficient gravity that she could be placed under interdict, specifically,

> The delicts of which Sister Louise Lears is accessed are: 1) the obstinate rejection, after written admonition, of the truth of the faith that it is impossible for a woman to receive ordination to the Sacred Priesthood (cann. 750, para. 2; and 1371, No. 1); 2) the public incitement of the faithful to animosity or hatred toward the Apostolic See or an Ordinary because of an act of ecclesiastical power of ministry (can. 1373); 3) the grave external violation of Divine or Canon Law, with the urgent need to prevent and repair the scandal involved (can. 1399); and 4) prohibited participation in sacred rites (can. 1365).[37]

As a result of his findings, Archbishop Burke placed Louise Lears under interdict—banning her from receiving sacraments—and barred her from holding any church position within his archdiocese. This ended her ministerial position at St. Cronan's Parish in suburban St. Louis. She moved to another diocese to care for her aged and ill mother.

Archbishop Burke left determination on Lears's fourth delict—"prohibited participation in sacred rites"—to the Congregation for the Doctrine of the Faith, which had published a Decree on May 29, 2008, announcing automatic excommunication for anyone who attempted the ordination of a woman: "Without prejudice to the prescript of can. 1378 of the Code of Canon Law, both the one who attempts to confer a sacred order on a woman, and the woman who attempts to receive a sacred order, incur an excommunication *latae sententiae* reserved to the Apostolic See."[38] The Decree, signed by former San Francisco archbishop, now Cardinal William Levada, prefect of the Vatican's Congregation for the Doctrine of the Faith, states that anyone directly participating in the "delict" (crime) of woman's ordination—specifically the ordaining bishops and those ordained—incurs automatic excommunication.

What Lears apparently did, along with other members in the congregation, is participate in a post-ordination second round of "laying on of hands," in which all, or sometimes predesignated members of the assembly, are invited to come forth and lay hands on the newly ordained.[39]

Whether Lears's specific case is clear enough to merit excommunication or not, the Congregation for the Doctrine of the Faith's decree at the time indicates the seriousness with which the Vatican viewed the growing phenomenon of the Roman Catholic Womenpriests movement and presages later additional administrative actions against the ordination of women. The Congregation's sights seem set on two converging phenomena: potential belief among bishops of their personal power, and a growing public acceptance of women's ordination.

Interestingly, the Congregation's decree does not distinguish among orders: deacon, priest, or bishop. To include the diaconate among the other two could indicate an acknowledgement that priestly and episcopal orders could be valid for women, given the strong arguments for women's diaconal orders having been valid and licet in Christianity's past. Further, diaconal orders for women are valid and licet in other churches with which the Catholic Church has mutual recognition agreements.

Alternatively, to include the diaconate with the presbyterate and episcopate effectively precludes the ordination of women as deacons, a notion expressly left aside by earlier documents on the ordination of women as priests, and which was not finally determined in the 2002 statement of the International Theological Commission on the diaconate, *From the Diakonia of Christ to the Diakonia of the Apostles*.[40]

The Congregation's 2007 decree against women's ordination raised more questions than it answered in its two hundred words, and it did not directly speak to Lears's situation or interdict. As a "medicinal penalty" an interdict calls for an individual to recant and applies outside the boundaries of the diocese in which it was levied. Lears's current diocesan bishop can lift it on consultation with Burke, provided she recants her "crime." It is possible she could recant her action (or presumed action) within the ordination ceremonies without having to affirm that women are incapable of receiving ordination. That is, participation in a ceremony of another group or movement is distinct from stating the Catholic Church can ordain women. The problem is whether Lears insists the movement's members are Roman Catholic.

The perduring question, therefore, is whether the women ordained are excommunicated because they participated in an illegal Catholic ordination or because they have left the Catholic Church.

For whatever reason, the canon cited in the decree (C. 1378) does not directly speak to this particular situation. Rather, that canon levies *latae sententiae* interdict on non-priests who attempt to celebrate Eucharist or hear sacramental confession, impart sacramental absolution, or both. The following canon, C. 1379, calls for a "just penalty" for those who attempt other sacraments, but neither canon directly calls for excommunication of someone who either attempts to impose or attempts to receive holy orders. The requisite imposition of such a severe penalty for directly participating in the ordination of a woman could indicate to some that illegal ordinations are valid, if not licit.

Two and one-half years after the Congregation for the Doctrine of the Faith published its Decree, wielded in the Lears case, another document appeared that both solidified the legal ban on women's ordination and caused worldwide uproar by its very composition. On July 15, 2010, the Congregation for the Doctrine of the Faith issued "Modifications to *Normae de gravioribus delictis*." In 2005, the Congregation for the Doctrine of the Faith, under the presidency of Joseph Cardinal Ratzinger, had requested and received papal approval for substantial and procedural norms in canon law that would expand the effective jurisdiction of the Congregation. The 2005 revisions and the 2010 revision concern two topics: laicization of priests and the celebration of sacraments.

Within the catchment of protecting sacraments, the document restates the legal restriction regarding the celebration of Eucharist first documented in 1215 (in its Article 3) and restates as well the prior decree of the Congregation forbidding women's ordination, now "reserved to the Sacred Congregation for the Doctrine of the Faith" (in its Article 5).[41] That women's ordination was termed a "grave delict" along with priest pederasty, priest's collections of juvenile pornography, and violating the seal of confession raised a media storm. Even so, it is clear that a woman ordained to any grade of order—deacon, priest, or bishop—as well as her ordaining bishop is subject to excommunication *latae sententiae.*

Needless to say, the actions of the Roman Catholic Womenpriests movement have left its membership in a canonical and theological quagmire. There are several points at issue regarding women's ordination. First, there are theological and historical distinctions to be made between the ordination of women as deacons and the ordination of women as priests and bishops, now blurred by the Congregation for the Doctrine of the Faith's all-encompassing decree and subsequent norms. The former—the ordination of women as deacons—is demonstrably possible, but the latter, at least insofar as priesthood is concerned, has engendered a long and contentious debate since the close of the Second Vatican Council. (The episcopacy is understood to be forbidden as well.)

What is unusual is that law seems to be outstripping theology as far as the diaconate is concerned. While he steadfastly holds against women priests, Pope Benedict XVI, an historical theologian, apparently recognizes the historicity of the ordination of women as deacons. Individuals on both sides of the discussion might consider German television's interview with Benedict XVI either tantalizing or dismissive. In the interview, recorded shortly after the July 31, 2007 Roman Catholic Womenpriests ceremonies on a Pittsburgh riverboat, Benedict suggested that law or custom may change to allow women more power in the Catholic Church. He said, "We will have to try and listen to God so as not to stand in their [women's] way."[42] The pope's comments came on the heels of his March 2 response to an Italian priest who asked if women could have a role in governance and ministry. Benedict's short answer was "yes" but that women could not have a greater role as priests.[43]

Despite Benedict XVI's seeming openness to women—he named 25 women to the World Synod of Bishops, although not as voting members[44]—he is highly unlikely to sanction the Roman Catholic Womenpriests movement. Some bishops, including Archbishop Timothy Dolan of Milwaukee (now of New York), raised the specter of formal excommunication for movement members even before the decree of the Congregation for the Doctrine of the Faith.

In the cases of the two women ordained in St. Louis and of the ordaining woman bishop, Burke rendered a "Declaration of Excommunication of Patricia Fresen, Rose Hudson, and Elsie McGrath" in addition to placing Sister Louise Lears under interdict. These three women who directly participated in the St. Louis ceremonies belong to the Roman Catholic Womenpriests movement. Fresen, a former Dominican sister from South Africa, was ordained by the movement in 2003 as deacon and priest and in 2005 as bishop.[45] Hudson and McGrath, both US citizens, were ordained as priests by Fresen in the Central Reform Synagogue event in St. Louis on November 11, 2007, which Louise Lears attended.[46]

Immediately after the St. Louis ceremonies, as in the past, US bishops and their spokesmen said sacramentally nothing happened and that the women by their action left the Catholic Church. Prior to the Congregation for the Doctrine of the Faith's Decree, all who participated in the Roman Catholic Womenpriests ordinations were technically under interdict. Independent of Church penalties and restrictions, ordained members of the movement and those who profess to belong to it are considered as having left the Catholic Church. The question is whether they are, or are not, validly ordained deacons, priests, and bishops. Do they belong to, or constitute, another "church"?

THE SACRAMENT OF ORDER: HISTORY AND THEOLOGY

To recapitulate: the Catholic legal stipulations regarding ordination are as follows. In order to be validly ordained, a baptized male must receive orders from a validly ordained bishop, and the ritual of ordination must have proper "matter" (the words) and "form" (the laying on of hands). Further, the bishop must intend to do as the church does. In order to be licitly (legally) ordained, an individual must have his diocesan bishop's (or religious superior's) permission. The ordaining bishop likewise must either be the diocesan bishop or have his permission (a dimissorial letter) to ordain the individual as deacon or priest for service in a particular church (that is, a particular diocese). Episcopal ordinations—ordinations as bishop—must be authorized or acceded to by the pope.

Theologically, the stipulation that the subject of priestly ordination must be male is essentially an argument from authority bolstered by the iconic argument. Perhaps the best English-language presentation of the theological argument determining the necessity of male gender for the reception of priestly ordination is in Sara Butler, *The Catholic Priesthood*

and Women: A Guide to the Teaching of the Church. The core of her argument follows *Inter Insigniores:* the priest represents Christ "taking the
role of Christ, to the point of being his very image, when he pronounces
the words of consecration."[47] That is, following St. Thomas Aquinas,
the priest functions as a sign that required natural correspondence in
gender. Butler explains the declaration itself follows St. Bonaventure,
who argued that only a man can be the sign of Christ, who is male. She
quotes Bonaventure: "he [Christ] can only be represented by the male
sex; therefore the capacity for receiving orders belongs only to males."[48]

Butler's discussion, resting as it does on the necessity of signification
by the subject of priestly ordination, does not consider the fact that the
church has stated valid Masses do not necessarily require the "institution
narrative," at least in the case of the ancient Holy Qurbana or Anaphora
of Addai and Mari, which possibly dates to the third century and is used
in the Assyrian Church of the East, the Syro-Malabar Catholic Church,
and the Chaldean Catholic Church. In 2001, the Holy See affirmed
the validity of the Anaphora of Addai and Mari, citing three reasons:
(1) the Anaphora of Addai and Mari, one of the most ancient Anapho-
ras, dates to the early church; (2) the church of the East is "a true particular church built upon orthodox faith and apostolic succession"; and
(3) while the Words of Institution are present in a "dispersed euchologi-
cal way."[49] Quite simply, if the institution narrative is not required for
valid Eucharist, why must the priest physically represent Christ?

So in the matter of the Roman Catholic Womenpriests, did anything really happen? Was anyone really ordained? Theologians might
speculate that the actions were valid but illicit because the ordination
of women is a theological question (even though Rome has declared
it closed). Canon lawyers would respond that the actions were both
invalid and illicit, since the law reflects accepted theology.

Leaving the matter of gender aside for the sake of argument, since
the women bishops are neither diocesan bishops nor acting with
permission of diocesan bishops (or religious superiors), the ordination ceremony was surely illicit within Roman Catholicism. Liceity
aside, validity becomes the point of contention. As demonstrated
by the actions of Lefebvre, Milingo, and Davídek, even illicit orders
might be considered valid. The first women bishops of Roman Catholic Womenpriests, Christine Mayr-Lumetzberger (Austria) and Gisela
Forster (Germany), contend that they were validly ordained by at least
one active Roman Catholic bishop, information about whose identity
and episcopal lineage they have locked in a bank vault, in addition to

having been ordained by Romulo Antonio Braschi. It is possible their Catholic bishop was Dusan Spiner, whose ordination by Davidek has been deemed by Rome both valid and licet.

Patricia Fresen was subsequently ordained by those first two women bishops. These three belong to what their movement terms a virtual diocese, and they appear to continue their ministries in Europe.[50] A fourth woman bishop, Dana Reynolds, was among the first ordained as deacon and priest in the United States and is termed "Bishop for the Western Region." Additional bishops of Roman Catholic Women-priests trace their provenance to those first two women bishops, who in turn may trace their apostolic lineage to Davídek through Spiner.

Except that gender invalidates their ordinations—and that is a very big invalidation—valid lineage would make the women "vagan" bishops, technically able to confer valid sacraments, while not in communion with Rome. Also, since orders properly given by some churches, such as the Orthodox Churches, the Armenian Apostolic Church, or the Polish National Catholic Church,[51] are both valid and licit, some might argue that Roman Catholic Womenpriests should be—or might some day be--likewise recognized. Some recognized churches ordain women as deacons, but Rome has not spoken regarding the validity of the ordinations. It is doubtful that it could deny it.[52]

No matter, the orders conferred by bishops of the Roman Catholic Womenpriests movement, whether valid or invalid, are not orders within the Roman Catholic Church. Hence the Roman Catholic Womenpriests movement calling itself "an international initiative within the Roman Catholic Church" is specious, as by its actions its members separate themselves from communion with the Catholic Church.

The question is whether their argument that they are Roman Catholic is specious in the same way as that of the followers of Milingo, or is as that of the members of the Society of Saint Pius X, or whether their situation is similar to that of the priests and bishops of *Koinótés*. The distinction between the Roman Catholic Womenpriests movement and, for example, the Society of Saint Pius X is more than gender, but it is clearly gender, and despite any theological argumentation to the contrary, the gender barrier regarding women's ordination is not easily overcome. As noted previously, the principal magisterial resistance to ordaining women as priests comes from the "argument from authority": Jesus chose male apostles. However, the argument from authority only applies to priesthood and the episcopacy. In the Acts of the Apostles it is clear that the community—not the apostles—chose they who have come to be regarded as the first seven deacons. These seven subsequently received the laying on of hands from the apostles.[53] In Paul's letter to the Romans we meet the only person in Scripture to hold the title "deacon": Phoebe, deacon (not deaconess) of the church at Cenchrae (Rom. 16:1).

There is substantial additional evidence that women served in early church ministries. As Pope John Paul II pointed out:

> In the history of the Church, even from earliest times, there were side-by-side with men a number of women, for whom the response of the Bride to the Bridegroom's redemptive love acquired full expressive force. First we see those women who had personally encountered Christ and followed him. After his departure, together with the Apostles, they "devoted themselves to prayer" in the Upper Room in Jerusalem until the day of Pentecost. On that day the Holy Spirit spoke through "the sons and daughters" of the People of God, thus fulfilling the words of the prophet Joel (cf. Acts 2: 17). These women, and others afterwards, played an active and important role in the life of the early Church, in building up from its foundations the first Christian community—and subsequent communities—through their own charisms and their varied service. The apostolic writings note their names, such as Phoebe, "a deaconess of the Church at Cenchreae" (cf. Rom 16:1), Prisca with her husband Aquila (cf. 2 Tim 4:19), Euodia and Syntyche (cf. Phil 4:2), Mary, Tryphaena, Persis, and Tryphosa (cf. Rom 16:6, 12). Saint Paul speaks of their "hard work" for Christ, and this hard work indicates the various fields of the Church's apostolic service, beginning with the "domestic Church." For in the latter, "sincere faith" passes from the mother to her children and grandchildren, as was the case in the house of Timothy (cf. 2 Tim 1:5).[54]

Whether the earliest women were "ordained" to such ministries according to current understandings of Catholic sacramental theology is the knotty problem, but in any event, it is clear they served in capacities that would today mark them as deacons.

Despite protestations to the contrary, there is historical literary, epigraphical, and liturgical evidence that women were actually ordained—at least to the diaconate—in a manner that scholars uniformly recognize as sacramental. Historical studies, such as those of Kevin Madigan and Carolyn Osiek, of Gary Macy, and of many others also indicate that women served as priests and as bishops.[55] But theological inquiry is divided as to whether these women were "ordained" in the modern sense of the word. That is, the theological understanding of sacramental ordination developed over centuries, and so the theological question has arisen whether women were "ordained" as priests and bishops, or simply assumed roles as non-ordained persons and, once the theology of ordination developed, they were deemed unordainable by reason of their gender.

The determination of "unordainability" because of gender has in modern times been rooted in two arguments: the argument from authority (Jesus chose male apostles), as described briefly earlier, and the *in persona Christi* or "iconic" argument, which is reducible to "the male Jesus must be represented by a male." The further argument brought forward in modern times is that the constant tradition of the church has restricted priestly ordination to men.

However, the *in persona Christi* or "iconic" argument, so prominent in *Inter Insigniores,* the 1976 document on women priests from the Congregation for the Doctrine of the Faith, does not appear in Pope John Paul II's 1994 apostolic letter *Ordinatio Sacerdotalis.* John Paul II in 1994 depends principally on the question of authority: does the church have the authority to ordain women as priests, given that Jesus chose only male apostles? His determination is no, the church does not have any authority to ordain women as priests. However, we do not know whether Jesus chose only male apostles. We only know the Gospels record he chose male apostles.[56]

For whatever reason, until the advent of the Roman Catholic Womenpriests movement, *Inter Insigniores* appeared on the official Vatican website solely in Portuguese,[57] although the document had been widely translated, quickly appeared in the official documentation publication of the Holy See, *Acta Apostolicae Sedes,* in Latin and Italian, and later in Latin and in Spanish in a publication of the bishop's conference of Spain.[58] The document appeared in English in *Origins,* a documentary service of the US Catholic Bishops.[59] While *Inter Insigniores* is a document rendering an opinion of the Congregation for the Doctrine of the Faith and ranks well below documents produced by ecumenical councils or by pontiffs, its recent sudden appearance on the Vatican website in five additional languages (English, French, Italian, Latin, Spanish) also speaks to the Congregation's concerns about women priests.[60]

The Congregation for the Doctrine of the Faith is the oldest of the Curia's nine congregations and the direct descendant of the Sacred Congregation of the Universal Inquisition founded in 1542 to root out heresy. From 1908 until 1965, it was known as the Holy Office, and was renamed by Paul VI. From 1971 to 1995, the Congregation issued only nine documents related to holy orders. Eight are classed as documents on sacraments: three concern "reduction" to the lay state of clerics, two concern dispensations from celibacy, and one concerns form in ordination ceremonies. Two others regard the ordination of women as priests: *Inter Insigniores* (1976) and, finally, its 1995 "*Responsum ad Dubium*," which presents the Congregation's opinion regarding John Paul II's apostolic letter *Ordinatio Sacerdotalis* (1994).[61] It is the opinion of the Congregation that the teachings of *Ordinatio Sacerdotalis* are to be definitively held.

Only this last document, the 1995 "*Responsum ad Dubium*," was published while Joseph Cardinal Ratzinger (now Pope Benedict XVI) was the Congregation's Prefect.[62] Since Ratzinger's election as Pope Benedict XVI, the sole additional document regarding ordination, a "Disciplinary Document", is the 2007 General Decree on the ordination of a woman discussed previously, the text of which appears on the Vatican website in seven languages.[63] In 2010, the decree was codified to church law, by means of modifications to *Normae de gravioribus delictis*, also published by the Congregation for the Doctrine of the Faith.

Inter Insigniores (1976) and *Ordinatio Sacerdotalis* (1994) remain the two best known contemporary documents that touch on the theology of the ordination of women. The story of *Inter Insigniores* and *Ordinatio Sacerdotalis* is more than a tale of two documents. As mentioned earlier, following the Second Vatican Council the ordination of women as priests was one among many reforms blowing into those open windows from many—if not most—parts of the world. Secular women's rights movements were well under way in developed nations, a theology of liberation was percolating in Latin America, and discussion literally exploded about the papal encyclical letter *Humanae Vitae*, which condemned what it terms "artificial" means of birth control.[64] To this ecclesial and ecclesiastical stew was added the theological notion that women—equally with men—could represent Christ as iconic of the fully human person and therefore could be ordained as priests.

What has become apparent since the publication of these two principal documents on women's ordination is their change in emphasis. *Inter Insigniores* relies on two points, one apparently theological (the iconic argument) and the other apparently juridical (the argument from authority). *Ordinatio Sacerdotalis* relies on the argument from authority.

The shift in emphasis took place in the years intervening between *Inter Insigniores* and *Ordinatio Sacerdotalis*, which saw growing assertions of the equally human creation of women to men and increased discussion and theological analysis about the ordination of women as priests in many quarters.

ANGLICAN WOMEN PRIESTS AND THE
VALIDITY OF ANGLICAN ORDERS[65]

In the 1970s, the movement toward the ordination of women as priests in the Anglican Communion was becoming stronger. The Anglican Communion had a longstanding tradition of ordained women deacons, which it fully restored in 1987. An Anglican woman had been ordained as priest in Hong Kong in 1944.[66] The 1968 Lambeth Conference passed five resolutions regarding women priests, stating that arguments for and against women priests were inconclusive, but provinces should refrain from ordaining women as priests until after wider consultation, including with other denominations that do ordain women and those that do not.[67]

Discussions ensued, but the Lambeth Conference meets only every ten years. Then, in 1974, the movement to include women priests in the Anglican Communion was jumpstarted, as three retired bishops of the Episcopal Church in the USA (ECUSA) ordained 11 women as priests in Philadelphia without the approbation of the Episcopal House of Bishops, or, presumably, the Anglican Consultative Council (or the Lambeth Consultative Body). This is roughly equivalent to Catholic bishops ignoring both the USCCB and the magisterium. Recall, women were theoretically accepted as ordained deacons, at least one woman had been ordained a priest in modern times, and the 1968 Lambeth Conference formally stated the matter was not settled, although it asked that "any national or regional Church or province" to refrain from ordaining women until after receiving the "advice" of the Anglican Consultative Council.[68]

These internally valid, but illicit, ordinations were joined the following year with more, as four additional women were ordained in Washington, DC. Deemed "irregular," the ordinations were reconciled at the 1976 General Convention of ECUSA, which authorized the ordination of women as priests and their consecration as bishops. Two years later, the 1978 Lambeth Conference noted that the Anglican provinces of Canada, Hong Kong, the United States and New Zealand had ordained women as priests but recommended against the ordination of women as bishops, even while noting the legal autonomy of the various provinces to admit women to holy orders.[69] The 1978 Lambeth Conference specifically recommended all provinces admit women to the diaconate (as opposed to a separate order of deaconesses) but refrain from ordaining women as bishops.[70] By allowing women priests, the Anglican Communion knew it had embarked on a difficult path and had added a serious point of fraction and discussion for its ecumenical relations:

> We recognise that our accepting this variety of doctrine and practice in the Anglican Communion may disappoint the Roman Catholic, Orthodox, and Old Catholic Churches, but we wish to make it clear (a) that the holding together of diversity within a unity of faith and worship is part of the Anglican heritage; (b) that those who have taken part in ordinations of women to the priesthood believe that these ordinations have been into [sic.] the historic ministry of the Church as the Anglican Communion has received it; and (c) that we hope the dialogue between these other Churches and the member Churches of our Communion will continue because we believe that we still have understanding of the truth of God and his will to learn from them as together we all move towards a fuller catholicity and a deeper fellowship in the Holy Spirit.[71]

If Anglican women priests were allowed in 1978, could Anglican women bishops be far behind? The carefully worded 1978 Lambeth recommendation recognizes the essential problem and states, "no decision to consecrate be taken without consultation with the episcopate through the primates and overwhelming support in any member Church and in the diocese concerned, lest the bishop's office should become a cause of disunity instead of a focus of unity."[72]

By the 1988 Lambeth Conference, the ordination or consecration of women bishops had moved to the top of the resolutions list. The final vote (423 for; 28 against; 19 abstentions) passed a resolution that provinces respect the decisions of other provinces, bishops with differing opinions exhibit courtesy toward each other, that the Archbishop of Canterbury appoint a commission to examine and monitor ongoing interprovincial relations as well as ecumenical relations, and that individual bishops continue dialogue and make pastoral provision for people and clergy who differ. Finally, the conference resolved it "recognises the serious hurt which would result from the questioning by some of the validity of the episcopal acts of a woman bishop, and likewise the hurt experienced by those whose conscience would be offended by the ordination of a woman to the episcopate. The church needs to exercise sensitivity, patience and pastoral care towards all concerned."[73]

The first Anglican woman bishop, Penny Jamieson, was consecrated in 1989 by the Anglican Church of New Zealand as seventh bishop of Dunedin. In the United States, the first Episcopal woman bishop was Barbara Clementine Harris, consecrated suffragan bishop of Massachusetts in 1989. A few years later, in 1994, the Episcopal General Convention reaffirmed that both men and women were eligible for ordination and consecration but that dioceses could refuse to ordain and consecrate women. That exclusion ended in 1997 when the Episcopal General Convention made eligibility of women for ordination as priests and bishops mandatory in every diocese. The 1998 Lambeth Conference included 11 women bishops: eight from the United States, two from Canada, and one from New Zealand. In 2006, Katherine Jefferts Shori, then Bishop of Nevada, was elected Primate of the Episcopal Church, and by 2010 there were 17 active and retired Episcopal women bishops in the United States.[74]

Things went equally well for women in the Church of England, the mother church of Anglicanism. In 2008, the General Convention of the Church of England, immediately prior to the 2008 Lambeth Conference, voted to allow women bishops, even against the dire warnings of Cardinal Walter Kasper. Cardinal Kasper, then-President of the Pontifical Council for Promoting Christian Unity, told the Lambeth Conference that Anglican woman bishops would fracture Anglican-Catholic ecumenical relations and dialogue, stating that the movement of Rome toward accepting Anglican orders would grind to a halt. Quoting from *Ordinatio Sacerdotalis*, Kasper said,

> Regarding the ordination of women to the priesthood and episcopate . . . the Catholic position as follows: "Priestly ordination . . . in the Catholic Church from the beginning has always been reserved to men alone," and that "this tradition has also been faithfully maintained by the Oriental Churches." He [Pope John Paul II] concluded: "I declare that the Church has no authority whatsoever to confer priestly ordination on women and that this judgment is to be definitively held by all the Church's faithful." This formulation clearly shows that this is not only a disciplinary position but an expression of our faithfulness to Jesus Christ. The Catholic Church finds herself bound by the will of Jesus Christ and does not feel free to establish a new tradition alien to the tradition of the Church of all ages.[75]

The Cardinal, however, was speaking to an assemblage belonging to a communion with a modern history of women clergy increasingly welcoming to women bishops.

Cardinal Kasper continued,

> Since it is currently the situation that 28 Anglican provinces ordain women to the priesthood, and while only 4 provinces have ordained women to the episcopate, an additional 13 provinces have passed legislation authorizing women bishops, the Catholic Church must now take account of the reality that the ordination of women to the priesthood and the episcopate is not only a matter of isolated provinces, but that this is increasingly the stance of the Communion. It will continue to have bishops, as set forth in the Lambeth Quadrilateral (1888); but as with bishops within some Protestant churches, the older churches of East and West will recognise therein much less of what

they understand to be the character and ministry of the bishop in the sense understood by the early church and continuing through the ages.

I have already addressed the ecclesiological problem when bishops do not recognize other's episcopal ordination within the one and same church, now I must be clear about the new situation which has been created in our ecumenical relations. While our dialogue has led to significant agreement on the understanding of ministry, the ordination of women to the episcopate effectively and definitively blocks a possible recognition of Anglican Orders by the Catholic Church.[76]

The gauntlet thrown down by Kasper before the Anglican Communion comprises this: either get rid of ordained women priests and bishops or forget reunion with Rome. Kasper's prediction that ordaining women as bishops in Anglicanism's mother church would derail their ecumenical efforts with other churches, arguing that apostolic lineage held by Anglican bishops would come to a screeching halt wherever a woman bishop was ordained. Recall, he said, "but as with bishops within some Protestant churches, the older churches of East and West will recognise therein [in the Church of England] much less of what they [the other Churches recognized by, but not in communion with, Rome] understand to be the character and ministry of the bishop in the sense understood by the early church and continuing through the ages." He also referred to the Lambeth Quadrilateral, which in turn refers to the institution narrative as central to Eucharist ("ministered with unfailing use of Christ's Words of Institution, and of the elements ordained by Him").[77] A central point of the Catholic iconic argument—independent of the recognition of the Anaphora of Addai and Mari examined earlier—is that the priest must physically represent Christ (as man) in the Mass.

The line in the sand Kasper draws is between churches recognized by Rome, which do not ordain women as priests, and "Protestant" bodies not recognized by Rome, which do. Such is a direct inference to the "Catholicity" of Anglicanism, which has been and remains a tangled web of provenance and practice. In a few cases, the apostolic lineage of some Anglican bishops is agreed to, and in some cases, their priestly ordinations are considered valid. Even so, since the Catholic Church generally does not recognize the validity of Anglican orders (or other sacraments beyond baptism and marriage), one could assume Anglican women ordained as priests and consecrated as bishops would not be a major bar to ecumenical relations and mutual recognitions, unless Kasper's words are portent to Rome's wishes for more regular, if often indirect, acceptance of Anglican ordination. That is, if, generally speaking, nothing happens in Anglican ordinations of men, what is Rome's difficulty with nothing happening in Anglican ordinations of women?

The Vatican clearly does wish to recognize Anglican women priests and bishops (deacons might be another matter), and it may see an opening to further divide the Anglican communion by accepting Anglican communion parishes (or even provinces) that refuse women's ordination excepting to the diaconate.

Even so, Rome does seem to willing to accept Anglican orders for men in a limited way and to create a "reunion" of sorts. For example, during a 2008 trip to the Catholic shrine at Lourdes, Rowan Williams, Archbishop of Canterbury, preached at a Mass celebrated by Cardinal Kasper, despite the Catholic canons that refuse anyone permission to preach at a Catholic Mass other than an ordained Catholic deacon, priest, or bishop.[78] Officially, at least, the Catholic Church does not generally view Anglican priests as validly ordained, nor does it see Anglican bishops as validly consecrated, excepting as noted earlier the few situations where the province of orders can be traced. The specter of validity of Anglican orders appears troublesome to Rome only where it must consider the validity of all those ordained, both male and female.

The magisterial view of Anglican priesthood, presented in Pope Leo XIII's 1896 bull *Apostolicae Curiae*, is that the Anglican rite of ordination does not effect ordination to a sacrificial priesthood. The bull definitively stated that Anglican ordination was not valid:

> To all rightly estimating these matters it will not be difficult to understand why, in the Letters of Julius III, issued to the Apostolic Legate on 8 March 1554, there is a distinct mention, first of those who, "rightly and lawfully promoted," might be maintained in their orders: and then of others who, "not promoted to Holy Orders" might "be promoted if they were found to be worthy and fitting subjects". For it is clearly and definitely noted, as indeed was the case, that there were two classes of men; the first of those who had really received Holy Orders, either before the secession of Henry VIII, or, if after it, and by ministers infected by error and schism, still according to the accustomed Catholic rite; the second, those who were initiated according to the Edwardine Ordinal, who on that account could not be "promoted," since they had received an ordination which was null.[79]

The nineteenth century Anglican Archbishops of Canterbury and of York responded to the papal bull with their own document, *Saepius Officio* (February 19, 1897), which in addition to defending Anglican practice at the time raises an interesting point: "For he seems to condemn the Orientals, in company with ourselves, on account of defective intention, who in the '*Orthodox Confession*' issued about 1640 name only two functions of a sacramental priesthood, that is to say that of absolving sins and of preaching; who in the '*Longer Russian*

Catechism' (Moscow, 1839) teach nothing about the sacrifice of the Body and Blood of Christ, and mention among the offices which pertain to Order only those of ministering the Sacraments and feeding the flock."[80] That is, the Catholic determination of nullity depends on the intent of the ordaining bishops to ordain to the sacrificial priesthood, and the Edwardine Ordinal did not so provide. But, the Anglican bishops note, members of the Eastern Churches must be similarly accused of improper intent, as both the *Orthodox Confession* (c. 1640) and the *"Longer Russian Catechism"* (Moscow, 1839) do not mention a sacrificial priesthood.

Even so, the papal bull appears to argue if there was no intent on the part of the first (in Catholic understanding) schismatic bishops of Anglicanism to ordain to the sacrificial priesthood: that is, to do as the whole Catholic Church did; then, in due time any valid episcopal lineage would die out. Catholicism would not recognize priests and bishops later ordained (and consecrated) as validly ordained (or consecrated).

A large part of Leo XIII's argument rests on Anglicanism's eliminating the precise emphasis on the sacrifice of the Mass, but the response of the Anglican Archbishops of Canterbury and of York, that Orthodox Christians in at least two cases pointed to (as earlier) ordain priests with rituals that say "nothing about the sacrifice of the Body and Blood of Christ,"[81] presents an interesting point. In the more than one hundred years since its publication, there has been no official Catholic response to that Anglican document.

The question of Anglican women's ordinations (and consecrations as bishops) only compounds the issue. On the one hand, the Anglican Communion would like Rome to admit to the valid lineage of Anglican episcopacy. Rome might wish to do that, but in so doing it would have to address more deeply the question of the women who have been ordained as deacons and priests and consecrated bishops. (Again, if nothing has happened—if there are no valid Anglican orders—then the matter should be a null issue. In fact, priests and bishops who now join Rome accept re-ordination, only rarely conditionally.)[82]

If the position is taken that the Anglican intent was to ordain "not to the priesthood, but to the ministry," then all ordained Anglicans, male or female, might still be considered validly ordained as deacons. In fact, Leo XIII's bull involves only priestly ordinations and episcopal consecrations, not diaconal ordinations. But it is impossible to forget that the Anglican Communion has, in addition to its long tradition of women deacons, women priests and, increasingly, women bishops.

In June 2006, two years prior to the Church of England's 2008 vote to admit women bishops, and two years prior to his comments cited earlier, Cardinal Kasper accepted at short notice an invitation to address a meeting of the bishops of the Church of England precisely on the topic of women bishops. Several senior women of the Church of England were present. Kasper reviewed the history of communications between the Catholic Church and the Anglican Communion, noting that Pope Paul VI addressed the question of the ordination of women in letters to Archbishop Donald Coggan (November 30, 1975, and March 23, 1976), followed by letters from Pope John Paul II to Archbishop Robert Runcie (December 20, 1984, and December 8, 1988). The question at hand was not the validity or invalidity of Anglican ordinations but the matter of women being accepted as priests and bishops in the Anglican Communion. As the pope put it, they presented "new obstacles in the way of reconciliation between Catholics and Anglicans."[83] Kasper then asserted a biblical basis for the Catholic Church's belief that women cannot be ordained as priests (and, therefore, as bishops): "The position of the Catholic Church can only be understood and evaluated if one recognizes that the argumentation has a biblical basis"[84] despite the fact that the Pontifical Biblical Commission did not find as such.

By way of response to Kasper's comments, Anglican Bishops Tom Wright, of Durham, and David Stancliffe of Salisbury, published a background paper for the projected discussions at the ensuing General Synod of the Church of England at York. They made several points, not the least of which is to point out Cardinal Kasper begins his argumentation from papal authority and only later moves to the authority of Scripture. Their argumentation, in some respects, comes close to that of the American Catholic movement Voice of the Faithful, or even Bishop Bruskewitz's nemesis, Call to Action, and of Roman Catholic Womenpriests:

> In discussing the source of the Church's authority, the Cardinal comes close at times to saying that it is only through the lens of the Church's tradition that scripture can be read. That has never been the Anglican position on the balance between scripture and tradition. Our formulation, carefully balanced, is that the faith we profess is a faith "uniquely revealed in the Holy Scriptures, set forth in the Catholic creeds, and to which the historic formularies of the Church of England bear witness." This commitment to proclaim the faith afresh is a challenge to pursue those developments in the Church's life that are consonant with scripture and are found to be life-giving. In the end, the arbiter is the *sensus fidei*, the entire body of the faithful, as was pointed out to Pius IX in 1848 by the Eastern Patriarchs in their Encyclical: "the protector of religion is the very body of the Church, even the people themselves." The faithful are the ultimate guardians of Tradition and the faith.[85]

Here, in the words of Wright and Stancliffe, we might hear echoes of the discussions and views of Davídek within *Koinótés*. Their challenge is one of balance: how does one balance revealed dogma with "developments in the Church's life that are consonant with scripture and are found to be life-giving"? For Wright and Stancliffe it is "the *sensus fidei*, the entire body of the faithful"—but that begs the further question: who makes up the "faithful"? Where the Nicene-Apostles Creed is the sole arbiter, there are many examples, even in this work, where through ignorance or willfulness another "creed" is substituted (witness the confusion over the profession of faith at the first Call to Action–Nebraska Mass at Mahoney State Park or the dissent presented by followers of Leonard Feeney).

What Wright and Stancliffe and were discriminating was dogma, which cannot evolve, and praxis, which can. For them, the matter of women bishops was an evolving praxis about which the faithful were capable of making a determination. This stands, of course, in stark relief against the Orsy-Ratzinger discussion about the relative weight and required assent to "definitive" but not clearly infallible teachings.

Within the Anglican context, it is possible Cardinal Kasper's 2006 intervention helped forestall the creation of women bishops in the Church of England, within which substantial resistance remains despite its 2008 vote to allow the consecration of women as bishops. Kasper's 2006 argument and his comments at the 2008 Lambeth Conference rest in part on the perception, although not the reality, that Canterbury is analogous to Rome in its position of leadership. While the Lambeth Conference is convened by the Archbishop of Canterbury, and there is significant external and internal recognition of the Archbishop of Canterbury's leadership, the Anglican Communion operates more on the "communal" (collegial, ecclesial) model as opposed to "juridical" (collaborative, political) model.

ORDAINED WOMEN DEACONS[86]

The separate issue of women deacons was neither discussed nor mentioned by Cardinal Kasper in either of his interventions before the Anglican bodies. Significant scholarship demonstrates that women served as deacons from the earliest centuries of Christianity until at least the eighth and possibly as late as the twelfth century in both the Eastern and Western Churches,[87] and the Anglican Communion uniformly accepts that women can be ordained as deacons. While some members or units of the Anglican Communion do not ordain women to the diaconate, most do.

The Catholic Church has made no definitive ruling on the readmission of women to the ordained diaconate. In 2001, three Vatican offices, the Congregations for the Doctrine of the Faith, for Divine Worship, and the Discipline of Sacraments and for Clergy, issued a notification directed mainly at the bishops of Germany and Austria directing them to stop forming women for ordination to the diaconate because they did not envision that the church would ordain them. The Notification, which was signed by the respective prefects, Cardinals Joseph Ratzinger (now Benedict XVI), and Jorge Arturo Augustin Medina Estévez and Darío Castrillón Hoyos (b. 1926 and b. 1929, respectively; both now retired), is a disciplinary document and as such is not considered to be legislative. That is, the Notification has not changed church law; it simply restates current practice.[88]

One could surmise that the Notification was issued, as it indicates, because some German-speaking bishops were preparing women for diaconal ordination.[89] It is entirely possible that some of the German-speaking women being so prepared eventually began the Roman Catholic Womenpriests movement. It is noteworthy that the document was issued jointly by the Congregation for the Doctrine of the Faith (which issued *Inter Insigniores*), along with the curial offices responsible for sacraments and for clergy. That is, if the matter were solely doctrinal in nature—if women could not (either because of an argument from authority or from the iconic argument) be ordained as deacons, the Congregation for the Doctrine of the Faith would more likely be the sole author. In fact, if a genuine doctrinal barrier existed against women deacons, the document *Ordinatio Sacerdotalis* would have already stipulated it. The fact that three different Vatican offices issued the document underscores the disciplinary—as opposed to doctrinal—nature of the Notification, which by definition is not legislative in nature.

As it stands, there is no formal argument that the ordination of women as deacons would be invalid. There remains, however, the question of liceity. The Notification is disciplinary, and hints of, but does not promise, disunion from Rome on the part of a bishop who ordained a woman as deacon. That changed with the two documents issued by the Congregation for the Doctrine of the Faith mentioned earlier, which have essentially legislated on the matter of both women priests and women deacons and declared *latae sententiae* excommunication for anyone participating in the ordination of a woman.

The newest legislation changes the trajectory of the discussion. Since women have in the past been ordained as deacons, so then at least a diocesan bishop might wish to ordain a woman as such, or at least petition (or advise) Rome that he would like to do so. Today, some churches with sacraments and orders recognized as valid by the Catholic Church, but not under the authority of the pope, can and do ordain women deacons. As noted earlier, the Armenian Apostolic Church has ordained women as deacons, and the Orthodox Church of Greece has voted to do so. These churches are separated juridically, but not doctrinally, from the Catholic Church, and maintain multiple mutual recognition agreements with the Catholic Church including and especially on the matter of holy orders.[90]

The vexed question of the ordination of women in the Catholic Church contains deep implications for ecumenical dialogue between and among churches that ordain women to the diaconate. Of the Eastern churches, two—the Armenian Apostolic Church and the Orthodox Church of Greece—are able to ordain women as deacons. Of Western churches, certain Old Catholic Churches (signers to the Union of Utrecht) are able to ordain women as deacons. While the Catholic Church definitely recognizes the validity of sacraments and orders in these Eastern churches and somewhat more technically recognizes the validity of sacraments and orders in these Western churches, it is unclear whether the validity of the ordination of women deacons in these churches would be equally recognized. There have been no Catholic statements regarding them.[91]

The Armenian Apostolic Church appears to have an unbroken tradition of ordaining monastic women deacons and today has women deacons in active ministries.[92] The Orthodox Church of Greece voted to return to its tradition of women deacons in 2004. At least four Union of Utrecht Old Catholic Churches ordain women deacons and priests: the Old Catholic Churches in Germany (1996),[93] Austria (1998), Netherlands (1998), and Switzerland (2002).[94] The Old Catholic Church in the Czech Republic ordained a woman deacon in 2003 but does not appear to have ordained a woman priest.[95]

These ordinations of women, whether as priests or as deacons, are licit and valid according to the requirements of their respective churches. Hence the question: does the Catholic Church also recognize these ordinations of women as valid? The restrictions of the Catholic Church are not binding in these churches. Further, it might be argued that Catholic teaching does not necessarily hold that gender is a determinant of validity. Writing within the context of Canon 968[96] of the 1917 or "Pio-Benedictine" Code of Canon Law, 1024, Pius XII with the apostolic constitution *Sacramentum Ordinus* (1947) determined "the matter of the holy orders of diaconate, presbyterate, and episcopate is the laying on of hands alone, and the sole form is the words determining the application of the matter."[97] Even prescinding from any argumentation regarding Catholic priesthood or episcopacy, two things must be noted: (1) the prior trajectory of the 1917 Canon 968 (subsequently, the 1983 Canons 1024 and 1024) attempts to restrict priesthood, not the diaconate, which by 1917 had faded to a step along the way to priesthood, and (2) hence male gender is assumed, and not part of Pius XII's final determination of matter or form. But male gender appears to be assumed for priestly and episcopal orders, not for ordination to the diaconate.

But Pius XII's unambiguous statement on the matter and form of holy orders has not been overcome, and those who hold otherwise are in anathema. Hence, assuming the ordinations in at least the Eastern churches noted, and possibly the Western churches, are carried out with proper matter and form, then their ordinations of men are both sacramentally valid and ecclesiastically licit within their respective churches. Further, because of the long history of women deacons (East and West), there seems no barrier to Rome's recognizing the validity of the diaconal orders of women in these churches.[98]

To examine the implications of the ordinations of women to the diaconate in these Eastern and Western churches, it is best to proceed at this juncture prescinding from the ordination of women as priests for two reasons: first, the ordination of women deacons is demonstrably possible (i.e., it does not meet the objections of either the iconic argument or the argument from authority, while it does demonstrate a constant tradition); second, the churches under scrutiny here, those Union of Utrecht Churches that ordain women as priests, depart significantly from Catholic Doctrine in other areas, much as the Roman Catholic Womenpriests movement.

While the permanent diaconate is not so clearly defined by the Western churches mentioned (Union of Utrecht), the Eastern churches here examined (Armenian and Orthodox Church of Greece) view women deacons as members of a permanent order. Such concurs with Rome's view. The permanence of diaconal orders is crucial, since an argument against the ordination of women deacons in the Catholic Church, as noted previously, is that such ordination would thereby qualify women for priestly ordination: if you can ordain a woman deacon then you can ordain a woman priest. However, no tradition—Eastern or Western—guarantees priestly orders for an ordained deacon, male or female, and the Catholic Church's modern restoration of a permanent diaconate militates against the notion of automatic "promotion" of a deacon to priesthood.[99] Further, given the documented history of women deacons in Christianity, the ordination of women deacons in these three churches—or even in the Catholic Church—departs from neither custom nor tradition.[100]

Conjoining the questions of women deacons and women priests serves neither side of the discussion. Those who ask for the restoration of the female diaconate are not necessarily asking for the ordination of women to priesthood. And they who argue for ordination of women priests are not necessarily asking for ordination of women to the diaconate as a permanent ministry but rather (as with the Roman Catholic Womenpriests movement) only seek ordination of women as transitional deacons awaiting priestly ordination. The question of women's ordination is ill served by conjoining the two.

It is important to recall that the two modern Catholic documents about these questions speak solely to the ordination of women to priesthood. The first, the Declaration of the Congregation for the Doctrine of the Faith *Inter Insigniores* (1976), presents both the "iconic argument" (Jesus must be represented by a male) and the "argument from authority" (Jesus chose only male apostles).[101] The second, the apostolic letter of John Paul II *Ordinatio Sacerdotalis* (1994), presents only the "argument from authority." It is addressed to the bishops of the Catholic Church and, as an apostolic letter, is not legislative in nature.[102] While the opinion of infallibility rendered by the Congregation for the Doctrine of the Faith regarding *Ordination Sacerdotalis* appears to have more weight given the election of Benedict XVI, it must be again underscored there is neither a *de jure divino* assertion of infallibility nor any clear papal statement relative to the document. Recall that nothing is infallible unless it is clearly defined as such.[103] However, given the argued strength of the document, there ought be no question that the ordination of women as deacons endangers accepted theology and law regarding women priests.

The question of women deacons was taken up by multiple quinquennenia—bodies appointed for five year terms—of the International Theological Commission of the Congregation for the Doctrine of the Faith under the presidency of Cardinal Joseph Ratzinger. The International Theological Commission concluded that the ordination of women deacons would require a decision of the magisterium, the full teaching office of the church.[104] Early ecumenical councils allow for the ordination of women to the diaconate (councils agreed to by all four churches in the present discussion), but later local councils sought to curb the practice.[105] Even so, in the Catholic Church, as late as the eleventh century the right to ordain women deacons was explicitly confirmed to a bishop in the West.[106] Aside from the restrictions of Canon 1024, there has been no modern ruling specifically against the ordination of women deacons in the Catholic Church and no ruling that overrides the conciliar documents or historic practice.[107]

Other documents of a higher order, specifically the Vatican II Decree On Ecumenism (*Unitatis Redintegratio*), speak directly to another point of this discussion. The 1993 Ecumenical Directory of the Pontifical Council for Promoting Christian Unity implies that Eastern Orthodox Churches have demonstrated apostolic succession, valid orders, and sacraments, without specifically naming any one[108] and correspondence regarding the Polish National Catholic Church specifically acknowledges its recognized status.[109]

CONCLUSIONS REGARDING THE DIACONATE

The Catholic Church has attempted to limit the significance of the history and possibility of women deacons through various curial statements and with the 2002 document of the International Theological Commission, "*Le Diaconate: Evolution et Perspectives,*" which argues that the rite of institution and functions of the women deacons of the ancient church were not identical to those of the men deacons of the ancient church.[110] Yet in churches that retain ancient tradition, women have been and are being ordained to the diaconate. The likely ritual for the Orthodox Church of Greece is derived from the Apostolic Constitutions[111] and comprises a ritual deep in the history of the Catholic Church as well. For a church recognized as having valid orders by the Catholic Church to use this ritual—nearly identical for men and for women—in modern times with the authority of tradition brings forth multiple questions regarding interchurch relations and could move forward the internal discussion of restoring the tradition of women deacons in the Catholic Church. This is especially true in the cases of the churches discussed earlier.

The ecumenical dimension of the female diaconate is crucial to the resolution of the question in the Catholic Church. Clearly, should a Catholic curial office declare the orders of women deacons in the Armenian Apostolic Church, the Orthodox Church of Greece, and Old Catholic Churches invalid, such could force a serious fracture in ecumenical relations. The Catholic reaction to the ordination of women priests (but not women deacons) in Anglicanism sets precedents for a reaction, but not for a reaction regarding women deacons.[112] The

Catholic Church has made no official comment on the ordination of women deacons in Anglicanism.

Independent of whether the ordained women of Eastern churches have been or are to be ordained as monastic women deacons, only to serve within their monasteries, or as women deacons in service to the larger community, their ordinations are to major orders and imply service at the altar. The Catholic Church's response can solidify or explode the ecumenical balance between and among the various churches involved. Granted, other issues divide Christianity with equal energy and emotion, but none has such clear support of the ancient tradition of the church.[113]

There are very few Christian denominations that do not ordain women as deacons or priests. If the Catholic Church chose to recognize and return to the larger and longer tradition of ordaining women deacons, it might solidify its position on the ordination of women priests. As noted earlier, the Catholic Church argues it does not have the authority to ordain women to the priesthood. If that argument is correct, the Catholic Church could easily return to the tradition of ordaining women deacons. If that argument is not correct, then the delay in a return to the tradition is not theological but political.

It would seem logical that a decision by the Catholic Church to return to its tradition of ordaining women deacons might better foster Christian unity as well as help the Catholic Church regain its perceived lost authority in matters of human rights and equality. A recurring theme in calls for the ordination of women, at least in the United States, is the lingering effects of the priestly sex abuse scandal. A tsunami of media reports and opinions has connected the worldwide sex abuse scandal with the dearth of women in leadership roles in the Catholic Church, specifically in ordained ministries. The linkage has given energy to the movements examined here—from Call to Action to Roman Catholic Womenpriests—and is mentioned at every juncture in argumentation for women's ordination. Maryknoll Father Roy Bourgeois, who took part in the St. Louis Roman Catholic Womenpriests ordinations, responded to the Vatican's disciplinary letter, linking a male-only priesthood to the scandal. He wrote, in part,

> Having an all male clergy implies that men are worthy to be Catholic priests, but women are not.
>
> According to USA TODAY (Feb. 28, 2008) in the United States alone, nearly 5,000 Catholic priests have sexually abused more than 12,000 children. Many bishops, aware of the abuse, remained silent. These priests and bishops were not excommunicated. Yet the women in our Church who are called by

God and are ordained to serve God's people, and the priests and bishops who
support them, are excommunicated.

Silence is the voice of complicity. Therefore, I call on all Catholics, fellow
priests, bishops, Pope Benedict XVI and all Church leaders at the Vatican, to
speak loudly on this grave injustice of excluding women from the priesthood.[114]

While it is not useful to commingle the arguments relative to
women deacons and women priests, certain common themes appear
and reappear in the discussion. Without question, the ordination of
women deacons is one of singular interest and import in ecumenical
discussion. Prior to the election of Benedict XVI, Cardinal Kasper told
a reporter in New York that the question of ordaining women to the
diaconate is "not settled."[115] His comment could be read as recognition of apparent unwillingness or inability of the requisite curial offices
to render a decision, but the fact that he commented on the record at
all supports the import of the topic.

The reasons given for the continued refusal to render a decision on
restoring the female diaconate obliquely (and perhaps unintention-
ally) present the Catholic Church's needs for ministry by women deacons. In the same meeting, Cardinal Kasper added that women were
already performing ministerial functions of ordained as deacons.[116]
Such is not wholly the case. The historic role of women deacons is
certainly maintained—the care of the poor, the dying, the homeless
and the hopeless. Women serve in disproportionate numbers as catechists, liturgists, sacristans, and administrators. These functions can
all be fulfilled by laypeople.[117]

While by exceptional rescripts women sometimes can fulfill some
duties of the office of deacon (witnessing marriages, solemnly baptiz-
ing), there are canonical restrictions against lay persons preaching or
sharing authority. It is here that women are shut out from licit participation in the formal work of the church. The Code of Canon Law
(as well as the Code of Canons of the Eastern Churches) specifically
forbids unordained persons to preach at Eucharistic liturgies or have
any ordinary juridical authority.[118] So while women may be the engine
of the church's praxis, they may not speak about it to the assembly.
And while women may manage funds, be trained as canon lawyers,
and prepare and even witness sacraments by rescript, they cannot have
ordinary jurisdiction.

So while a woman may be a member of a marriage tribunal, as a
lay person she cannot be a single signer of an opinion, even an opinion
she has written. Such would evidence ordinary juridical authority
of a woman over a man. Similarly, preaching or otherwise formally

functioning in diaconal capacity at liturgy, particularly at the liturgy of the Eucharist, is expressly forbidden. While each prohibition maintains the division between clergy and laity (something Call to Action–Nebraska railed against) each could be resolved through the restoration of ordained women deacons in the Catholic Church.

Although a number of diaconal ministries are performed by unordained persons, and certain diaconal juridical and sacramental authority can be delegated to unordained persons, despite Cardinal Kasper's opinion that women are already doing what they would do as deacons, no Catholic woman in full communion with Rome genuinely functions as a deacon.[119]

The 2002 International Theological Commission document states that the functions of women deacons of the ancient church are not the same as the functions of the deacon today.[120] Still, the document does not deny that women were sacramentally ordained.[121] In fact, the seventy-page French text concludes:

> Regarding the ordination of women to the diaconate, it should be noted that two important points emerge from what has been set forth until now: 1) the deaconesses mentioned in the ancient tradition of the Church—as suggested by their rite of institution and the functions they exercised—are not purely and simply the same as deacons; 2) The unity of the sacrament of order, in the clear distinction between the ministries of the bishop and the priests on the one hand and the ministry of the deacon on the other, is strongly underscored by ecclesial tradition, above all in the doctrine of Vatican Council II and the postconciliar teaching of the Magisterium. In the light of these elements, supported by the evidence of the present historical-theological research, it will be up to the ministry of discernment, which the Lord has established in his Church, to speak authoritatively on this question.[122]

The document, formally a "working paper," may go before the plenarium of the Congregation for the Doctrine of the Faith, which in turn may issue its own statement. Presenting a seven-chapter chronological exploration of the history and theology of the diaconate, the document leans away from returning women to the diaconate without issuing a definitive finding.

For many years commission subcommittees considered the theological role and identity of permanent deacons; the document never left subcommittee in the previous iteration of the commission (1992–1997). The current subcommittee unsuccessfully presented papers for approval in annual meetings in 1999, 2000, and 2001,[123] and finally gained approval in October 2002.[124] Portuguese priest Henrique de Noronha Galvão headed this most recent commission subcommittee on the diaconate.[125]

The as yet unanswered question of the restoration of the tradition of women deacons in the Catholic Church languished for at least twenty years, since the suppression of the original International Theological Commission study on women deacons, requested by Paul VI. As a natural complement to his *motu proprio* On the Order of Deacons (*Ad Pascendum*) (August 15, 1972) restoring the permanent diaconate, Paul VI asked about women deacons. While no official document appeared, its supporting research apparently appeared in 1974 as an article by Cipriano Vagaggini in *Orientalia Christiana Periodica*. Vagaggini demonstrated that women deacons were ordained by the bishop in the presence of the presbyterate and within the sanctuary by the imposition of hands. Vagaggini concluded the historic ordination of women deacons was sacramental.[126] Other scholars have reached similar conclusions, but the 2002 commission document strenuously avoids agreeing that women were ever validly ordained.[127] In this respect, the document proceeds from a foregone conclusion. It makes careful distinctions between what it terms "*diacres*" and "*diaconesses*," eschewing the term "woman deacon" and avoiding linguistic analysis of the titles and roles of women ministers of history.

Despite selective use of history and theological opinion, the document does not completely exclude women from diaconal ordination. While it alludes to the larger body of historical-theological evidence and opinion that concludes women were sacramentally ordained, it does not acknowledge the strength of the argument.

While historical claims are not normative in either direction, what the church once did the church can do again. This is a basic point in the development of tradition, as pointed out by Terrence W. Tilley in his 1998 Presidential Address to the College Theology Society, "normative theological claims cannot stand or fall solely on the basis of historical warrant."[128]

However, the commission implies as best it can that the diaconate's participation in the sacrament of orders eliminates women, latching on to language that implies but does not specifically state that the deacon is configured to Christ precisely as the priest is configured to Christ. Adopting language from *Ad Pascendum*, the document repeatedly states the deacon is "sign or sacrament of Christ himself."[129] Benedict XVI's recent modifications to the Code of Canon Law serve to explicate this point in favor of women deacons.[130]

Regarding women deacons, the document looks at the functions of women deacons, their rites of ordination, the question of sacramental ordination, and the relationship of the diaconate to priesthood.

Functions of Women Deacons

While the works of women deacons of history—always rooted in the Word, the liturgy, and charity—differed regionally, the International Theological Commission's document on the diaconate recognizes that St. Paul called Phoebe a deacon (not deaconess) of the church at Cenechrae.[131] Even so, it ignores or relegates to footnotes substantial literary and epigraphical evidence. For example, one sixth-century tombstone in Turkey reads, "Here lies the deacon Maria of pious and blessed memory." Other markers abound in the East and in the West.[132]

The scattershot approach is supported by a general attitude that all persons called "deacon" are male. The determination that women deacons—"deaconesses"—do not appear until the third century or so is an advantage because in the early church, women deacons were called by their job title, "deacon." In deciding that there is no simple equivalence between women deacons and men deacons, the commission breaks no new ground.[133] Many scholars have demonstrated that the female diaconate of the early church differed across time and space; it was not identical to men's ministry except that it was a true ministerial diaconate. In various instants women deacons preached the Word, assisted at the liturgy, and ministered in charity to women, all tasks somewhat available to women now where the diocesan bishop allows. Like Kasper, the document states that now there is no diaconal service that cannot be done by any member of the laity.[134] But as has been demonstrated previously here, several tasks are available only to clerics: for example preaching at Mass and serving as a single judge.

Citing Cardinal Walter Kasper's argument that it is impossible to take a few historical facts and make an argument, the document proceeds to do just that.[135] It subtly discounts historical mentions of the functions of women deacons, even as it recognizes deaconesses as one of "the two branches of the diaconate."[136] Over forty years ago, French Jesuit Jean Daniélou delineated four areas of ministry specific to women deacons: (1) evangelization, catechesis, and spiritual direction; (2) liturgical roles equivalent to porter, acolyte, lector, and deacon; (3) care of the sick, including anointing; and (4) liturgical prayer.[137] Depending on the era and the locale, women had more or less an active role in the developing sacramentality of the church. Daniélou's finding that women sacramentally anointed the sick depends on Epiphanius: "the woman deacon is delegated by the priest to perform his ministry for him" and raises a deeper question that underlies the quandary embedded in the document: can women be given the power of orders?[138]

Ordination Rituals

Women were ordained to the diaconate in rituals identical to those used for men. The diaconal ordination ritual of the Apostolic Constitutions, codified by the Councils of Nicea (325) and Chalcedon (421) appears identical for males and for females and begins: "O bishop, you shall lay hands on her in the presence of the presbytery."[139] Perhaps the oldest known complete rite of ordination for women deacons, a mid-eighth-century Byzantine manuscript known as "Barberini gr. 336," requires that women be ordained by the bishop within the sanctuary, the proximity to the altar indicating the fact of a true ordination.[140] Diaconal orders were publicly given in the sanctuary; the orders of subdiaconate and below were privately given in the sacristy.

While ecclesiastical law since the end of the fourth century forbids the wearing of the stole to anyone other than bishops, priests, and deacons, and subdeacons were not allowed to handle the chalice, the bishop gave the stole and the chalice to the woman ordained.[141] Similarly, the eleventh-century Bessarion Manuscript,[142] Vatican Manuscript, gr. 1872,[143] and others point to the sacramental nature of the ordination of women deacons.[144] Even so, the document suggests any ceremonials for women presented "minor orders"—e.g., subdeacon, lector—and retroactively questions the intent of the ordaining bishops of history.[145]

The sole recognition of the ordination of women is the laying on of hands for "deaconesses," by implication a fourth and "minor order." The concept of the fourth order of women "deaconesses" forms the core of the entire document and was reportedly present in the 18-page 1999 draft.[146] The commission neither considers nor disputes the "ordainability" of women not involving itself in the distinguishing argument—the question of the subject of ordination—against women priests. Gender is neither form nor matter in the sacrament of orders.[147] The document does not conclude either for or against sacramental ordination of women deacons, nor refer to the scholarship of Cipriano Vagaggini, except in a footnote referring to debate among and between Vagaggini, Roger Gryson, and Aimé Georges Martimort, the latter of whom it appears to depend upon. The Martimort-Gryson repartee in articles and in two books in French (each later translated into English) comprises a complete conversation on the question of sacramental ordination of women deacons, updating the 1926 work of A. Kalsbach.[148] Gryson led with a definitive exploration of texts and concluded that women were sacramentally ordained.[149] Martimort, in his rejoinder, argued specifically against that interpretation.[150] It is telling that Martimort's work was published after the first unpublished ITC document and after the work of Daniélou, Vagaggini, and Gryson. It is also telling how carefully the commission follows Martimort as well as more recent writings by subcommittee member Gerhard Müller.[151]

Are Deacons Sacramentally Ordained?

Echoing the Council of Trent, the document finds the majority theological opinion since the twelfth century supports the sacramentality of the diaconate and states such must be considered in propositions regarding women deacons, perhaps implying that if diaconal ordination is sacramental, then a woman cannot receive it. It does not examine the ecumenical implications of the denial of sacramental diaconal ordination of women. In addition to the modern examples in prior sections of this monograph, scholarship by Evangelos Theodorou and K. K. FitzGerald discusses the continued tradition in Orthodoxy.[152]

While the ITC document may intend to exclude women from the diaconate, its distinctions may serve to support inclusion. As the document repeats several times, the deacon is ordained not to the priesthood but to the ministry (*"non ad sacerdotium sed ad ministerium"*). The real question is not whether, but how, the diaconate participates in the sacrament of orders.[153] However, given that Vatican II presupposes the sacramentality of both modes of the diaconate, the document creates distinctions between *"in persona Christi capitis Ecclesiae"* (how the priest acts—in the person of Christ, head of the church) and a term new in this document, *"in persona Christi servi"* (how the deacon acts—in the person of Christ-servant). By implication, *"in persona Christi"* with any extension cannot be applied to a woman.[154]

Splitting and then rejoining the concept of Christ-Head and Christ-Servant does not contribute to an understanding of the diaconate as a separate and permanent vocation and part of the sacrament of orders. Relentlessly, the conclusion of the ITC document notes that the Catechism of the Catholic Church (n. 1008) affirms "the three grades of ordained ministry are exercised *in persona Christi capitis,*" and in a footnote observes that the relative canons are under revision.[155] As it happened, when the relative canons were revised with Benedict XVI's *motu proprio*, the distinction between bishop and priest (*"in persona Christi capitis Ecclesliae"*) and deacons (*"in persona Christi servi"*) were codified to the advantage of the restoration of women deacons.

Deacons and Priests

If the priesthood debate regarding women is definitively closed, then no woman deacon would be "advanced" to priesthood.[156] The writers may have redacted early draft arguments toward stating the diaconate shared in the sacerdotal priesthood.[157] While such a finding might preclude women from the diaconate, it could also redound to the advantage of the argument for women priests because of the inarguable presence of ordained women deacons in history and today.

The widespread media coverage of worldwide psychosexual dysfunction and malfeasance among Catholic clergy underscores a difficulty of the ITC document. Its attempt to narrowly define the sacrament of orders at any level as part of the (male) priesthood of Christ, excluding women, undermines church teachings about the equality of all persons. The humanity of Christ overcomes the limitations of gender; there is no church document that insinuates or states an ontological distinction among humans except among documents that address the question of ordination.[158]

Further, the ecumenical implications of the distinctions of the ITC document must be considered. Beyond the specific instance of the Anaphor of Addai and Mari explicated earlier, the notion of the ordained minister acting "*in persona Christi*" does not apply in the Eastern Church, where the priest invokes the Holy Spirit, who does all the sacramental work. (The Eastern priest does not say "I absolve you," but rather "May you be absolved"; even the Latin Rite requires an epiclesis—an invocation of the Holy Spirit—for the effecting of a sacrament.)

The final pages of the ITC document state the question is not one of "doing" but of "being," not of function, but of essence, and implying that women, already eliminated from acting "*in persona Christi capitis*," cannot be deacons because of what the document finds as indivisible and necessary symbolism of Christ-Head and Christ-Servant: "in diaconal action would be realized a particular presence of Christ Head and Servant proper to sacramental grace, to the configuration to Christ and to the communal and public dimension of works which are exercised in the name of the church. Belief in this perspective and in the sacramental reality of the diaconate would permit discovery and affirmation of its proper characteristic, not in relation to its functions, but in relation to its theological nature and its representative symbolism."[159]

Such limiting of Christ to his maleness essentially denies the action of Christ in his church, which remains 50 percent female. The genuine question "why not?" has remained constant since Vatican II.[160] Cardinal

Carlo Maria Martini (b. 1927), archbishop emeritus of Milan, called for women deacons at the 1994 Eucharistic Congress in Siena, Italy.[161] Five years later, ordination of women deacons was the second of Martini's seven points before the European Bishops' 1999 Synod.[162]

Mother Hrip'sime, a woman deacon ordained by the Armenian Patriarch of Constantinople and who assisted in liturgies in the United States many years ago, is alive today.[163] The current Armenian Patriarch of Constantinople, His Beatitude Archbishop Mesrob II, has spoken favorably of ordaining more women deacons. The Greek Orthodox Church ordained monastic women deacons through the 1950s, and the Orthodox Church of Greece has voted to restore the practice. Bartholomew, Ecumenical Patriarch of Constantinople, said in 1996 it is possible to return to this "ancient tradition of the Church."[164]

ORDINATION, EXCOMMUNICATION, AND ROMAN CATHOLIC WOMEN

It is not likely the Catholic Church will change its perspective on women priests or bishops, even as it must more carefully examine and explain its position regarding the actions of some segments of Christianity. It is possible, even advisable, that the Catholic Church restore its older tradition of women deacons. It is also possible and advisable that the Roman Catholic Church expands its acceptance of married priests. All of these are already present in one form or another within communions with a claim to Catholic legitimacy and validity. Women deacons and married priests are also present in churches in communion with Rome. How will the magisterium respond to the actions of valid and legitimate bishops that stretch the parameters of the possible, beyond excommunicating them? Will it make any definite determination regarding the validity of the ordinations carried out legitimately outside its boundaries?

Lacking definitive determinations regarding the infallibility of the church's ban on women priests, how will ordained women be formally considered? Specifically, what precisely is the status of women ordained as priests by a valid and legitimate bishop in the Czech underground church? The question, if not of legitimacy at least of validity, remains regarding those originally ordained in the Roman Catholic Women-priests movement, particularly regarding who may have been ordained by a recognized Roman Catholic bishop. Union of Utrecht Old Catholic Church women priests present fewer theological questions because Old Catholic clergy are typically received as laymen when they ask to be received by the Catholic Church, although some Old Catholic Churches have arguable claims to apostolic succession.

The matter of women deacons is less complicated. The women ordained only as deacons in modern times in Orthodox Churches and in the Czech underground church appear to be validly and legitimately ordained deacons. Even the first six women ordained as deacons in the Roman Catholic Womenpriests movement by a valid Roman Catholic bishop have a claim to validity, if not legitimacy. It is possible as well that some legitimately ordained women deacons in some Union of Utrecht Old Catholic Churches and in some Anglican provinces may indeed meet the tests of validity Rome would levy in order to recognize their status.

It is critically important to distinguish ordination of women as priests or bishops and ordination of women as deacons, for both the theological and juridical reasons examined here and in light of other contemporary issues. Most arguments for women's ordination do not carefully distinguish ordination as priests or bishop and ordination of women as deacons, in part because these arguments begin from the position of rights and power, rather than from the needs of the church. Despite internal discussions and actions regarding women deacons within the Roman Catholic Church and those churches in communion with it, there remains a "loyal opposition" that calls for women priests. The loyal opposition, for example in Call to Action and in Roman Catholic Womenpriests, is not totally "loyal" in the eyes of Rome, as it often digresses from dogma in other areas. It is these groups that caught the attention of Bishop Bruskewitz in Nebraska, and which often advance women's ordination only as part of a wider agenda of issues.

It is precisely because the loudest calls for the ordination of women as priests come from the quarters of the church seemingly also on a collision course on other issues that the question of women priests and bishops grinds to a frozen halt within circles of power. The problem is clear: it appears that they who support the ordination of women as priests also oppose specific teachings of the church. Conjoining all the arguments gives the impression that women priests would dilute dogma in many other areas, specifically areas of human sexuality.

There is further diminution of interest in women deacons in light of arguments for women priests and bishops that are rooted in a call for access to power, in part because the diaconate as lived by the over 35,000 (predominantly married) men worldwide does not appear to enter into the power structure of the church sufficiently to effect any real change. Such ignores the reason for diaconal service. The point is not "power," but service, although a genuine restoration of ancient diaconal practices, particularly restoration of the control of church funds and charity to the deacons, would engender a certain amount of power.

Even so, reopening the diaconate to women and admitting ordained women to proper governance and ministry would have a startling effect on the public perception of the official church, now suffering from an increasing erosion of moral authority. The concurrent implosions of systems, as diocese after diocese collapses into bankruptcy, combined with the international media spotlight on what multiple diocesan bishops and the Vatican (specifically, Benedict XVI) did or did not do regarding the pederast scandal, actually presents an opportunity for the official church to preach brilliantly on the value of the human person as male and female and climb out of the mud left by its own mistakes.

Prescinding from the concept of women priests, the hierarchy's inherent dysfunctional responses to women can be addressed and perhaps in part cured by the restoration of the ancient tradition of women deacons, even as related issues in other churches and communions surface. As Union of Utrecht Old Catholic Churches, other Old Catholic bishops and movements (for example, those related to Milingo), Roman Catholic Womenpriests, Call to Action and multiple other organizations and movements gain equal footing with the Catholic Church headquartered at the Vatican on the newly leveled worldwide media stage, Catholicism can act to both retain its dogma and recall its older traditions. Both women deacons and a wider acceptance of married priests could meet the needs of the whole church for ministry and for substantiation of Catholicism's evangelical message. What the church once did, the church can do again.

As for the already ordained women, whether as priests or bishops or as deacons, whether legitimately within their own churches or illegitimately within the Roman Catholic Womenpriests movement or other ecclesial communions unrecognized by Rome, the question remains whether, theologically, "the church" has done anything at all. Again, the world's perception is clouded and confused. While Pope Benedict XVI seems ready to welcome women into positions of governance and ministry that require ordination (but not priestly ordination), the formal excommunication of the priests, deacons, and bishops of Roman

Catholic Womenpriests supports the notion that something sacramental has already happened. Who else has been excommunicated and why? Archbishop Marcel Lefebvre was, and those whom he ordained validly and illicitly. Archbishop Emmanuel Milingo, who did the same, was also excommunicated. The validity of their sacramental actions is not questioned. The substantiation of their excommunications is juridical; they are accused of having abused their sacramental powers.

As for the ordination of women as priests, it is not possible to perform a sacrament and do as the Catholic Church does if the Catholic Church does not believe it can do it. That is, Rome in its official teachings does not believe women can be ordained as priests. Therefore, Rome cannot do what it does not believe it is able to. Yet in some very clear and public instances the church as the people of God, claiming to be in communion with Rome, says it can ordain women to priesthood. Some groups demonstrating this belief, *Koinótes* and certain Union of Utrecht churches, appear to have followed the pattern of the Anglican communion in determining the question. Others, such as the Roman Catholic Womenpriests movement, which also claims communion with Rome, assume the official teachings of the Catholic Church are merely juridical and can be overcome by sacramental authority. (So also, regarding married priests and bishops, in the case of Married Priests Now! and the further activities of Emmanuel Milingo.)

Independent of these actions there seems little question about the restoration of the tradition of ordained women deacons. Rome has said nothing regarding the diaconal ordinations of women deacons in *Koinótes*, Orthodoxy, in Churches of the East, or in Union of Utrecht Old Catholic Churches. If the diaconal ordinations in Orthodoxy, in Churches of the East, and in Union of Utrecht Old Catholic Churches are valid within these other recognized Churches, with which the Catholic Church hopes for reunion at some distant point, what does that imply for the diaconal ordinations of the Roman Catholic Womenpriests movement, which does not have a permanent diaconate? If ordinations are invalid and part of another recognized Church, what does that imply for ecumenical relations, especially in light of *Unitatis Redintegratio*? If the ordinations in Orthodoxy, in Churches of the East, and in Union of Utrecht Old Catholic Churches retain the historical provenance of the Catholic Church, what does that imply for their validity?

Neither the form nor the matter, the words nor the actions, will go away. Despite multiple efforts in modern times to tamp down and close the still open book on women's ordination, scholars continue to debate it, even as some women have taken matters, literally, into their own hands. Too many questions survive the efforts to end the discussion, and the possibility that women can be validly ordained, if not as priests, at least as deacons, begs for resolution and action. Until then, the discussion will continue, but should it?

It is well to recall the words of Benedict XVI on the subject, spoken in 1997 while he was prefect of the Congregation for the Doctrine of the Faith, particularly regarding to discussion of women's ordination and remaining within communion with the Rome: "However, in late January, Cardinal Joseph Ratzinger, who oversees church doctrine said at a news conference that Catholics who reject certain teachings, including the church's ban on women priests, are 'not necessarily heretics.' Their perspective is 'not grounds for excommunication' under church law, he said, although 'they are making a serious error against the faith.'"[165] If those who reject teachings on women priests are making a "serious error," but are not "heretics," the implication is that the teachings, perhaps at some distant point in the future, can be changed.

If the teaching on women priests is irreformable, Rome must clearly state the theological parameters and finalize the discussion. So also with women deacons. Ongoing discussion at this point seems circular, even as it is aimed at withdrawing what juridical authority diocesan bishops seemed to have had over restoring women deacons. The recent changes in canon law emanating from the Congregation for the Doctrine of the Faith make the ordination of a woman to the diaconate a "crime" worthy of excommunication. Yet there remains no clear doctrinal statement regarding women deacons beyond the early conciliar decrees and papal letters expressly giving bishops the juridical authority to ordain women as deacons for their dioceses. For good or for ill, fairly or unfairly, the Vatican appears like the litigator who is losing a case on its merits and who can only challenge the substance of the case administratively.

The questions are serious enough to deserve definitive teaching. Until then, they remain open.

NOTES

INTRODUCTION

1. Moon, a Presbyterian from North Korea, founded the Holy Spirit Association for the Unification of World Christianity in Korea on May 1, 1954.
2. Benedict XVI, post-synodal apostolic exhortation *Saramentum Caritatis* (February 22, 2007), http://www.vatican.va/holy _father/benedict_xvi/apost_exhortations/documents/hf_ben-xvi _exh_20070222_sacramentum-caritatis_en.html (accessed January 26, 2011).
3. Patrician Friesen, Rose Hudson, and Elsie McGrath were subjects of a formal decree of excommunication by Archbishop Burke, now a Cardinal Prefect of the Supreme Tribunal of the Apostolic Signatura (the Roman Catholic Church's Supreme Court). Burke left St. Louis nearly immediately following his actions. See *St. Louis Review*, "Declaration of Excommunication of Patricia Friesen, Rose Hudson, and Elsie McGrath," March 12, 2008, http://stlouisreview .com/article/2008-03-12/declaration-0 (accessed February 8, 2011).

PART I

1. S. L. Hansen, "Vatican Affirms Excommunication of Call to Action Members in Lincoln," *Catholic News Service* (December 8, 2006), http://www.catholicnews.com/data/stories/cns/0606995.htm (accessed November 2, 2010).
2. Weakland had previously served in Rome as fifth Abbot Primate of the Benedictine Confederation (1967–1977) and is now retired. See Rembert G. Weakland, *A Pilgrim in a Pilgrim Church: Memoirs of a Catholic Archbishop* (Grand Rapids, MI: W. B. Eerdmans, 2009).
3. Facts are from Bruskewitz's curriculum vitae at http://www .dioceseoflincoln.org/Archives/about_curriculum-vitae.aspx (accessed February 10, 2011).

4. The office is now called Vicar General.

5. His principal consecrator was the late Daniel E. Sheehan, then Archbishop of Omaha; his co-consecrators were the late Leo J. Burst, then a Milwaukee auxiliary bishop, and Glennon P. Flavin, his predecessor as bishop of Lincoln.

6. The national average is approximately 1 priest per 1,640 Catholics. Center for Applied Research in the Apostolate. See http://cara .georgetown.edu/CARAServices/requestedchurchstats.html (accessed November 2, 2010).

7. As of 2011, Lincoln's 95,000 Catholics live in 136 parishes; Omaha counts 220,000 Catholics and 148 parishes and missions; Grand Island counts 49,544 Catholics and 69 parishes and missions.

8. Paul VI, Decree Concerning the Pastoral Office of Bishops in the Church *Christus Dominus*, (October 28, 1965), no. 38. http://www .vatican.va/archive/hist_councils/ii_vatican_council/documents/ vat-ii_decree_19651028_christus-dominus_en.html (accessed November 2, 2008).

9. There are 178 Latin or Roman Catholic (arch)dioceses; 17 Eastern Catholic eparchies (dioceses), and one apostolic exarchate (the Syro-Malankara Catholic Exarchate in the United States). Only the 258 active bishops and eparchs have a vote; retired members have a voice but no vote. Auxiliary bishops cannot vote on budget matters. See http://www .usccb.org/comm/catholic-church-statistics.shtml (accessed November 2, 2010)

10. See http://www.usccb.org/whoweare.shtml (accessed August 10, 2010). The Archdiocese of Baltimore was founded in 1789.

11. The recommendations of *Christus Dominus* were made law by Paul VI, *motu proprio Ecclesiae Sanctae* no. 41. (1), "Bishops of countries or territories which do not yet have an episcopal conference according to the Norms of the Decree *Christus Dominus* are to see to its establishment as soon as possible, and to the drawing up of its statutes which are to be confirmed by the Apostolic See." http://www .vatican.va/holy_father/paul_vi/motu_proprio/documents/hf_p-vi _motu-proprio_19660806_ecclesiae-sanctae_en.html (accessed November 2, 2008).

12. Paul VI, Decree *Christus Dominus*, no. 37.

13. Ibid., no. 38.

14. The five-member bishops' committee for this statement comprised Cardinal Joseph L. Bernardin, Archbishop of Chicago, Chair; John J. O'Connor, Auxiliary Bishop of the Military Ordinariate of the U.S.A.;

Thomas J. Gumbleton, Auxiliary Bishop of Detroit; Daniel P. Reilly, Bishop of Norwich; George A. Fulcher, Bishop of Lafayette (Indiana).

15. Paul VI, Decree *Christus Dominus*, no. 38.

16. Ibid., no. 44; emphasis added.

17. For example, the USCCB statements "On Embryonic Stem Cell Research" (2008), "Forming Consciences for Faithful Citizenship" (2007), "Global Climate Change" (2001).

18. Joseph Cardinal Ratzinger and Vittorio Messori, *The Ratzinger Report: An Exclusive Interview on the State of the Church* (San Francisco: Ignatius, 1985), 59.

19. Phyllis Zagano and Terrence W. Tilley, *The Exercise of the Primacy: Continuing the Dialogue* (New York: Crossroad/Herder, 1998), ix–x.

20. See Ibid. See also Patrick Granfield, *The Limits of the Papacy: Authority and Autonomy in the Church* (New York: Crossroad, 1987); "Pope," *s.v.*, *New Dictionary of Theology*, ed. Joseph A. Komanchak, Mary Collins, and Dermot A. Lane (Wilmington, DE: Michael Glazier, Inc., 1987), 779–81.

21. Multiple works have appeared regarding these difficulties. See, for example, Philip Jenkins, *Pedophiles and Priests: Anatomy of a Contemporary Crisis* (New York: Oxford University Press, 2001); Thomas G. Plante, *Sin against the Innocents: Sexual Abuse by Priests and the Role of the Catholic Church* (NY: Praeger Publishers, 2004); Paul R. Dokecki, *The Clergy Sexual Abuse Crisis: Reform and Renewal in the Catholic Community* (Washington, DC: Georgetown University Press, 2004); Mary Gail Frawley-O'Dea, *Perversion of Power: Sexual Abuse in the Catholic Church* (Nashville: Vanderbilt University Press, 2007). See also Mark M. Gray and Paul M. Peri, "Catholic Reactions to the News of Sexual Abuse Cases Involving Clergy," Working Paper 8 (Washington, DC: Center for Applied Research in the Apostolate, 2006); Thomas P. Doyle, A. W. Richard Sipe, and Patrick J. Wall, *Sex, Priests, and Secret Codes: The Catholic Church's 2,000 Year Paper Trail of Sexual Abuse* (Los Angeles: Volt, 2006); Myra L. Hildago, *Sexual Abuse and the Culture of Catholicism: How Priests and Nuns Become Perpetrators* (New York: Routledge, 2007); Anson Shupe and A. W. Richard Sipe, *Spoils of the Kingdom: Clergy Misconduct and Religious Community* (Champaign: University of Illinois Press, 2007).

22. The USCCB actions essentially but not explicitly criticized Bernard Cardinal Law's oversight of the horrific Boston cases that bled across the national media, as well as the lesser-known problems in other dioceses. No matter the public statements of the USCCB about oversight

and reform, it did not sanction bishops who managed past cover-ups. Within the year, after a stunning vote of no confidence by his priests, Cardinal Law resigned as Archbishop of Boston and removed himself to a convent of ultraconservative nuns in Maryland before accepting the plum position of archpriest of the Patriarchal Basilica of St. Mary Major in Rome. He retained membership on numerous Vatican committees, his participation made all the more convenient by his change of residence despite numerous public calls that he be dismissed.

23. John Jay College of Criminal Justice of the City of New York, "The Nature and Scope of Sexual Abuse of Minors by Catholic Priests and Deacons in the United States 1950–2002" (February 2004).

24. The USCCB has released seven annual reports, the most recent "2009 Annual Report—Report on the Implementation of the Charter for the Protection of Children and Young People" (Washington, DC: USCCB, 2010). Various reports and studies appear on the USCCB website.

25. Paras. 6, 9, 12 and note 1. Both the 2002 and the 2006 Norms specifically note, "Due regard must be given to the proper legislative authority of each Eastern Catholic Church." The Norms address allegations of sexual abuse of minors by priests or deacons.

26. Congregation for the Doctrine of Faith's (CDF) revision gained extreme media attention, as it listed the ordination of women as grave crimes in the midst of others, such as clerical pederasty, violating the seal of confession, and clerical possession of child pornography. The text states that the pope approved the document on May 21, 2010, but it does not bear his signature and remains a promulgation of the CDF. See http://www.usccb.org/mr/Norms-English.pdf (accessed January 21, 2011).

27. The widespread belief among experts and activists is "the hierarchy in general continue to deny the essential role their own actions have played in creating this nightmare." Thomas Doyle, OP, Letter to the Editor, *National Catholic Reporter* (March 30, 2007). While a staffer at the Apostolic Delegation in Washington, DC, Doyle was among the first to directly warn the bishops of the burgeoning scandal. (The Delegation became a Pro-Nuntiature when President Ronald Regan established diplomatic relations with the Holy See and a Nuntiature when John Paul II dropped the distinction between those countries that recognized the Holy See's ambassador as head of the diplomatic corps and those that did not.)

28. The Portland, Tucson, Spokane, Davenport, San Diego, Fairbanks, Wilmington dioceses and the Archdiocese of Milwaukee filed for

bankruptcy protection. Alan Cooperman, "Archdiocese of Portland, Ore. Declares Bankruptcy" *Washington Post* (July 7, 2007) A01; Arthur H. Rothstein, "Roman Catholic Diocese of Tucson Files for Bankruptcy over Abuse Cases" *Associated Press* (September 20, 2004); Janet I. Tu, "Spokane Diocese Files for Bankruptcy" *The Seattle Times* (Spokane, WA) (December 7, 2004); Thomas Geyer, "Davenport Diocese Files for Bankruptcy" *Quad City Times* (October 11, 2006); Michael Fischer, "On Eve of Trial, San Diego Diocese Files for Bankruptcy Protection" *The Press-Enterprise* (San Diego, CA) (February 27, 2007); Matt Miller, "Alaska Diocese files for Ch. 11" *Daily Deal* (March 4, 2008); Brian Witte, "Catholic Diocese of Wilmington Files Bankruptcy" *Associated Press* (October 18, 2009); Annysa Johnson and Paul Gores, "Archdiocese of Milwaukee Files for Bankruptcy Protection" *Journal Sentinel* (January 4, 2011). See http://www.bishop-accountability.org/bankruptcy.htm#Portland (accessed January 27, 2011).

29. Ashbel Green and Steve Woodward, "Judge OKs Portland Archdiocese Bankruptcy Deal," *Religion News Service* (April 17, 2007).

30. USCCB Office of Media Relations "Governor Keating Resigns from National Review Board" (June 16, 2003) http://www.usccb.org/comm/archives/2003/03-128.shtml (accessed January 21, 2011).

31. The (Arch)dioceses of Boston, Massachusetts; Manchester, New Hampshire; Davenport, Iowa; Portland, Maine; and Fort Worth, Texas, are the most notorious in this respect. See http://www.bishop-accountability.org/.

32. "The Archives Past and Present." See http://asv.vatican.va/en/arch/1_past.htm.

33. See, for example, Gregory Kesich, "Lauzon Lawsuit Opens Church's 'Secret Archive'" *Portland Press Herald* (Maine) (March 27, 2002) http://www.bishop-accountability.org/news3/2002_03_27_Kesich_LauzonLawsuit_Lauzon_AND_Robitaille_1.htm (accessed February 8, 2011).

34. Robert Hrdlicka pled guilty to indecent acts with minors while a US Navy chaplain, was court-martialed, and was sent to prison in 1993. He had been additionally accused of abusing four boys in the Lincoln diocese in 1978. Paul Margand was convicted and given three years in jail for similar crimes. One other priest was accused. According to Call to Action–Nebraska, at least two accusers entered into a confidentiality agreement in November 2004 with the diocese and accepted payments for dropping charges against Jerome C. Murray. See http://bishopaccountability.org/, which gives citations to contemporary news stories on these matters.

35. According to the 2009 report, the Diocese of Lincoln and five Eastern Catholic Eparchies refused to be audited and are not in compliance with the charter. See http://www.usccb.org/ocyp/annual_report/6 _CH1.pdf (accessed August 11, 2010).

36. "2006 Annual Report—Report on the Implementation of the Charter for the Protection of Children and Young People" (Washington, DC: USCCB, March 2007), viii. At the time of that writing, only 2 of 195 US dioceses and eparchies did not respond to the 2006 CARA survey: the Archdiocese of Indianapolis, which did not respond, and the Diocese of Lincoln, which refused to participate (ibid., 8).

37. The Commission ruled on June 30, 1992, and Pope John Paul affirmed the ruling July 11, 1992. See *Acta Apostolicae Sedes* 86 (1994), 541; *Origins* 23 (April 28, 1994), 777–79.

38. By a letter addressing both questions, Arlington Bishop Loverde allowed female altar servers and extended permission to use the 1962 Latin Mass. See letter of Bishop Paul S. Loverde , March 21, 2006. (A bishop's "letter" is a means of his exercising jurisdiction.) http:// www.arlingtondiocese.org/bishop/documents/liturgy-loverdeletter .pdf (accessed January 21, 2011); and *The 1996 Synod of the Diocese of Lincoln: A Journey of Faith into the 21st Century: Statutes for the Diocese of Lincoln, Nebraska Resulting from the Collaborations of the Bishop, Priests, Religious, and Laity of the Diocese* (August 5–7, 1996), chap. 5, sect. 4, "The Holy Eucharist."

39. "CHD Reports Conflicting," *CALL Spirit* (September/October 1985), 1, 4.

40. "Lincoln Catholics Reveal Petition Attempt," *CALL Spirit* (September/October 1985), 1, 6–9.

41. "Sequel to Campaign for Human Development Story," *CALL Spirit* (January/February 1986), 8.

42. "Response to 'Partners in the Mystery of Redemption,'" *CALL Spirit* (Fall 1988), 10.

43. "Lay Women and Men in Service to the Church," *CALL Spirit* (Summer 1989), 2–13.

44. "A Sad Footnote," *CALL Spirit* 10:4 (1991), 6.

45. "Giggles From the Past," *CALL Spirit* 10:4 (1991), 7

46. Flavin was a priest, then auxiliary bishop, of Saint Louis, until he acceded to Lincoln at the age of 51.

47. "To Everything There is a Season," *CALL Spirit* 12:2 (1993), 1.

48. Donna Steichen, *Ungodly Rage: The Modern Face of Catholic Feminism* (San Francisco: Ignatius, 1991); Helen Hull Hitchcock, *The Politics of Prayer: Feminist Language and the Worship of God* (San Francisco:

Ignatius, 1992); Manfred Hauke, *Women in the Priesthood: A Systematic Analysis in the Light of the Order of Creation and Redemption* (San Francisco: Ignatius, 1988).

49. Steichen, *Ungodly Rage*, 118.

50. Secretariat for the Liturgy, USCCB "Suggested Guidelines Regarding Servers Prepared by the Committee on the Liturgy" (June 1994). No. 70.1 of the *General Instruction of the Roman Missal* restricted liturgical functions in the sanctuary only to men. This document specifically noted those restrictions no longer applied.

51. The sequence of legislative texts is as follows: 1917 Code of Canon Law; apostolic letter *Pastorale Munus* (November 30, 1963); Decree of Vatican II *Christus Dominus* (October 28, 1965); apostolic letter *Ecclesiae Sanctae* (August 6, 1966); and 1983 Code of Canon Law.

52. Stevens became president of the College of Saint Mary in Omaha in 1996.

53. Telephone interview, Dr. Maryanne Stevens, March 28, 2007.

54. For single events, such as weddings and funerals at the invitation of a pastor, by custom priests have, or had, sacramental faculties in contiguous dioceses. Following the widespread priest pederasty problems, guidelines from the UCSSB and the Conference of Major Superiors of Men now state a letter of suitability must be sent to a particular diocese whenever a priest asks to exercise public ministry within another diocese.

55. Richard Maciejewski was ordained for Grand Island in June 1967. Following disagreements with his bishop, he was left without assignment in the early 1970s and was suspended from priestly ministry in June 1973.

56. Copies of the "Affirmation of Faith" used at the event were provided by the Diocese of Lincoln and Call to Action–Nebraska; the Eucharistic Prayer was provided by the Diocese of Lincoln.

57. "Joseph, our bishop" is mentioned, a probable reference to Chicago's Cardinal Joseph Bernardin.

58. Telephone interview. Father Jack McCaslin, March 22, 2007.

59. Telephone interview, Richard Maciejewski, March 28, 2007.

60. Email correspondence from John Krejci to author, March 18, 2007.

61. Letter of J. A. McShane to Monsignor Thorburn, March 4, 1996.

62. Letter of Lori Darby and John Krejci, co-chairs, Call to Action–Nebraska, to Most Rev. Fabian Bruskewitz, March 6, 1996.

63. Letter of Monsignor Timothy J. Thorburn to J. A. McShane, March 7, 1996.

64. Letter of Fabian W. Bruskewitz to Lori Darby and John Krejci, March 18, 1996.

65. *Southern Nebraska Register* (March 22, 1996). The organizations named were Planned Parenthood, Society of Saint Pius X (Lefebvre Group), Hemlock Society, Call to Action, Call to Action–Nebraska, Saint Michael the Archangel Chapel, Freemasons, Job's Daughters, DeMolay, Eastern Star, Rainbow Girls, and Catholics for a Free Choice.

66. Six lay persons in Hawaii invited Bishop Richard Williamson of the breakaway Society of Saint Pius X of Canada to perform confirmations in their chapel and were subsequently excommunicated by Honolulu Bishop Joseph A. Ferrario (d. 2003) on May 1, 1991, following a formal canonical warning January 18, 1991. On June 28, 1993, the Apostolic Pro-Nuncio of the United States, Archbishop Agostino Cacciavillan, misrepresented the decree of the Congregation for the Doctrine of the Faith, intimating that its head, Cardinal Ratzinger, suggested the person in question be placed under interdict. The petitioner pursued the matter and in February 1994 received the June 4, 1993, Decree of the Congregation, which affirmed that the case did not merit *latae sententiae* excommunication and made no mention of interdict. http://www.sspx.org/diocesan_dialogues/honolulu_&_hawaii6.htm (accessed November 2, 2010).

67. Thornburn cited Canons 208, 209, 210, 212, 221, 223, 375, 381, 391, 392, 749, 752, 753, 754, 1313, 1314, 1317, 1318, 1319, 1320, 1369, 13793, 1374, and 1375. Letter of Monsignor Timothy Thorburn to James A. McShane, April 1, 1996.

68. Canon 305.1.

69. Call to Action conferences grew steadily during the 1990s. In 1993, 2,800 persons attended; in 1994, 3,100; in 1995, 4,000; and in 1996, over 5,000. In 1995, it established a website at http://www.call-to-action.org.

70. The self-published history of Voice of the Faithful is by James E. Muller and Charles Kenney, *Keep the Faith, Change the Church* (New York: Rodale/St. Martin's Press, 2004).

71. By way of contrast, Cardinal Joseph Ratzinger had just turned 78 when elected pope on April 19, 2005. No one saw his as a "caretaker papacy."

72. Paul VI, encyclical letter *Octogesima Adveniens* (May 14, 1971), para. 48. He cites his encyclical letter *Populorum Progresso* (March 26, 1967) at 81: *AAS* 59 (1967), 296–97. *Populorum Progresso* does not use the term "call to action."

73. Leo XII, encyclical letter *Rerum Novarum* (May 15, 1891), http:// www.vatican.va/holy_father/leo_xiii/encyclicals/documents/hf_l -xiii_enc_15051891_rerum-novarum_en.html (accessed November 2, 2008).

74. Homily of Pope Paul VI to the Second Synod of Bishops, September 30, 1971. http://www.vatican.va/holy_father/paul_vi/homilies/1971/ documents/hf_p-vi_hom_19710930_it.html (accessed November 2, 2010).

75. Para 6.

76. The Synod's "Justice in the World" is posted on the Vatican web site only in Portuguese. http://www.vatican.va/roman_curia/synod/doc- uments/rc_synod_doc_19711130_giustizia_po.html (accessed Febru- ary 8, 2011). An official translation is posted by the Office for Social Justice (Minneapolis-St. Paul) at http://www.osjspm.org/majordoc _justicia_in_mundo_offical_test.aspx (accessed February 8, 2010).

77. Para. 5.

78. Recommendations of Vatican II published in *Christus Dominus* were made law through *Ecclesiae Sanctae*.

79. http://www.cta-usa.org/reprint07-01/25years.html (accessed Sep- tember 2, 2010). Rev. Charles Curran, a priest of the Diocese of Roch- ester, New York, digressed from Vatican teaching on birth control and was removed from his teaching position at Catholic University; Rev. William Callahan, SJ (d. 1998), was a founder of the activist Quixote Center; Theresa Kane, RSM, publicly asked Pope John Paul II to admit women to "all the ministries of our church"; Matthew Fox is a former Dominican priest known for creation spirituality; Edwina Gateley is a feminist preacher; Sister Carmel McEnroy, RSM, was removed from her tenured position at St. Meinrad's Seminary in 1995 for advocat- ing ordination of women priests; Barbara Fiand, SNDdeN, was similarly removed from her seminary teaching post in the late 1990s because she advocated women's priestly ordination; Paul Collins, MSC, is an ecclesi- ologist who challenged the notion of "infallibility" attached to the 1994 *Ordinatio Sacerdotalis* on women priests; Michael Morwood is a former religious priest who lives in Australia and lectures widely in the United States; Lavinia Byrne is a former Catholic sister whose book *Women at the Altar* (London: Continuum, 1994) was pulped by US Catholic pub- lishers on order of the Vatican; Sister Jeannine Gramick and Rev. Rob- ert Nugent were officially silenced in their lesbian/gay ministry; Bishop Jacques Gaillot is a French bishop who began a diocese without walls; Sri Lankan priest Tissa Balasuriya was silenced due to his views on women's ordination.

80. For example, Bishop Dennis Browne of Hamilton, New Zealand said, "We as church need to be continually open to finding ways in which the Eucharist can become easily available to all of our faithful people. We need to be sensitive to the questions that the faithful often ask us, e.g., 'Why does it seem to be possible for former married priests of the Anglican Communion to be ordained and function as Catholic priests, while former Catholic priests who have been dispensed from the vow of celibacy are unable to function in any pastoral way?'" See the following Part II on this point.

81. In a book written to quell questions among seminarians, International Theological Commission member Sara Butler, MSBT, argues that the fundamental reason women cannot be ordained priests is that Jesus chose male apostles. Sara Butler, *The Catholic Priesthood and Women: A Guide to the Teaching of the Church* (Chicago: Hillenbrand Books, 2007).

82. From modifications made in the *Normae de gravioribus delictis*, reserved to the Congregation for the Doctrine of the Faith, art. 5, http://www.usccb.org/mr/Norms-English.pdf (accessed February 19, 2011).

83. Reuters, "Hungary's Military Bishop Resigns for Love," March 23, 2007. Rome typically refuses to laicize bishops. Bishop Tamás Szabó is still listed among Catholic hierarchy but has apparently renounced the priesthood. http://www.catholic-hierarchy.org/bishop/bszabo .html (accessed November 2, 2010).

84. "In the discussion which followed the publication of the Declaration, however, an overly benign interpretation was given to the homosexual condition itself, some going so far as to call it neutral, or even good. Although the particular inclination of the homosexual person is not a sin, it is a more or less strong tendency ordered toward an intrinsic moral evil; and thus the inclination itself must be seen as an objective disorder." Congregation for the Doctrine of the Faith, "Letter to the Bishops of the Catholic Church on the Pastoral Care of Homosexual Persons" (October 1, 1986), no. 3, clarifying the Congregation's "Declaration on Certain Questions Concerning Sexual Ethics" (December 29, 1975).

85. Temporary or permanent infertility within marriage does not bar sexual relations. Also, a woman need not become pregnant against her will, and any woman can protect herself if her partner will not agree to abstain during fertile times. By "objectively disordered" the Catholic Church does not make a psychological judgment, despite media assertions to the contrary. See, for example, the misstatement in *The New York Times*: "The church views gay sex as a sin and homosexual

tendencies as a psychological disorder, but it does not bar chaste gay men from participating in the sacraments." Paul Vitello, "With Scandal Vatican Shifts its Screenings," *The New York Times* (May 31, 2010), A1. Both statements are incorrect. Homosexual activity is, morally speaking, objectively disordered and therefore always wrong. Whether a sinful act constitutes a "sin" moves to a different order of thought because to commit sin an individual must have full knowledge of the gravity of and grant free consent to the given act.

86. Laurie Goodstein, "Bishops Denouce Writings of a Catholic Theologian" *The New York Times* (March 23, 2007), A15. The USCCB presented an unusually long and detailed dissection of Maguire's views, which essentially provide a gloss on the "personally opposed" concept and expand it to argue that because Catholic opinion is divided, church teaching is not normative. Eight bishops and two cardinals (Dulles and George) signed the USCCB statement. USCCB Office of Media Relations, "Doctrine Committee Offers 'Public Correction' of Theologian's Pamphlets on Contraception, Abortion, and Same-Sex Marriage" (March 22, 2007) http://www.usccb.org/comm/archives/2007/07-051.shtml (accessed January 21, 2011). Dolan was named archbishop of New York by Pope Benedict XVI in February 2009.

87. Call to Action, "Milwaukee archbishop dismisses liturgy by women priests at CTA conference" http://www.cta-usa.org/News200609/dolan.html (accessed January 21, 2011).

88. Call to Action, "A Call for Reform in the Catholic Church" http://www.cta-usa.org/cta-ad.html (accessed January 21, 2011).

89. Bozek was involuntarily laicized in 2009 and remains head of the parish, which voted in August 2010 to reject the reconciliation plan with the archdiocese that would have removed him. See Michele Munz, "St. Stanislaus Steps Back from Unification," *St. Louis Post-Dispatch* (August 9, 2010), http://www.stltoday.com/lifestyles/faith-and-values/article_f9836b51-f292-5e04-8ff4-d58edbc55bd3.html (accessed August 16, 2010); and Malcolm Gay, "Renegade Priests Leads a Split St. Louis Parish," *The New York Times* (August 14, 2010), A10, A13.

90. Call to Action Media Release, August 16, 2010.

91. "Statement of Joseph Cardinal Bernardin Re: Call to Action Group" (March 26, 1996).

92. Bob Reeves, "Priests Won't Review Group Memberships," *Lincoln Star-Journal* (March 26, 1996), 1-A, 4-C.

93. Daniel C. Maguire's The Religious Consultation on Religion, Reproductive Health, and Ethics website is at http://www.religious consultation.org/index.html (accessed January 21, 2011).

94. The CTA website has been redesigned since founders Sheila and Dan Daley retired in 2008, and at this writing it no longer links to the preponderance of liberal to radical Catholic advocacy groups, particularly those centered on women's ordination, homosexuality, and abortion: Catholics Speak Out, part of the Quixote Center and called a movement for justice, equality, and democracy in the Roman Catholic Church; FutureChurch, which defines itself as a coalition of parish-based Catholics who are committed to preserving the Eucharist as the core of Catholic worship; The Federation of Christian Ministries, which certifies competent women and men to do public ministry such as presiding at weddings, funerals, liturgies; and several pages dedicated to women's issues, particularly ordination, including: Irish-based Brothers and Sisters in Christ (BASIC); Mary's Pence; WATER (Women's Alliance for Theology, Ethics and Ritual); Women and the Australian Church (WATAC); Catholic Women's Ordination (UK); Women's Ordination Conference (WOC; US); InclusiveChurch; Catholic Network for Women's Equality—(Canada); Women's Desk—We (Asia and The Philippines) CORPUS (Corps of Resigned Priests United for Service); Epiphany (Australia)—from an association of Catholic priests in Australia who have left official church ministry; features Celibacy Is the Issue and Rent a Priest; ARCC (Association for the Rights of Catholics in the Church); North American Conference of Separated and Divorced Catholics; Soulforce; The Humanita Foundation—(Australia); Catholic Pastoral Committee on Sexual Minorities (CPCSM); Always Our Children; OUTreach ND; Straight Spouse Network; Catholics For a Free Choice; Save Our Sacrament; New Ways Ministry; Dignity USA; Dignity Canada-Dignité; California Catholics For a Free Choice; The Rainbow Sash. Call to Action appears to retain its support of these many causes.

95. Letter of Dan Daley and Nicole Sotelo to Archbishop Harry Flynn, March 16, 2007. New Ways Ministry website: http://mysite.verizon.net/~vze43yrc/.

96. "NOMINATION FORM—CALL TO ACTION BOARD OF DIRECTORS
    The Call to Action Board of Directors has determined to move toward a more inclusive process for nomination and selection of new Board members. As a first step in this direction, we are inviting current Call To Action members to nominate candidates for two of four current Board

seats and for consideration in future Board selection processes. Board members will be selected in relation to the following criteria, although it is understood that no one person will likely fulfill all criteria: Candidates that embrace the Call To Action agenda (e.g., the Anti-racism initiative, NextGen activities, the JustChurch project) Candidates that move forward the Board's goal of greater diversity, giving priority to 1) persons of color, 2) persons from within the NextGen profile, 3) persons from the GLBT community. Candidates that bring specific skills/expertise to Board work: fund-raising, finances, communications, public relations, or theology. Candidates who are committed to the work of anti-racism and active non-violence (e.g., principles and strategies of Christian non-violence) and are willing to be transformed by this commitment. Candidates who are comfortable dealing with media (television/radio/print)", http://www.cta-usa.org/boardofdirectors/nominations.html (accessed August 13, 2010).

97. "Rachel Pecora on the Fall 2006 National CTA Conference, with an addendum from Teresa Hawk," *Voices of Nebraska Catholics* 9:4 (December 2006) http://www.calltoactionnebraska.org/voices0904/frmseguevoices0904.html (accessed January 21, 2011).

98. Telephone conversation, James A. McShane, March 16, 2007.

99. Donna Steichen, *Ungodly Rage*, 276–77. Presentation Sister Cafferty, 1984 president of the Leadership Conference of Women Religious and its former executive director, died in 1997; the Catholic Campaign for Human Development annual award is named in her honor. Her work with Monsignor John Joseph "Jack" Egan of Chicago is chronicled in Margery Frisbie, *An Alley in Chicago.*

100. The way the "call" was answered does not seem to have met the approval of Paul VI, who referred to the "*cosi detta*" ("so-called") call to action.

101. Margery Frisbie, *An Alley in Chicago: The Ministry of a City Priest* (New York: Sheed & Ward, 1991).

102. Canon 1374. A person who joins an association which plots against the Church is to be punished with a just penalty; however, a person who promotes or directs an association of this kind is to be punished with an interdict.

103. Canon 305.1 All associations of the Christian faithful are subject to the vigilance of competent ecclesiastical authority which is to take care that the integrity of faith and morals is preserved in them . . .

104. *The 1996 Synod of the Diocese of Lincoln: A Journey of Faith into the 21st Century: Statutes for the Diocese of Lincoln, Nebraska resulting from the collaborations of the Bishop, Priests, Religious, and Laity of the Diocese*

(August 5–7, 1996), chap. 1, sect. 7. "Forbidden Societies" includes "Call to Action (in its various forms)," page 16.

105. Krejci's ordination class was two years behind Bruskewitz's.

106. *Ferrendae sententiae* interdicts and excommunications can be appealed. While under appeal, the penalty (interdict or excommunication) remains, but the effects (inability to participate in sacraments) are suspended.

107. *State v. Coomes*, 170 Neb. 298, 302 (1960). Breach of the peace is a common law offense. The term "breach of the peace" is generic and includes all violations of the public peace, order, decorum, or acts tending to the disturbance thereof. In June 2007, the diocese refused to allow CTA-N members access to its chancery buildings, and threatens they will be arrested as trespassers should they attempt to deliver a petition to Bishop Bruskewitz on their behalf. http://www.callto actionnebraska.org/segue.html (accessed August 16, 2010).

108. Unsigned editorial, "Catholics of Lincoln Deserve Better than This," *National Catholic Reporter* (May 5, 2000), 32, quoting unsigned "Ask The Register," *Southern Nebraska Register* (November 7, 1997), 5.

109. Letter of Archbishop Piergiorgio S. Nesti, CP, then secretary of the Congregation for Institutes of Consecrated Life and Societies of Apostolic Life, to Sister Doris Gottemoeller, RSM, president of Sisters of Mercy of the Americas, April 10, 1999. Also, telephone interview, Sister Theresa Kane, RSM, May 1, 2007. In January 2009, the congregation, under the leadership of Slovenian Cardinal Franc Rodé, CM, called for an "Apostolic Visitation" of all active religious institutes of women in the United States. Cardinal Rodé was replaced by Brazilian Archbishop João Bráz de Avizin early in 2011.

110. Letter of Marie Chin, RSM, to Archbishop Piergiorgio S. Nesti, April 15, 1999.

111. Letter of Fabian W. Bruskewitz to Jeannine Gramick, March 21, 2000. Gramick responded that she was not speaking in violation of the May 31, 2000, Notification from the Congregation for the Doctrine of the Faith but rather on its then 12-year investigation of her. Her topic would be "Conscience and Development of Doctrine: Whose Responsibility?" She wrote, "I would welcome the opportunity to meet with you so that we can better understand the issues that affect the people of God we both are called to serve. Please let me know if this would be possible." Letter of Jeannine Gramick to Fabian W. Bruskewitz, April 7, 2000. Bishop Bruskewitz did not reply. See also Tom Roberts, "Gramick on conscience in Lincoln," *National Catholic Reporter* (May 5, 2000). Both Gramick and Nugent were summoned to their

respective orders' headquarters in Rome on May 23–24, 2000. Pamela
Schaeffer, "Gramick, Nugent summoned to Rome," *National Catholic
Reporter* (June 2, 2000). Also, telephone interview, Sister Jeannine
Gramick, SL, May 1, 2007.

112. When Joan Chittister, OSB, accepted an earlier invitation to give two
talks at a men's Benedictine Monastery in Schuyler, Nebraska, within
the Archdiocese of Omaha, his chancellor, Monsignor Thorburn, wrote
its abbot: "Because of the scheduled program with Chittister, I shall be
obliged in conscience to do all that I can to discourage anyone from
considering a religious vocation in your community, from frequent-
ing the St. Benedict Center, to repent for my past speaking favorably
about it and to do what I can to prevent the advertising of your facility
in the diocese of Lincoln." Thorburn sent a copy to the archabbot of
the Missionary Benedictine Congregation of St. Ottilien in Germany.
Concurrently, the Lincoln vocation director rescinded an invitation for
the abbey to be represented at the Lincoln annual vocation day. Teresa
Malcolm, "Chittister Visit Irks Neighboring Chancellor (Benedictine
Sr. Joan Chittister Invited to Speak at Retreat Center)," *National
Catholic Reporter* (June 4, 1999).

113. Letter of Cardinal Giovanni Battista Re (b. 1934) to Bishop Bruskewitz, November 24, 2006.

114. Unsigned editorial, "Excommunication," *The Pilot* 167:14 (April 5,
1996), 12.

115. *The Charter for the Protection of Children and Young People* was established by the USCCB in June 2002 as a means for addressing allegations of sexual abuse of minors by Catholic clergy (deacons and priests,
not bishops).

116. National Review Board for the Protection of Children and Young People, *A Report on the Crisis in the Catholic Church in the United States*
(February 27, 2004), footnote 49, 138–39.

117. http://www.catholicculture.org/news/features/index.cfm?rec
num=43317; http://www.bettnet.com/blog/index.php/weblog/
comments/bruskewitz_pulls_no_punches/; http://thebishopfabian
bruskewitzfanclub.blogspot.com/2006/04/fraternal-correction.html
(accessed January 27, 2011).

118. Email from Deacon Timothy McNeil, Chancellor of the Archdiocese
of Omaha, to author, August 17, 2010.

119. Voice of the Faithful was initially banned in Rockville Centre, New
York, by its diocesan bishop William F. Murphy, one of Boston Car-
dinal Law's former auxiliary bishops. Muller and Kenney, *Keep the
Faith*, 237. See also John Bookser Feister, "Voice of the Faithful 'Keep

the Faith, Change the Church,'" *St. Anthony Messenger* 111:1 (June 2003), 28–33.

120. This is unless, of course, Call to Action is not considered an association of the Christian Faithful, whose criteria it appears to meet.

121. Canon 1316, "Insofar as possible, diocesan bishops are to take care that if penal laws must be issued, they are uniform in the same city or region."

122. Telephone conversation, Monsignor Timothy Thorburn, August 13, 2010.

123. Richard Gaillardetz, "Shifting Meanings in the Lay-Clergy Distinction," *Irish Theological Quarterly* 64 (1999), 115–39.

124. Avery Dulles, *Models of the Church* (Garden City, NY: Doubleday, 1978).

125. Yves Congar, *Lay People in the Church* (Westminster, MD: Newman, 1965).

126. Paul Lakeland, *Liberation of the Laity* (New York: Continuum, 2004) and *Catholicism at the Crossroads: How the Laity Can Save the Church* (New York: Continuum, 2007).

127. The USCCB has no official policy regarding either CTA or VOTF, and each diocese sets its own policies. Email from Sister Mary Ann Walsh to author, August 16, 2010.

PART II

1. Anglican-Roman Catholic International Commission joint statement, "The Gift of Authority" (Authority in the Church III), 1998, no. 49.

2. Lincoln has three married permanent deacons, only because they relocated from other dioceses, and 151 Latin Rite priests, none of whom is married.

3. Groups represented at the ceremony reportedly included the Old Catholic Church, Orthodox, Liberal Catholic Church of Spain, Charismatic Church of Brazil, Independent Catholic and others from the United States of America and other parts of the world. "Milingo to be installed as patriarch," *Lusaka Times* (August 13, 2010), http://www.lusakatimes.com/?p=28565 (accessed January 22, 2011).

4. The property once belonged to the Canons of Saint Bernard and contained a popular shrine to Our Lady of the Fields. It was purchased in 1968 by a group of businessmen who had hoped to establish a seminary there, but who later donated it to the fledgling Society of Saint Pius X.

5. By incardination (also called "enrollment") a secular bishop, priest, or deacon becomes in theory a member of the diocesan bishop's household and is considered "attached" to his diocese. See Canons 265–272. Religious priests are incardinated in their respective orders or institutes.

6. Canon 1382. "A bishop who consecrates someone a bishop and the person who receives such a consecration from a bishop without a pontifical mandate incur an automatic (*latae sententiae*) excommunication reserved to the Apostolic See." Those ordained are Bernard Fellay, Bernard Tissier de Mallerais, Richard Williamson, and Alfonso de Galarreta. Bishop Antônio de Castro Mayer (1904–1991), retired diocesan bishop of Campos, Brazil, was co-consecrator with Lefebvre. Both de Castro Mayer and Lefebvre were Rome-educated. Pope Benedict XVI's lifting of their excommunications caused worldwide news in 2009, when Williamson was discovered to be a Holocaust denier.

7. There are two Latin forms of the Roman Rite: the ordinary form (1962) and the extraordinary form (1570). The latter, in the missal promulgated by Pius V and reissued by Bl. John XXIII, is referred to as the Tridentine Rite. The 1962 form is generally permitted. See Benedict XVI, apostolic letter *motu proprio Summorum Pontificum* on the use of the Roman Liturgy prior to the reform of 1970 (July 7, 2007), http://www.vatican.va/holy_father/benedict_xvi/motu_proprio/documents/hf_ben-xvi_motu-proprio_20070707_summorum-pontificum_lt.html (accessed January 22, 2011).

8. Among their major concerns are liturgy and ecumenism.

9. A Toronto Catholic priest was suspended for celebrating the Tridentine Mass for the Society of St. Pius X because they are not in communion with Rome. See "Priest Who Ministered to Gibson Is Disciplined," *Christian Century* 121:19 (September 21, 2004), 16.

10. Conversation with Archbishop Milingo, December 6, 2006, Belvedere, Tarrytown, NY. Much recent historical and theological scholarship addresses Catholic women deacons. See, for example, Roger Gryson, *The Ministry of Women in the Early Church* (Collegeville, MN: Liturgical, 1976); the translation of *Le ministère des femmes dans L'Église ancienne. Recherches et synthèses, Section d'historire 4* (Gembloux: J. Duculot, 1972); Aimé George Martimort, *Deaconesses: An Historical Study* (San Francisco: Ignatius, 1986); the translation of *Les Diaconesses: Essai Historique* (Rome: Edizioni Liturgiche, 1982); Phyllis Zagano, *Holy Saturday: An Argument for the Restoration of the Female Diaconate in the Catholic Church* (New York: Crossroad, 2000); Ute Eisen, *Women Officeholders in Early Christianity: Epigraphical and Literary Studies*

(Collegeville, MN: Liturgical, 2000); the translation of *Amsträgerinnen im frühen Christentum. Epigraphische und literarische Studien* (Göttingen: Vandenhoeck & Ruprecht, 1996); Kevin Madigan and Carolyn Osiek, *Ordained Women in the Catholic Church: A Documentary History* (Baltimore: Johns Hopkins University, 2005); and Gary Macy, *The Hidden History of Women's Ordination: Female Clergy in the Medieval West* (New York: Oxford University Press, 2008).

11. Facts about Milingo's life are from Mona Macmillan's introduction to E. Milingo, *The World in Between: Christian Healing and the Struggle for Spiritual Survival*, ed. Mona Macmillan (London: C. Hurst and Company, 1984), 1–13; and from Gerrie Ter Haar, *Spirit of Africa: The Healing Ministry of Archbishop Milingo of Zambia* (London: Hurst, 1992).

12. The Archdiocese of Zambia was erected April 25, 1959.

13. Macmillan's introduction to Milingo's edited writings states that Milingo received a diploma from the one-year Institute of Pastoral Sociology in Rome and studied education at University College, Dublin, in 1962–63. *World in Between*, 3.

14. In 2010, Milingo sued the Catholic Archdiocese of Zambia, alleging it illegally changed title to the land on which the hospital rests from his personal ownership to the Zambian Helpers Society.

15. Ter Haar, *Spirit of Africa*, 178. The others are the Brothers of Saint John the Baptist, the male counterpart to the Daughters, and the Divine Providence Community in 1978. Prior to these, in 1966, he founded the Zambia Helpers Society to aid the rural poor. Ter Haar, *Spirit of Africa*, 2, 10–11, 30, 93. Much of the information in this section depends on Ter Haar's definitive study of the period. See also Ter Haar and Stephen Ellis, "Spirit Possession and Healing in Modern Zambia: An Analysis of Letters to Archbishop Milingo," *African Affairs* (Great Britain), 87, no. 347(1988) 185–206.

16. Bruno Wolnik, SJ, was Prefect from 1927 to 1950; Adam Kozlowiecki, SJ (1911–2007), was named apostolic vicar in 1955 and its first archbishop in 1959. He served until Milingo took possession of the archdiocese on May 29, 1969, having resigned in favor of a native African. From 1970 to 1989, Kozlowiecki, a survivor of Auschwitz and Dachau, continued to live in Lusaka and served as director of the Pontifical Missionary Society of Zambia. He was created Cardinal by fellow Pole John Paul II at the age of 86. He is buried in Lusaka.

17. Macmillan, Introduction, *World in Between*, 5.

18. Macmillan, *World in Between*, 22. The Word of God was founded in 1967 as a Catholic outreach to University of Michigan students by

Ralph Martin, Steve Clark, Jim Cavnar, and Gerry Rauch. Martin now runs Renewal Ministries, a Catholic outreach in Ann Arbor. See Stanly M. Burgess, Gary B. McGee, and Patrick H. Alexander, *Dictionary of Pentecostal and Charismatic Movements* (Grand Rapids, MI: Zondervan, 1998); and Vinson Synan, *The Century of the Holy Spirit: 100 Years of Pentecostal and Charismatic Renewal* (Nashville: Thomas Nelson, 2001).

19. Norbert Brockman, "Milingo, Emmanuel," *An African Biographical Dictionary*, Amenia, NY: Grey House Publishing, 1994.
20. Macmillan, Introduction, *World in Between*, 5.
21. Macmillan, *World in Between*, 39.
22. Ter Haar, *Spirit of Africa*, 26–27.
23. Ibid., 27, quoting open letter of February 5, 1979, p. 6.
24. Ibid., quoting letter to Archbishop Lourdusamy, December 5, 1979.
25. Ibid., 232–33.
26. Macmillan, Introduction, *World in Between*, 5.
27. Macmillan. 36–37.
28. Ter Haar, *Spirit of Africa*, 31–32.
29. Macmillan, Introduction, *World in Between*, 5–6.
30. A. O. Igenoza, "African Weltanschauung and Exorcism: The Quest for the Contextualization of the Kerygma," *Africa Theological Journal* 14:3 (1985), 179–93, 182, citing E. B. Idowu, *African Traditional Religion: A Definition* (London: S. C. M., 1973), 139.
31. Igenoza, "African Weltanschauung and Exorcism," 189.
32. Ibid..
33. Ibid., 190, citing handwritten notes of Rev. Patrick Kalilombe of Malawi.
34. Macmillan, 48.
35. Ter Haar, *Spirit of Africa*, 33.
36. Ibid., 33–34, and 34 n74.
37. Ibid., 38, quoting Letter No. 2269 from the Apostolic Nunciature, April 12, 1982. See also Richard Sales "Why was Milingo Recalled to Rome," *The Christian Century* 99:36 (November 17, 1982), 1157.
38. Ter Haar, *Spirit of Africa*, 41.
39. Ibid., 41, n92, citing Milingo letter, March 16, 1983.
40. Ibid., 62, citing *Newsweek* (September 27, 1982); *Time* (October 25, 1982); and the London *Times* (October 25, 1982) and (August 8, 1983).
41. Ter Haar, *Spirit of Africa*, 42, citing private correspondence.
42. Pope Paul VI established the "Pontificia Commissio de Spirituali Migratorum atque Itinerantium Cura" with the *motu proprio Apostolicae*

Caritatis to provide for "people on the move," such as seafarers, tourists, displaced persons, nomads, and others without fixed places of residences or who were away from their homes.

43. Zambia Episcopal Conference, "A Letter from members of Zambia Episcopal Conference to the Catholics of Zambia on Recent Events in the Archdiocese of Lusaka," *AFER (African Ecclesial Review)* 25:1 (February 1983), 51–57.

44. Reviews include those by Laurenti Magesa, *AFER (African Ecclesial Review)* 27:4 (August 1985), 252–54; Hans-Jürgen Becken, *Missionalia* 13:2 (August 1985), 84; Stephen Chan, *Africa* 55:3 (1985), 345–46; Richard Gray, *African Affairs* 84 (1985), 295–96; James J. Stamoolis, *Themelios* 12:1 (Spring 1986), 31–32; Paul G. Hiebert, *Pneuma* 9:2 (Fall 1987), 194–96; and Lawrence S. Cunningham, *National Catholic Reporter* 21 (August 30, 1985), 17. Reviews also ran in *Times Literary Supplement* (June 28, 1985), 729; *Best Sellers* 45 (August 1985), 192; *CHOICE: Current Reviews for Academic Libraries* 22 (June 1985), 1458; among others.

45. Chan, *Africa*, 346.

46. "The Roman Ritual of Exorcism," in Malachi Martin, *Hostage to the Devil: The Possession and Exorcism of Five Living Americans* (San Francisco: HarperSanFrancisco, 1976, 1992), 460.

47. Vittorio Lanternari, "From Africa into Italy: The Exorcistic-Therapeutic Cult of Emmanuel Milingo," in *New Trends in Development in African Religion*, ed. Peter B. Clarke (Connecticut: Greenwood Press, 1998), 263–283, 271–72.

48. Niels Christian Hvidt, "Interview with Archbishop Immanuel Milingo," February 14, 1998. http://www.tparents.org/Library/Unification/Talks/Milingo/Malingo-980214.htm (accessed November 2, 2010).

49. Presentation of the revised Rite of Exorcism by Cardinal Jorge A. Medina Estévez, January 26, 1999, http://www.vatican.va/roman_curia/congregations/ccdds/documents/rc_con_ccdds_doc_1999-01-26_il-rito-degli-esorcismi_it.html (accessed February 8, 2011). Trans. *L'Osservatore Romano*.

50. "I belonged to a category that finished at 70 years old. I am not the only one. On the other hand, the Pope may extend the retirement age according to the needed service of a person. So there have been some who have gone over 75 years. In this category there are those who expect a prolongation of office. But unfortunately they were not given the prolongation. They suffered a lot to find themselves one day, with a letter, 'your work is finished in Vatican from today on.' They were

totally discouraged as they went about looking for new settlement. I have seen the torments of these people, who thought that they would leave their work with a sumptuous banquet, while they are just told that 'Your work in the Vatican is over.' I did not suffer much, because I was stronger in my vocation in the healing ministry." Email from Emmanuel Milingo to Peter Paul Brennan, March 12, 2008.

51. Blessing ceremonies of the Unification Church (now called the Family Federation for World Peace and Unification) are said to remove the couple from sinful humanity and, consequently, from original sin. Children born of these marriages are said to be free from original sin.

52. "The Words of Rev. Sun Myung Moon from 1993" http://www.tparents.org/Moon-Talks/sunmyungmoon93/UM930128.htm (accessed January 22, 2011).

53. Canon 1071 states that diriment impediments are automatically invalidating impediments and render persons incapable of contracting valid marriages. Canon 1078 lists these impediments to marriage, which include "sacred orders." Only the Apostolic See can dispense the ordained.

54. The warning, called a public canonical admonition, is provided for in Canon 1347 §1 of the Code of Canon Law.

55. "Public Canonical Admonition Issued to Archbishop Milingo," Vatican Information Service News (July 17, 2001) http://visnews-en.blogspot.com/2001/07/public-canonical-admonition-issued-to.html (accessed February 8, 2011).

56. Ibid.

57. For timeline and links to news stories, see Mary Jane Despres, "2001 Timeline of Events Surrounding Archbishop Emmanuel Milingo and Maria Sung." http://www.tparents.org/Library/Unification/Talks/Despres/Despres-MalingoTimeLine-1.htm (accessed January 22, 2011).

58. Michele Zanzucchi, *El pez rescatado del pantano* (Madrid: Ciudad Nueva, 2002). Earlier, relatively conservative takes on the story also appeared, before and after these publications. See "Archbishop Milingo's Voyage," *Catholic Insight* 9:8 (October 1, 2001), 23; and Camilo José Cela Conde, "Lo que diga el Vaticano," *Siempre!* 48:2513 (August 15, 2001), 45.

59. *Times of Zambia*, "I Am Still a Catholic—Insists Milingo," September 11, 2007. http://allafrica.com/stories/200709110366.html (accessed January 22, 2011).

60. Rocco Palmo, "Milingo, Missing Again" Whispers in the Loggia (July 4, 2006) http://whispersintheloggia.blogspot.com/2006/07/milingo-missing-again.html (accessed January 22, 2011).

61. According to the Archdiocese of Washington, Stallings was a priest-candidate from another diocese who became a priest of Washington at the recommendation of his North American College seminary rector, Bishop James A. Hickey, who later became Archbishop of Washington. In 1989, then-Father Stallings announced his intention to establish his own church. His disagreements with Catholicism centered on abortion, birth control, homosexuality, and remarriage following divorce, which he announced on the "Phil Donohue Show." Richard Ostling, "Catholicism's Black Maverick," *Time* (May 14, 1990). Following his televised announcement, on February 5, 1990, then Vicar General, Msgr. William Kane, said, "by his public declaration that he has separated himself from the Church and by his renunciation of Church teaching, Father Stallings has excommunicated himself." *Catholic Standard* (February 8, 1990), 1–6, 16.

62. The CORPUS website is at http://www.corpus.org

63. Email from Peter Paul Brennan to author September 28, 2010.

64. John L. Allen, Jr., "Zambian Archbishop Breaks with Rome; Wants to Help Reconcile Married Priests with the Catholic Church, He Says," *National Catholic Reporter* (July 14, 2006).

65. Carol Glatz, "Vatican Says Archbishop Milingo, Four Others Incur Excommunication," *Catholic News Service* (September 26, 2006), http://www.catholicnews.com/data/stories/cns/0605467.htm (accessed November 2, 1010).

66. Stallings' Temple web pages report "George Augustus Stallings, Jr. is the Archbishop and Founder of an autonomous, independent and African-centered Catholic Church, known as Imani Temple under The African-American Catholic Congregation, headquartered on Capitol Hill in Washington, DC," but do not list the provenance of his episcopal or priestly orders. http://imanitempleaacc.com/GA_Stallings_Bio.pdf (accessed September 29, 2010).

67. As archbishop of Lusaka, Milingo was Principal Consecrator of Archbishop Medardo Joseph Mazombwe, now Archbishop Emeritus of Lusaka. Milingo was Principal Co-consecrator of Archbishop Elias White Mutale (1929–1990), of Kasama, Zambia; Bishop Patrick Augustine Kalilombe, M. Afr., of Lilongwe, Malawi; Archbishop Patrick Fani Chakaipa (1932–2003), of Harare, Zimbabwe; and Archbishop Adrian Mung'andu (1920–2002), of Lusaka, Zambia.

68. Those ordained were Raymond Grosswirth of Rochester, New York, and Deacon Dominic Riccio of Newark, New Jersey. The ceremony took place at Trinity Reformed Church in West New York, New Jersey. "Milingo 'Ordains' Two Married Men, Confirms Links with Man

who Claims to be Messiah," *Catholic News Agency* (February 2, 2007), http://www.catholicnewsagency.com/new.php?n=8246&PHPSESS ID=9aad19d43151b39d17634e19da09b5cb (accessed November 2, 2010).

69. Paul VI, encyclical letter On the Celibacy of the Priest (*Sacerdotalis Caelibatus*) (June 24, 1967), no. 42.

70. The Married Priests Now! website appears to have been taken down. This quote was accessed December 12, 2007.

71. http://www.marriedpriestsnow.org statement dated March 11, 2007 (accessed December 13, 2007).

72. Brighton Phiri, "Milingo Accuses Catholics of Illicit Sex, Homosexuality," *Lusaka Post* (August 8, 2001), http://www.wewillstand.org/media/20010808_9.htm (accessed November 2, 2010).

73. Bruce Chooma, "Is Married Priests Movement Beginning of Catholic Church Reformation?" *Times of Zambia* (August 9, 2007).

74. His pension was once again cut off following his January 9–27, 2008, visit to Rome.

75. Catholic Information Service for Africa/All Africa Global Media, "Korean Bishops Warn Against Ex-Bishop Milingo" (September 18, 2007).

76. The school offers three areas of study: True Parents Studies, Unification Spirituality Studies, and Church Administration Studies (Master of Theology, Th.D., and D. Min.). See http://www.cheongshim .ac.kr/en/index.htm (accessed September 27, 2010).

77. As of July 2007, Worldwide Communion of Catholic Apostolic National Churches (Igrejas Católicas Apostólicas Nacionais) member churches included the following: Argentina: Iglesia Católica Apostólica Argentina (joined 1972); Australia: Australian Catholic Church (1992); Belgium: Gemeenschap van de Goede Herder (http://www .goedeherder.be/); Bolivia: Catholic Apostolic Church of Bolivia; Brazil: Igreja Católica Apostólica Brasileira (founded 1945); Canada: La Fraternité Sacerdotale Saint Jean l'Évangéliste (1990); Colombia: Iglesia Católica Nacional (2005); Costa Rica: The Catholic Apostolic Church of Costa Rica; Czech Republic: The Catholic Apostolic Church of the Czech Republic; Ecuador: The Catholic Apostolic Church of Ecuador; France: The Catholic Apostolic Church of France; Guatemala: Fr. Eduardo Aguirre and followers (received as of July 2007); Italy: The Catholic Apostolic Church of Italy; Mexico: Iglesia Católica Apostólica Mexicana; Philippines: Congregacao de Sao Carlos do Brasil (1985); Spain: The Catholic Apostolic Church of Spain; United

Kingdom: Catholic Apostolic National Church; United States: Communion of Christ the Redeemer (2007).

78. Vivian Sequera, "Excommunicated Archbishop Celebrates Marriage of Former Priest in Brazil," Associated Press (April 1, 2007). "The couple now belong to Milingo's advocacy group Married Priests Now!, which has 18,600 married priests in Brazil, according to Jose Moura." Formally, relations with non-Christian bodies are termed "interreligious," not "ecumenical."

79. Tom Hennigan, "The Archbishop, His Wife, the Pope and the Moonies," *Irish Times* (April 14, 2007).

80. Ibid.

81. Emmanuel Milingo, email correspondence from Emmanuel Milingo, "Action and Reaction, a Report from Abp. Milingo on His African Pilgrimage," September 22, 2008.

82. David Wiley, "Rebel Priest Publishes Life Story," *BBC News* (January 18, 2008), http://news.bbc.co.uk/2/hi/africa/7195377.stm (accessed September 27, 2010).

83. http://www.catholiczambia.org.zm/index.php?sid=1724 (accessed September 20, 2007.) No longer available.

84. Letter of Emmanuel Milingo to Archbishop (later Cardinal) Simon Lourdusamy, then secretary of the Congregation for the Evangelization of Peoples, December 5, 1979, as quoted in Ter Haar, *Spirit of Africa*, 31.

85. See, for example, Marie McDonald, MSOLA, "The Problem of the Sexual Abuse of African Religious in Africa and in Rome," Paper for the Council of "16," November 28, 1998, which blames celibacy as a foreign value, the inferior position of women, the AIDS pandemic, financial difficulties of women's congregations, and generally poor understanding of consecrated life combined with a "conspiracy of silence" regarding abuse of women religious by priests and seminarians.

86. Milingo, *World in Between*, 16. *Mashawe* is typically believed to be manifest by agitation, anxiety, and other psychological disturbances, and is thought to lead to nervous breakdowns.

87. Founded in 1955 by Archbishop McCarthy of Nairobi. Mother Gacambi was named superior general in 1970. See http://soeurs-blanches.cef.fr/eng/100_kenyaa.htm (accessed September 27, 2010).

88. Details of her healing are reported in Adrian Hastings, "Emannuel Milingo as Christian Healer," in *African Medicine in the Modern World*, ed. U. Mclean and C. Fyfe, University of Edinburgh Seminar, December 10–11, 1986 (Edinburgh: University of Edinburgh, 1987),

147–71; Lanternari, "From Africa into Italy," 263–83, 273; and, to a lesser extent, Ter Haar, *Spirit of Africa*, 23–24.

89. See Milingo, *World in Between.*

90. "The Pontifical Commission 'Ecclesia Dei' was established by John Paul II with the *Motu Proprio* of 2 July 1988 with the 'task of collaborating with the bishops, with the Departments of the Roman Curia and with the circles concerned, for the purpose of facilitating full ecclesial communion of priests, seminarians, religious communities or individuals until now linked in various ways to the Fraternity founded by Archbishop Lefebvre, who may wish to remain united to the Successor Peter in the Catholic Church.'" See http://www.vatican.va/roman_curia/congregations/cfaith/ced_documents/rc_con_cfaith_20090930_ecclesia-dei_en.html (accessed September 20, 2010).

91. Email from Peter Paul Brennan, an archbishop of Married Priests Now!, to author, January 9, 2008. Assuming the correct intent was present and the proper ritual was used, all might be considered validly ordained.

92. The Archdiocese of Washington settled a lawsuit involving allegations about Stallings for $125,000 in 2009. William Wan, "Washington Archdiocese Reaches Settlement in Sexual Abuse Lawsuit," *Washington Post* (October 14, 2009), B-2.

93. The recent Decree of the Congregation for the Doctrine of the Faith regarding the "delict," or crime, of the sacred ordination of a woman" (December 19, 2007) states in part, "both the one who attempts to confer a sacred order on a woman, and the woman who attempts to receive a sacred order, incur an excommunication *latae sententiae* reserved to the Apostolic See." *Acta Apostolicae Sedis* 100 (2008), 403, published in *L'Osservatore Romano* (May 30, 2008). The Decree's intent was later restated by the Congregation within a long list of grave delicts, or "crimes" published in July 2010 with the approval of Pope Benedict XVI, but not bearing his signature. "The more grave delict of the attempted sacred ordination of a woman is also reserved to the Congregation for the Doctrine of the Faith: 1° With due regard for can. 1378 of the Code of Canon Law, both the one who attempts to confer sacred ordination on a woman, and she who attempts to receive sacred ordination, incurs a *latae sententiae* excommunication reserved to the Apostolic See." http://www.usccb.org/mr/Norms-English.pdf (accessed September 10, 2010).

94. The matter and form for valid ordination were defined the Pius XII, apostolic constitution On the Sacrament of Order (*Sacramentum Ordinis*) (November 30, 1947), which does not specify a required gender

for the ordinand. The default assumption of the document would be male gender.

95. Among the others that use the term "Old Catholic" in the United States are the Old Catholic Church of America, the Old Catholic Church in North America, the Catholic Apostolic National Church, and the Independent Old Catholic Church of America. The Catholic Church also technically recognizes the validity of orders in the Autocephalous Church Movement (The Catholic Apostolic Church).

96. The international Old Catholic community comprises the autonomous Old Catholic Churches in the Netherlands, Germany, Switzerland, Austria, Poland, the United States, Canada, Croatia, France, Sweden, Denmark, and Italy, associated by the Union of Utrecht. The Old Catholic Church in the Czech Republic has mutual recognition of sacraments with the Old Catholic Church of Mariavites, the Independent Catholic Church in the Philippines, and with the Anglican Communion. The Union of Utrecht rejects the dogma of the Immaculate Conception promulgated by Pius IX in 1854 and rejects the disciplines (but not the doctrine) of the Council of Trent. Not all Union of Utrecht Churches are recognized by the Holy See.

97. The Second Vatican Council's Decree on Ecumenism, *Unitatis Redintegratio* (November 21, 1964), unequivocally recognizes the sacraments (and specifically Eucharist and orders) of the Oriental Orthodox Churches. The Code of Canon Law allows Catholics outside of danger of death to receive the sacraments of the Orthodox Churches. Canon 844. §2. Whenever necessity requires it or true spiritual advantage suggests it, and provided that danger of error or of indifferentism is avoided, the Christian faithful for whom it is physically or morally impossible to approach a Catholic minister are permitted to receive the sacraments of penance, Eucharist, and anointing of the sick from non-Catholic ministers in whose Churches these sacraments are valid.

98. The provenance of various orders can be traced through Gary L. Ward, Bertil Persson, and Alan Bain, eds., *Independent Bishops: An International Directory* (Detroit: Apogee Books, 1991).

99. *The Times of Zambia* (Ndola) (December 26, 2007).

100. Assist News Service, Journal Chrétien, "Zambia: Catholic Church to sue splinter group" (December 26, 2007). http://www.spcm.org/Journal/spip.php?breve5779 (accessed January 22, 2011).

101. Many of the facts in this section depend on the website of the Apostolic Catholic Church, http://www.oldcatholic.com/costa.html (accessed January 2, 2008), which domain is no longer operative. It reported, "When he learned of the excommunication, Dom Carlos Duarte Costa,

responded, establishing the Brazilian Catholic Apostolic National Church (ICAB) on July 6, 1945. The extract of the statutes of the new church was published in Federal official gazette, page 12, 637, July 25, 1945. The Brazilian Catholic Apostolic Church was registered in book No 2 of the Civil Societies, under Number 107.966 of the Book A, Number 04." See also http://www.hrcac.org.uk/icab-founded-1913 .html (accessed January 26, 2011).

102. "The college of bishops for the enthronement was led by Bishop Paul Deblock Yede of the Gallicanes Catholic Church assisted by Bishop Jean Ndjewel and Bishop Dika of Congo Brazzaville, both of the Old Catholic Church." See http://upfsouthernafrica.org.za/content/view/51/1/ (accessed September 21, 2010).

103. Allen, "Zambian Archbishop Breaks with Rome."

104. "CORPUS membership is now inclusive of the following: 1.) Married priests; 2.) Wives of married priests, who may or may not be called to ordination themselves; 3.) Married men who have never been ordained, but are nevertheless called; 4.) Single and married women who have never been ordained, but are nevertheless called; 5.) Diocesan and religious order priests, deacons and women religious who support the inclusive goals of CORPUS." http://www.corpus.org/ page.cfm?Web_ID=588 (accessed January 8, 2008.)

105. Minutes of February 2007 CORPUS board meeting.

106. Hickman ultimately traces the provenance of his orders to Dominicus Marie Varlet (1719), Roman Catholic Bishop of Babylon, through Johannes Van Stiphout (1745), Old Catholic Bishop of Haarlem, but there is no Catholic record of Varlet's ordination, which according to Hickman's website followed the following legitimate provenance. The Dutch Church had been without a Bishop for 18 years as a punishment from Rome because the Dutch Church refused to cooperate in the persecution of the "Jansenists" in Holland. Following the election of Comelius Van Steenhoven to serve as Archbishop of Utrecht, Varlet consecrated Van Steenhoven the seventh Archbishop of Utrecht, creating the Old Catholic Church.

107. *Episccopi vagantes*—"wandering bishops"—were consecrated in one or another line of apostolic succession traced by the Catholic Church but are not in communion with Rome. They received "absolute ordination"—ordained to the service of no one. Two main lines of vagan bishops are the Old Catholic and the traditionalist Pierre Martin Ngô-dinh-Thuc (1897–1984), who was Archbishop of Huê, Việt Nam from 1960 until his resignation in 1968. A political exile, he consecrated four bishops of the Palmar movement in 1976. He left the

group, which became the Palmarian Catholic Church, and reconciled with Rome. In the early 1980s, while in retirement in Toulon, France, he consecrated several members of the Sedevacantist movement as bishops, including Catholic diocesan and religious priests.

108. Angela Bonavoglia, "One Woman Who Refused to Wait: The Ordination of Mary Ramerman," *Good Catholic Girls: How Women Are Leading the Fight to Change the Church* (New York: HarperCollins, 2005), 239–56.

109. I do not believe Salomão Barbosa Ferraz's daughter is Esther de Figueiredo Ferraz, a prominent Brazilian jurist and former minister of education born in São Paulo on February 6, 1916.

110. See http://www.catholic-hierarchy.org/bishop/bferraz.html (accessed September 27, 2010). CatholicHierarchy.org lists Barbosa Ferraz's two ordinations within a month of each other.

111. In 1940, prior to his break from Rome, Duarte Costa also consecrated Bishop Eliseu Maria Coroli (1900–1982).

112. The reasons for permitting remarriage of a deacon have varied in recent times. From 1984 to 1997, the deacon had to (1) be performing a significant ministry; (2) have children who needed care; *and* (3) have elderly close relatives who needed care. By a 1997 Circular Letter from the Congregation for Divine Worship and the Discipline of the Sacraments (Prot. N. 263/97), then Archbishop (later Cardinal) Jorge Medina Estévez, Prefect of the Congregation, declared deacons could remarry if only one of the three conditions was met. A few months after John Paul II's death in 2005, a letter from Medina Estévez's successor, Cardinal Francis Arinze (Prot. N. 1080/05) adapted the conditions slightly and declared all three must be met: (1) vital ministry; (2) need attested to by diocesan bishop; (3) presence of minor children. The provision for care of elderly relatives has apparently been dropped. There seem to have been a number of dispensations from 1997 to 2002, once Cardinal Arinze took office, and even more from 2002 to 2005. After Arinze's 2005 Circular Letter, dispensations became significantly more difficult to obtain. Anecdotally, the dispensation practices from 1997 to 2002–2005 seem to have upset the Orthodox, who stand firmly against remarriage of clerics (although priest-candidates are sometimes permitted ordination to the transitional diaconate prior to marriage and ordination to priesthood following marriage).

113. "Mistico come padre Pio o rivoluzionario come Martin Lutero? Qual è la vera missione dell'arcivescovo Milingo? Perché combatte per l'abolizione del celibato sacerdotale?" http://www.libreria

universitaria.it/confessioni-uno-scomunicato-milingo-emmanuel/ libro/9788887509830 (accessed September 27, 2010).

114. Fernando Lugo interview with Andrés Schipani, *The Guardian* (August 14, 2008).

115. Emmanuel Milingo, "Priests Should Be Allowed to Marry," in *Introducing Issues With Opposing Viewpoints: Christianity*, ed. Mike Wilson (Farmington Hills, MI: Greenhaven Press, 2008), 54–59, 54. From "Press Statement: The Holy Spirit is Creating a New Church for a New Day," Married Priests Now!, November 28, 2006.

116. Milingo Responds to Benedict XVI on Celibacy, Press Release, November 16, 2006.

117. Holy See Press Office, Synodus Episcoporum Bulletin, XI Ordinary General Assembly of the Synod of Bishops, October 2–23, 2005 http://www.vatican.va/news_services/press/sinodo/documents/ bollettino_21_xi-ordinaria-2005/02_inglese/b11_02.html (accessed January 22, 2011).

118. Eastern Catholic Churches were forced to give up the tradition beyond their patriarchal territories, including and especially in the United States.

119. Holy See Press Office, Synodus Episcoporum Bulletin, XI Ordinary General Assembly of the Synod of Bishops, October 2–23, 2005 http://www.vatican.va/news_services/press/sinodo/documents/ bollettino_21_xi-ordinaria-2005/02_inglese/b11_02.html (accessed January 22, 2011).

120. Stacy Meichtry, "Coverage of Bishops Synod on the Eucharist: Report #3 Priest Shortage Continues to Roil Synod of Bishops," *National Catholic Reporter* (October 4, 2005). Patriarch Laham was born in 1933, Cardinal Scola in 1941.The summaries of interventions as published by the *Vatican Information Service* omits their reported exchange.

121. Now known as the Prelature of the Holy Cross and Opus Dei, the organization was founded in Spain in 1928 and first given approbation in 1950 by Pius XII. John Paul II made it a personal prelature in 1982.

122. John Paul II, apostolic letter *Ecclesia Dei* (July 2, 1988), para. 3, citing can. 1382. http://www.vatican.va/roman_curia/pontifical _commissions/ecclsdei/documents/hf_jp-ii_motu-proprio_02071988 _ecclesia-dei_en.html (accessed September 23, 2010).

123. Ibid., para. 6 (c), citing Congregation for Divine Worship, letter *Quattuor Abhinc Annos*, October 3, 1984: *Acta Apostolicae Sedis* 76 (1984), 1088–89.

124. Andrea Tornielli, "L'ultimatum del Vaticano ai ribelli di Lefebvre: pace se accettate il Concilio," *Il Giornale* (June 23, 2008), http://www.ilgiornale.it/a.pic1?ID=271075 (accessed September 23, 2010). See also "Personal Prelature Mooted for Lefevrists," *Catholic News,* June 25, 2008. http://www.cathnews.com/article.aspx?aeid=7811 (accessed September 23, 1010).

125. Website of Society of Saint Pius X, *Documentation Information Catholiques Internationales,* "Concerning the Ultimatum of Cardinal Castrillon Hoyos" (July 1, 2008), http://www.sspx.org/discussions/concerning_ultimatum_cardinal_castrillon_hoyos.htm (accessed September 27, 2010). Emphasis in original.

126. Benedict XVI, apostolic letter *motu proprio Summorum Pontificum* (July 7, 2007). The text is only available in Latin and Hungarian on the Vatican website.

127. *Quicumque vult salvus esse, ante omnia opus est, ut teneat catholicam fidem . . . Haec est fides catholica, quam nisi quisque fideliter firmiterque crediderit, salvus esse non poterit. Amen.*

128. Since there is no Eastern tradition of conditional re-ordination, the Congregation for the Oriental Churches asked Robert F. Taft, SJ, Professor Emeritus of Oriental Liturgy at the Pontifical Oriental Institute in Rome to write a liturgy specifically for this purpose. Interview with R. F. Taft, SJ, October 13, 2008.

129. Congregation for the Doctrine of the Faith, *"Dichiarazione sulla 'chiesa clandestine' nella repubblica ceca"* (February 11, 2000). See also Václav Drchal, *"Ženatý muž se stal kn?zem"* (June 4, 2008), http://www.lidovky.cz/zenaty-muz-se-stal-knezem-0y5-/ln_domov.asp?c=A080603_204807_ln_domov_fho (accessed September 24, 2010).

130. Gouthro, a former Dominican, has retired to Nevada; Trujillo is a former priest of Cheyenne, Wyoming; Stallings, a former priest of the Archdiocese of Washington, remains head of his Imani Temple (the National Cathedral of the African-American Catholic Congregation) in Northeast Washington, DC. Stallings was consecrated a bishop by Independent Old Catholic bishop Richard W. Bridges in 1990 and has six additional temples attached to his movement, five in the United States and one in Nigeria. His followers profess both the Nicene and the Apostles' Creeds.

131. The ordinations of women will be discussed in a following section.

INTERLUDE

1. *New Commentary of the Code of Canon Law*, J. P. Beal, J. A. Corriden, T. J. Greed, eds. (New York and Mahwah, NJ: Paulist, 2000), 1543.
2. John Tagliabue, "Czechoslovak Church's Quandary: Married Priests," *The New York Times* (November 22, 1990), http://query.nytimes.com/gst/fullpage.html?res=9C0CE1DA1F3BF931A15752C1A966958260 (accessed October 2, 2010).
3. Arthur Jones, "Secret No More," *National Catholic Reporter* (May 11, 2001).
4. Miriam Therese Winter, *Out of the Depths: The Story of Ludmila Javorova, Ordained Roman Catholic Priest* (New York, Crossroad, 2001), 248.
5. This section depends on Petr Fiala and Jiří Hanuš, "Women's Ordination in the Czech Silent Church," *The Month* 31(1998), 282–88, which appeared in the second printing of Petr Fiala and Jiří Hanuš, *Koinótés: Felix M. Davídek and the Hidden Church* (Brno: CDK, 1997). See also Petr Fiala and Jiří Hanuš, *Skrytá církev: Felix M. Davídek a společenství Koinótés* (Brno: Centrum Pro Studium Demokr. A Kultury, 1999); Petr Fiala and Jiří Hanuš, *Die Verborgene Kirche* (Paderborn: Schöningh, 2004).
6. Fiala and Hanuš, "Women's Ordination," 284–85.
7. Ibid., 287, citing Ludmila Javorová's private archives.
8. Bendřich Provazník (consecrated by *Koinótés* bishop Eugen Kocis), Josef Dvořák, and Jiří Pojer objected at the Synod. Dvořák, Pojer, and Stanislav Kratky, who also left *Koinótés*, were consecrated by Davídek. None was ever recognized as a bishop by Vatican authorities, although two others—Oskar Formánek, SJ (1915–1991), and Dusan Spiridion Spiner (b.1950) are recognized as valid Catholic bishops. Nevertheless, the underground church has been decreed as no longer necessary or extant by a Declaration of the Congregation of the Doctrine of the Faith "On Bishops and Priests Ordained Secretly in the Czech Republic" (February 14, 2000).
9. Fiala and Hanuš, "Women's Ordination," 283, citing recording of Davídek's closing synod remarks, December 26, 1970, from the private archives of Ludmila Javorová.
10. Seven women were ordained priests: Ludmilla and three others, by Davídek; in Slovakia, two by Basilian Bishop Nikodem Krett and one by "a Jesuit bishop." Winter, *Out of the Depths* 145–46. I assume the "Jesuit bishop" is recognized Roman Catholic Bishop, Oskar Formánek, SJ, consecrated by Davídek for *Koinótés*. Nikoem (or Nicodemus) Krett

(or Kreta) was a Basilian priest, possibly ordained secretly by Davídek, although his name does not appear on official lists. Davídek ordained approximately 68 priests, 17 bishops, and at least one woman deacon, Libuse Hornanska, in addition to Javorová as deacon and priest. Winter, *Out of the Depths*, 248–49.

PART III

1. Davídek's point is crucial. He said, "The Pope is not the whole Church just as you and I are not the whole Church. Therefore, canonical excommunication only concerns individuals in the state of *contra dogmatum*, not the extending of orthodox practices." Fiala and Hanuš, "Women's Ordination," 283, citing recording of Davídek's closing synod remarks, December 26, 1970, from the private archives of Ludmila Javorová.

2. Congregation for the Doctrine of the Faith, Dichiarazione *Sulla "Chiesa Clandestine" Nella Repubblica Ceca*.

3. The texts and documentation are published in English in Congregation for the Doctrine of the Faith, *From "Inter Insigniores" to "Ordinatio Sacerdotalis": Documents and Commentaries* (Washington, DC: United States Catholic Conference, 1998).

4. "*Dubium*: Whether the teaching that the Church has no authority whatsoever to confer priestly ordination on women, which is presented in the Apostolic Letter *Ordinatio Sacerdotalis* to be held definitively, is to be understood as belonging to the deposit of faith.

   Responsum: Affirmative.

   This teaching requires definitive assent, since, founded on the written Word of God, and from the beginning constantly preserved and applied in the Tradition of the Church, it has been set forth infallibly by the ordinary and universal Magisterium (cf. Second Vatican Council, Dogmatic Constitution on the Church Lumen Gentium 25, 2). Thus, in the present circumstances, the Roman Pontiff, exercising his proper office of confirming the brethren (cf. Lk 22:32), has handed on this same teaching by a formal declaration, explicitly stating what is to be held always, everywhere, and by all, as belonging to the deposit of the faith.

   The Sovereign Pontiff John Paul II, at the Audience granted to the undersigned Cardinal Prefect, approved this Reply, adopted in the Ordinary Session of this Congregation, and ordered it to be published.

   Rome, from the offices of the Congregation for the Doctrine of the Faith, on the Feast of the Apostles SS. Simon and Jude, October 28, 1995. Joseph Card. Ratzinger, Prefect, Tarcisio Bertone, SDB, Archbishop

EmeritusofVercelli, *Secretary*," http://www.vatican.va/roman_curia/
congregations/cfaith/documents/rc_con_cfaith_doc_19951028
_dubium-ordinatio-sac_en.html (accessed January 25, 2011)

5. Canon 749.3 "No doctrine is understood to be infallibly defined
   unless this is manifestly demonstrated." See Francis Morrissey, *Papal
   and Curial Pronouncements: Their Canonical Significance in Light of
   the Code of Canon Law*, 2nd ed. (Ottawa: Faculty of Canon Law, Saint
   Paul University, 1995.)

6. In October 1967, the Synod of Bishops voted to establish an international theological commission, whose membership was officially
   announced in May 1969. *Herder Correspondence* pungently commented on who did—and did not—appear on the list. Those omit-
   ted were Edward Schillebeeckx, Hans Küng, John L. McKenzie,
   J. B. Metz, and Piet Schoonenberg. Three of 38 theologians who
   signed a letter in *Herder Correspondence* in December 1968 "calling
   for freedom of theological inquiry and a reform of the procedures of
   the Doctrinal Congregation" and asking for formation of the commission were eventually appointed: Karl Rahner, Yves Congar, and Joseph
   Ratzinger. *Herder Correspondence* called Ratzinger perhaps "the most
   respectable of the younger progressive school of German theologians."
   "The Thirty Theologians," *Herder Correspondence* 6:7 (July 1969),
   2120–214.

7. Pontifical Biblical Commission, "Report," *Origins* 6 (1976), 92–96, at
   96.

8. The first postdefinition use of papal infallibility is Pope Pius XII's 1950
   solemn declaration that the Assumption into Heaven of the Blessed
   Virgin Mary was an article of faith for Catholics.

9. See, for example, Joachim Salaverri, *De Ecclesia Christi, Sacrae Theolo-
   giae Summa*, 5th ed., Vol. 1 (Madrid: Biblioteca de Autores Cristianos,
   1962).

10. Geoffrey Robinson writes of the "tendency to move many matters from
    the realm of the doubtful and not strictly necessary, where freedom
    reigned, to the realm of the necessary, where unity was demanded."
    *Confronting Power and Sex in the Catholic Church: Reclaiming the
    Spirit of Jesus* (Collegeville, MN: The Liturgical Press, 2008), 121.
    See also *The HarperCollins Encyclopedia of Catholicism*, ed. Richard
    P. McBrien (New York: HarperCollins, 1995), 665; and John E. Thiel,
    Senses of Tradition: Continuity and Development in Catholic Faith
    (New York: Oxford University Press, 2000), 48.

11. The Congregation for the Doctrine of the Faith published a supersed-
    ing *Professio fidei* with commentary on it in *L'Osservatore Romano*,

Weekly Edition in English (July 15, 1998), 3–4. Canon 833 gives details regarding those required to take the oath.

12. L. M. Orsy, *Receiving the Council: Theological and Canonical Insights and Debates* (Collegeville, MN: Liturgical Press, 2009), 119–20.

13. Davídek and Lefebvre died and Milingo became a bishop before the new profession of faith came about. Bruskewitz obtained office in 1992.

14. Petr Fiala and Jiří Hanuš, "Women's Ordination in the Czech Silent Church," *The Month* 31 (1998), 282–88; 283, citing recording of Davídek's closing Synod remarks, December 26, 1970, from the private archives of Ludmila Javorová.

15. J. P. Beal, J. A. Coriden, T. J. Green, *New Commentary on the Code of Canon Law* (Mahwah, NJ: Paulist, 2000), 913. The note refers to Catholic Theological Society of America, "Tradition and the Ordination of Women," *Origins* 27:5 (June 19, 1997), 75–79.

16. Orsy, *Receiving the Council*, 119–20.

17. Ibid., 126; emphasis in the original.

18. Ibid., 127, citing Gérard Philips, *L'Eglise et son mystère*, vol. 1 (Paris: Decslée, 1967), 327–28.

19. Ibid., 127.

20. Congregation for the Doctrine of the Faith, *Profession of Faith and Oath of Fidelity*, Acta Apostolicae Sedis 81 (January 9, 1989), 104–6.

21. *L'Osservatore Romano*, Weekly Edition in English (July 15, 1998), 3, http://www.ewtn.com/library/curia/cdfoath.htm (accessed October 14, 2010).

22. Orsy, *Receiving the Council*, 115.

23. Ibid., 116–41. The original essays are in *Stimmen der Zeit* 216 (1998), 735–40; 217 (1999), 169–72, 305–16, and 420–32.

24. The *Motu proprio* also modifies the Code of Canons for the Eastern Churches, adding a similar paragraph to Canon 598, also allowing for "just penalties."

25. Congregation for the Doctrine of the Faith, *Profession of Faith and Oath of Fidelity*. The document's footnotes are (1) Congregation for the Doctrine of the Faith, *Profession of Faith and Oath of Fidelity*, AAS 81 (January 9, 1989), 105, and (2) Cf. *Code of Canon Law*, Canon 833.

26. Congregation for the Doctrine of the Faith, "Doctrinal Commentary on the Concluding Formula of the *Professio fidei*" (June 29, 1998). The three documents are available at http://www.vatican.va/roman _curia/congregations/cfaith/documents/rc_con_cfaith_doc_1998 _professio-fidei_en.html (accessed January 25, 2011).

27. Orsy, *Receiving the Council,* 141
28. *"Sacram ordinationem valide recipit solus vir baptizatus."* The history of Canon 1024 is really a history of eliminating women from priestly office and only after the thirteenth century was final pronouncement made that only ordained priests could celebrate Eucharist. Therefore, it is possible the barring of women from priesthood is mainly directed at their not being permitted to say Mass, which seems directly related to objections regarding women touching the sacred. For example, regarding women deacons, fourteenth-century canonist Matthew Blastares wrote, "They were forbidden access and performance of these services by later fathers because of their monthly flow that cannot be controlled." Kevin Madigan and Carolyn Osiek, *Ordained Women in the Catholic Church: A Documentary History* (Baltimore: Johns Hopkins University, 2005), 138.
29. See, for example, Adolf Kalsbach, *Die altkirchliche Einrichtung der Diakonissen bis zu ihrem Erlöschen* (Freiburg: Herder, 1926); Roger Gryson, *The Ministry of Women in the Early Church* (Collegeville, MN: Liturgical, 1976); the translation of *Le ministère des femmes dans L'Église ancienne. Recherches et synthèses, Section d'historire* 4 (Gembloux: J. Duculot, 1972); Aimé George Martimort, *Deaconesses: An Historical Study* (San Francisco: Ignatius, 1986); the translation of *Les Diaconesses: Essai Historique.* (Rome: Edizioni Liturgiche, 1982); Phyllis Zagano, *Holy Saturday: An Argument for the Restoration of the Female Diaconate in the Catholic Church* (New York: Crossroad, 2000); Ute Eisen, *Women Officeholders in Early Christianity: Epigraphical and Literary Studies* (Collegeville, MN: Liturgical, 2000); translation of *Amtsträgerinnen im frühen Christentum. Epigraphische und literarische Studien* (Göttingen: Vandenhoeck & Ruprecht, 1996); Gary Macy, *The Hidden History of Women's Ordination* (New York: Oxford University Press, 2008); and Madigan and Osiek, *Ordained Women.*
30. Macy, *Hidden History,* 46–47.
31. "Irregularities" and "impediments" block the reception of sacraments. Irregularities make a valid sacrament illicit; impediments must be overcome or dispensed. Diriment impediments can neither be overcome nor dispensed. However, not all impediments are invalidating. The current official Catholic theology regarding the ordination of women as priests is presented in Sara Butler, *The Catholic Priesthood and Women: A Guide to the Teaching of the Church* (Chicago: Hillenbrand Books, 2007) and, less extensively but similarly regarding women as deacons, in Gerhard Müller, *Priesthood and Diaconate* (San Francisco: Ignatius, 2002) (Originally *Priestium und Diakonat: Der Empfänger des Weihesakramentes*

in schöpfunungstheologischer und christologischer Perspektive [Frieburg: Johannes Verlag, 2000]). Butler mentions "impediment" only once, citing Thomas Aquinas's affirmative answer that female sex is an impediment to receiving orders. Butler, *Catholic Priesthood,* 46.

32. See "Women Ordained as Catholic Priests in Austria," *AFP* (June 30, 2002), http://www.smh.com.au/articles/2002/06/29/1023864 671182.html (accessed October 5, 2010.)

33. Roberto Garrido Padin (b. 1945), was ordained bishop in 1989 by Bishop Manoel Ceia Laranjeira (1903–1994), who had been consecrated bishop in 1951 by Roman Catholic Bishop Salomão Barbosa Ferraz (1880–1969). Hilarios Karl-Heinz Ungerer, who leads the Free Catholic Church in Germany, was consecrated bishop by a bishop of the Polish Mariavite Church, part of the Old Catholic Church of the Netherlands.

34. Spiner, the eldest of three brothers, was born in Vydrnike and graduated from the Theological Faculty in Bratislava University. 17 1976 (http://krotov.info/spravki/persons/20person/1950_spiner.htm (accessed October 13, 2010). "After the fall of Communism Spiner agreed not to practise as a bishop and today works as a parish priest in Slovakia. He clandestinely ordained the women as deacons in Upper Austria on Palm Sunday this year and had promised to ordain them priests on the Danube boat." "Church in the World," *The Tablet* (July 6, 2002), 25–26. Dagmar Celeste, an American born in Austria, was unable to attend the diaconal ordinations and so was ordained both deacon and priest on the riverboat.

35. "The seven women claiming ordination June 29 were: Germans Iris Müller, Ida Raming, Gisela Forster, and Pia Brunner; Austrians Mayr-Lumetzberger and School Sr. Adelinde Theresia Roitinger; and an Austrian-born American who used the assumed name of 'Angela White.' [Dagmar Celeste] . . . While organizers declared themselves satisfied with Braschi's credentials, they acknowledged they had also expected a third bishop, a Czech, who allegedly ordained a handful of women as deacons in secret on Palm Sunday. Though she would not name the bishop, Mayr-Lumetzberger said the women ordained June 29 plan to ask him to re-ordain them in secret, sub conditione—a technical term meaning that the second ordination would be valid only if the first one is not." John L. Allen, Jr., "Seven Women 'Ordained' Priests June 29 in a Ceremony They Term 'Not Licit, but a Fact," *National Catholic Reporter* (July 1, 2002). http://www.natcath.org/NCR_Online/ archives/071902/ordinations.htm (accessed January 25, 2011).

36. All are from the United States, except where noted. 2002 Danube Seven: Christine Mayr-Lumetzberger (Austria), Adelinde Theresia Roitinger (Germany), Gisela Forster (Germany), Iris Muller (Germany), Ida Raming (Germany), Pia Brunner (Germany), Angela White/Dagmar Celeste (US); 2003: Bishops: Christine Mayr-Lumetzberger (Austria), Gisela Forster (Germany); Deacon and Priest: Patricia Fresen (South Africa); 2004: Deacons: Genevieve Benay (France), Monika Wyss (Switzerland), Astride Indrican (Latvia), Victoria Rue, Jane Via, Michele Birch-Conery (Canada); 2005: Ordained Bishop: Patricia Fresen; Priests: Genevieve Benay (France), Victoria Rue, Jean Marie Marchant, Michele Birch-Conery; Deacons: Marie David, Jean Marie Marchant, Rebecca McGuyver, Dana Reynolds, Kathleen Strack, Kathy Vandenberg, Regina Nicolosi; 2006: Bishop: Ida Raming (Germany); Priests: Eileen McCafferty DiFranco, (Merlene) Olivia Doko, Joan Clark Houk, Kathleen Strack Kunster, Rebecca McGuyver, Bridget Mary Meehan, Dana Reynolds, Kathy Sullivan Vandenberg, Monika Wyss (Switzerland), Jane Via, Regina Nicolosi; Deacons: Andrea Johnson, Judith McKloskey, Cheryl Bristol, Juanita Cordero, Janice Sevre-Duszynska, Mary Ellen Robertson; 2007: Priests: Marie Evans Bouclin (Canada), Cheryl Bristol, Juanita Cordero, Rose Marie Hudson, Alice Marie Iaquinta, Andrea M. Johnson, Elsie Hainz McGrath, Judith McKloskey, Mary Ellen Robertson; Deacons: Ruth Broeski, Gloria Ray-Carpenento, Rose Marie Hudson, Alice Marie Iaquinta, Jim Lauder, Elsie Hainz McGrath, Monica Kilburn Smith (Canada), Suzanne Thiel, Toni Tortorilla; 2008: Bishop: Dana Reynolds; Priests: Ruth Broeski, Gloria Carpenento, Suzanne Dunn, Jim Lauder, Judy Lee, Kathy Redig, "Marilyn Ruth," Janice Sevre-Duszynska, Monica Kilburn Smith (Canada), Rod Stephens (ordained 1974; "received into" RCWP 2008), Suzanne Thiel, Toni Tortorilla, Gabriella Ward, Barbara Zeman; Deacons: Sandra DeMaster, Mary Ann McCarthy Schoettly, Barbara Zeman, Alta Jacko, Mary Styne, Linda Wilcox; 2009: Bishops: Joan Houk, Andrea Johnson, Bridget Mary Meehan, Regina Nicolosi; Priests: Sandra DeMaster, Alta Jacko, Morag Liebert (Scotland), Marybeth McBryan, Mary Ann Schoettly, Mary Smith, Mary Styne, Linda Wilcox; Deacons: Theresa Novak Chabot, Janine Denomme, Mary Kay Kusner, [Marybeth McBryan], Rose Mewhort (Canada West), Marty Meyer-Gad, Dena O'Callaghan, Chava Redonnet, Kim Sylvester (Canada West), Diane Whalen, Katy Zatsick, Confidential Deacon 1-Midwest, Confidential Deacon 2-Midwest, Confidential Deacon 1-West, Confidential Deacon-1 Canada East; 2010: Bishop: Merlene Olivia Doko; Priests: Theresa Novak Chabot,

Janine Denomme, Mary Kay Kusner, Rose Mewhort (Canada West), Marty Meyer-Gad, Chava Redonnet, Pat Sandall, Kim Sylvester (Canada West), Diane Whalen, Confidential Priest 2–West, Catacomb Priest 1–Midwest, Catacomb Priest 2–Midwest; Deacons: Caryl Johnson, Patricia La Rosa, Ann Penick, Bertha Popeney, Mary Ellen Sheehan, Michael Tompkins, Monique Venne, Catacomb Deacon 1-East. http://www.romancatholicwomenpriests.org/history.htm (accessed October 2, 2010).

37. Raymond L. Burke, "Statement Regarding the Canonical Discipline of Sister Louise Lears, SC" (June 26, 2008), http://www.archstl.org/index.php?option=com_content&task=view&id=523&Itemid=150 (accessed November 2, 2010).

38. Congregation for the Doctrine of the Faith, "General Decree regarding the delict of attempted sacred ordination of a woman" (December 19, 2007, published 30 May 2008), http://www.vatican.va/roman_curia/congregations/cfaith/documents/rc_con_cfaith_doc_20071219_attentata-ord-donna_en.html (accessed January 26, 2011).

39. Lears immediately appealed the interdict to three Vatican congregations: Congregation for the Doctrine of the Faith, Congregation for Bishops, and Congregation for Institutes of Consecrated Life and Societies of Apostolic Life, effectively finding an administrative remedy to her situation as Canon law allows for a "suspensive effect" of canonical penalties. While Lears moved out of St. Louis, Burke's interdict remained in effect, barring her from the sacramental life of the Church (C. 1331 and C. 1332). Once imposed, an interdict remains with the person until it is lifted, either by the bishop who imposed it or the bishop where the person is present—after that bishop has consulted with the bishop who imposed the censure (C. 1355).

40. International Theological Commission, *From the Diakonia of Christ to the Diakonia of the Apostles* (Chicago: Hillenbrand, 2004) and (London: London Truth Society, 2003).

41. Congregation for the Doctrine of the Faith, *Normae de gravioribus delictis* (May 21, 2010). The document states Benedict XVI approved the Norms, but they do not bear his signature. See http://www.nccbuscc.org/mr/Norms-English.pdf (accessed October 5, 2010).

42. Benedict XVI's interview with broadcasters Bayerische Rundfunk, Deutsche Welle, ZDF and Vatican Radio at his summer residence at Castelgandolfo on August 5, 2006 was conducted in German and translated by the Vatican. http://www.dw-world.de/dw/article/0,2144,2129951,00.html (accessed January 26, 2011). See

also "Pope Says Church Not a String of 'Nos,'" *The New York Times* (Reuters) (August 13, 2006) and The Times of Malta (Reuters) (August 14, 2006) http://www.timesofmalta.com/articles/view/20060814/ local/pope-says-church-not-a-string-of-nos (accessed January 26, 2011).

43. Discorso improvvisato da Benedetto XVI al Clero romano, I temi dell'incontro: Vita, famiglia e formazione dei sacerdoti. CITTA' DEL VATICANO, venerdì, 3 marzo 2006 (Zenit.org) Il 2 marzo 2006, nell'Aula della Benedizione del Palazzo Apostolico Vaticano, Benedetto XVI ha incontrato il Clero della Diocesi di Roma per il tradizionale appuntamento di inizio Quaresima. http://www.zenit.org/ article-552?l=italian (accessed January 25, 2011). See Phyllis Zagano, "The Question of Governance and Ministry for Women," *Theological Studies* 68:2 (June 2007), 348–67 for analysis of these statements.

44. The 2008 World Synod of Bishops on the Bible includes six women of 41 experts and 19 women of 37 observers. See Cindy Wooden, "Pope Names More Women than Ever to Synod of Bishops on Bible," *Catholic News Service* (September 9, 2008), http://www.catholicnews .com/data/stories/cns/0804558.htm (accessed October 5, 2010). The women experts were Sister Sara Butler, MSBT then professor of dogmatic theology at St. Joseph's Seminary in Yonkers, New York (now of Mundelein Seminary, Illinois), one of two women Pope John Paul II named to the International Theological Commission in 2004; Spanish Sister Nuria Calduch-Benages, professor of the biblical theology of the Old Testament at Rome's Pontifical Gregorian University and a member of the Missionary Daughters of the Holy Family of Nazareth; Bruna Costacurta, an Italian professor of Old Testament theology at the Gregorian; Marguerite Lena, a professor of philosophy in Paris and director of theological formation for young adults at Paris's St. Francis Xavier Community; Sister Mary Jerome Obiorah, a member of the Sisters of the Immaculate Heart of Mary and professor of sacred Scripture at the University of Nigeria and at the major seminary of the Archdiocese of Onitsha, Nigeria; and Trappist Sister Germana Strola, a member of the monastery at Vitorchiano, Italy.

45. Patricia Fresen was not among the first six ordained deacon by Spiner nor among the seven ordained on the Danube. Fresen traces her apostolic succession through Christine Mayr-Lumetzberger (Austria) and Gisela Forster (Germany), who were ordained by Romulo Antonio Braschi. Brasci was ordained a Catholic priest in Argentina and established his own movement in 1975, which became the Catholic Apostolic Charismatic Church of Jesus the King in 1978. Braschi was ordained bishop in 1998 Munich by Roberto Garrido Padin (b. 1945), a bishop of the

Brazilian Catholic Apostolic Church, and Hilarios Karl-Heinz Ungerer, a German bishop of the schismatic Free Catholic Church. Padin was ordained priest in 1972 by Bishop Luigi Mascolo of the Brazilian Catholic Apostolic Church and consecrated bishop in 1989 by Manoel Ceia Laranjeira, who had been consecrated bishop in 1951 by Roman Catholic bishop Salomão Barbosa Ferraz. Although his episcopal lineage is distinct from that of Padin, Ungerer leads the Free Catholic Church in Germany, which is related to the Brazilian Catholic Apostolic Church. Braschi was ordained bishop again in 1999 by Bishop Jerónimo José Podestá (1920–2000), resigned bishop of Avellanda, Argentina, from 1962 to 1967. His second—if not his first—episcopal ordination could be considered valid because of the provenance of Davídek's orders.

46. See Pamela Schaeffer, "Though Church Bans Women Priests More and More Women are Saying "Why Wait?" *National Catholic Reporter* (December 7, 2007). http://natcath.org/NCR_Online/archives2/2007d/120707/120707a.htm (accessed January 25, 2011).

47. Butler, *Catholic Priesthood*, 80–81, citing *Inter Insigniores*, 5.

48. Ibid., 81–82, citing Bonaventure, *In IV Sent.* D. 25, a.2, q. 1, conclusion. Butler notes Bonaventure also eliminates the episcopate as proper to a woman because she is not "the bridegroom of the Church." Bonaventure is apparently silent regarding the diaconate.

49. Pontifical Council for Promoting Christian Unity, "Guidelines for Admission to the Eucharist Between the Chaldean Church and the Assyrian Church of the East" (July 20, 2001), http://www.vatican.va/roman_curia/pontifical_councils/chrstuni/documents/rc_pc_chrstuni_doc_20011025_chiesa-caldea-assira_en.html (accessed January 26, 2011). See also A. Gelston, *The Eucharistic Prayer of Addai and Mari* (Oxford: Clarendon, 1992), 48–55; and Mar Aprem Mooken, "Anaphora of Addai and Mari from the Perspective of the Church of the East," in *Studies on the Anaphora of Addai and Mari*, ed. Boscos Pothur (Kochi, India: LRC Publications, 2004) 205–6. Robert F. Taft, "Mass Without the Consecration? The Historic Agreement Between the Catholic Church and the Assyrian Church of the East Promulgated 26 October 2001," *Christian Orient* 26:1 (March 2005), 68–88; or *Worship* 77:6 (November 2003), 482–509; or *Centro Pro Unione Bulletin* 63 (Spring 2003), 15–27.

50. See http://www.virtuelle-dioezese.de/

51. The Polish National Catholic Church was begun in 1897 by Roman Catholic priest Francis Hodur, who founded a "National Church" and called for (1.) Legal ownership of church properties; (2.) Parish government in secular matters by parish committees elected by the

parishioners; (3.) Appointment to pastorates of priests approved by parishioners; (4.) Appointment of Polish Bishops in America by Rome with input by clergy and laity. Hodur was excommunicated by Rome in 1898.

52. See Phyllis Zagano, "Catholic Women's Ordination: The Ecumenical Implications of Women Deacons in the Armenian Apostolic Church, the Orthodox Church of Greece, and Union of Utrecht Old Catholic Churches," *Journal of Ecumenical Studies* 43:1 (Winter 2008) as corrected in Phyllis Zagano, *Women in Ministry: Emerging Questions on the Diaconate* (Mahwah, NJ: Paulist, 2012); and Phyllis Zagano, "Ecumenical Questions on Women and Church," in *Church and Religious Other: Essays on Truth, Unity and Diversity*, ed. Gerard Mannion (London: T. & T. Clark/Continuum, 2008), 23–40. Some Union of Utrech Old Catholic Churches and their derivatives also ordain women as priests.

53. Phyllis Zagano, "The Revisionist History of Benedict XVI," *Harvard Divinity Bulletin* 34:2 (Spring 2006), 72–77. Irenaeus retroactively calls Stephen, one of the seven, the first deacon.

54. John Paul II, apostolic letter On the Dignity of Women (*Mulierias Dignitatem*) (August 15, 1988), 27. Other translators of Romans 16:1 call Phoebe a deacon, not a deaconess, of the Church at Cenchreae. These include Benedict XVI.

55. Josephine Mayer, *Monumenta de viduis diaconissis virginibusque tractantia, Florilegium patristicum tam veteris quam medii aevi auctores complectens* (Bonn: Peter Hanstein, 1938); Eisen, *Women Officeholders*; Madigan and Osiek, *Ordained Women*; Macy, *Hidden History*; Cipriano Vagaggini, "L'ordinazione delle diaconesse nella tradizione greca e bizantina," *Orientalia Christiana Periodica* 40 (1974), 149–89.

56. Mary Magdalene is called "apostle to the apostles" and agreed to as a witness to the Resurrection. However, she is not recorded as a member of the Twelve and is not mentioned as being at the Last Supper.

57. The prefect of the Congregation at the time was Croatian Cardinal Franjo Šeper (1905–1981), who served as prefect from 1968 to 1981 and was succeeded by Cardinal Joseph Ratzinger (b. 1927), now Pope Benedict XVI. Šeper died one month after retiring.

58. *Dichiarazione circa la questione dell'ammissione delle donne al sacerdozio ministerial—Inter insigniores (Declaratio circa quaestionem admissionis mulierum ad sacerdotium ministeriale)*, October 15, 1976; *AAS* 69 (1977), 98–116; Documenta 30; Or 28.1.1977, 1–3 [Lat./Ital.]; Notitiae 13 (1977), 51–66; Communicationes 9 (1977), 36–50; CEE 97–131 [Lat./Hisp.]; DocCath 74 (1977), 158–64; EV 5,

1392–1423; LE 4471; Dokumenty, I, 30. (CEE is *Ocho Documentos Doctrinales de la Sagrada Congregación para la Doctrina de la Fe*, Conferencia Episcopal Española. Segretariado de la Comisión Episcopal para la Doctrina de la Fe (Ed.) (Biblioteca Doctrinal. Documenta, 1, Madrid 1981).

59. *Inter Insigniores*, "Declaration on the Admission of Women to the Ministerial Priesthood," *Origins* 6:3 (February 3, 1977), 517–24.

60. See Morrissey, *Papal and Curial Pronouncements*.

61. As of this writing, the *Responsum ad Dubium* does not appear on the Vatican's website in any language and is officially published in Italian and Latin as "Risposta circa la dottrina della Lettera Apostolica '*Ordinatio Sacerdotalis*'" (*Responsum ad dubium circa doctrinam in Epist. Ap. "Ordinatio Sacerdotalis" traditam*), October 28, 1995.

62. In 1969, Ratzinger was among the first men named to the International Theological Commission. He became a member of the Congregation for the Doctrine of the Faith in 1977, serving as its Prefect (President) from November 1981 until his election as pope in April 2005.

63. The document appears in English, French, German, Italian, Latin, Portuguese, and Spanish. See http://www.vatican.va/roman_curia/con gregations/cfaith/doc_dis_index.htm (accessed January 25, 2011).

64. Paul VI, encyclical letter *Humanae Vitae* (July 25, 1968), http://www.vatican.va/holy_father/paul_vi/encyclicals/documents/hf_p-vi _enc_25071968_humanae-vitae_en.html (accessed January 26, 2011).

65. This section recasts and updates portions of Zagano, "Ecumenical Questions," 23–40.

66. Florence Li Tim-Oi was ordained on January 25, 1944, by the Bishop of Hong Kong. See *Freedom Is a Dream: A Documentary History of Women in the Episcopal Church*, ed. Sheryl A. Kujawa-Holbrook (New York: Church Publishing, 2002). Anglican women priests are ordained in the following dioceses: Aotearoa, New Zealand and Polynesia; Australia, Bangledesh, Brazil, Burundi, Canada, Central America, England, Hong Kong, Ireland, Japan, Kenya, Korea, Mexico, North India, Philippine, Rwanda, Scotland, Southern Africa, South India, Sudan, Uganda, Wales, West Indies, and the Anglican Church of the Province of West Africa.

67. Anglican Consultative Council, "The Lambeth Conference Resolutions Archive, from 1968" (London: Anglican Communion Office, 2005), resolutions 34–38.

68. "The Conference recommends that, before any national or regional Church or province makes a final decision to ordain women to the

priesthood, the advice of the Anglican Consultative Council (or Lambeth Consultative Body) be sought and carefully considered." Ibid., resolution 37.

69. See Leslie J. Francis and Mandy Robbins, *The Long Diaconate 1987:1994: Women Deacons and the Delayed Journey to Priesthood* (Herefordshire, Wales: Gracewing, 1999).

70. Anglican Consultative Council, "The Lambeth Conference Resolutions Archive, from 1978" (London: Anglican Communion Office, 2005), resolution 20: "The Conference recommends, in accordance with Resolution 32(c) of the Lambeth Conference of 1968, those member Churches which do not at present ordain women as deacons now to consider making the necessary legal and liturgical changes to enable them to do so, instead of admitting them to a separate order of deaconesses."

71. Ibid., resolution 21.7.

72. Ibid., resolution 22.

73. Anglican Consultative Council, "The Lambeth Conference Resolutions Archive, from 1988" (London: Anglican Communion Office, 2005), resolution 1.5.

74. See http://www.episcopalchurch.org/88087_ENG_HTM.htm. Because the Episcopal Church headquartered in the United States includes other areas and territories, it has dropped "USA" and now refers to itself as the Episcopal Church. Its websites are, equally, http://www.ecusa .anglican.org and http://www.episcopalchurch.org. It is incorporated as the Domestic and Foreign Missionary Society of the Protestant Episcopal Church in the United States of America.

75. "Cardinal Kasper to Anglican Communion, 'The Aim of Our Dialogue Has Receded Further,'" *Zenit* (July 31, 2008), http://www.zenit .org/article-23384?l=english (accessed November 2, 2010).

76. Ibid. The Lambeth Quadrilateral is a resolution of the 1888 Lambeth Conference affirming Anglican belief to "supply a basis on which approach may be by God's blessing made towards home reunion: (a) The Holy Scriptures of the Old and New Testaments, as 'containing all things necessary to salvation,' and as being the rule and ultimate standard of faith. (b) The Apostles' Creed, as the Baptismal Symbol; and the Nicene Creed, as the sufficient statement of the Christian faith. (c) The two Sacraments ordained by Christ Himself—Baptism and the Supper of the Lord—ministered with unfailing use of Christ's Words of Institution, and of the elements ordained by Him. (d) The Historic Episcopate, locally adapted in the methods of its administration to the varying needs of the nations and peoples called of God into the Unity

of His Church." Anglican Consultative Council, "The Lambeth Conference Resolutions Archive, from 1888" (London: Anglican Communion Office, 2005), resolution 11.

77. Ibid.

78. "Archbishop Gives Lourdes Sermon," *BBC World News,* (September 24, 2008) http://news.bbc.co.uk/2/hi/uk_news/7631156.stm (accessed January 25, 2011). Williams was in renegade Anglican company. According to the *London Mail,* "He was also joined by an unprecedented pilgrimage of 10 Church of England bishops, some 60 Anglican priests and about 400 Anglican lay worshippers, a number of whom are considering becoming Catholics in protest at the decision of the General Synod in July to pave the way for the creation of women bishops." Simon Caldwell, "Rowan Williams Becomes First Anglican Leader to Accept Visions of Virgin Mary as Fact," *Mail Online,* (September 25, 2008) http://www.mailonsunday.co.uk/news/worldnews/article-1060951/ Rowan-Williams-Anglican-leader-accept-visions-Virgin-Mary-fact.html (accessed October 8, 2010).

79. Leo XIII, *Apostolicae curae,* "On the nullity of Anglican orders" (September 18, 1896), no. 9, http://www.papalencyclicals.net/Leo13/l13curae.htm (accessed October 9, 2010). See also Franklin Johnson, "Review of A Vindication of the Bull 'Apostolicae Curiae,' A Letter on Anglican Orders", *The American Journal of Theology* 2:4 (October, 1898), 931–32.

80. F. Cantuar and Willelm Ebor, *Saepius Officio,* Answer of the Archbishops of Canterbury and York to the Bull *Apostolicae Curae* of H. H. Leo XIII. http://www.ucl.ac.uk/~ucgbmxd/saepius.htm (accessed April 2, 2008).

81. Ibid.

82. Approximately one hundred Episcopal priests have joined the Catholic Church in the United States since the "pastoral provision" of accepting them as married men. Since that time about seven parishes (four in Texas and one each in Massachusetts, Pennsylvania, and Missouri) have joined the Catholic Church as "Anglican Rite" parishes, which retain much of their own liturgy along with the Book of Common Prayer. See http://www.pastoralprovision.org/ (accessed November 2, 2010). The "pastoral provision" was made possible by Paul VI, encyclical letter *Sacerdotalis Caelibatus* (June 24, 1967), no. 42: "a study may be allowed of the particular circumstances of married sacred ministers of Churches or other Christian communities separated from the Catholic communion, and of the possibility of admitting to priestly functions those who desire to adhere to the fullness of this communion and to

continue to exercise the sacred ministry." See Congregation for the Doctrine of the Faith, "Statement on behalf of some clergy and laity formerly or actually belonging to the Episcopal (Anglican) Church for full communion with the Catholic Church" (April 1, 1981) DOCU-MENTA 45 OR 1.4.1981; DocCath 78 (1981) 433 [Gall.]; EV 7, 1110–1113; LE 4836; Dokumenty, I, 45, available online in Italian at http://www.vatican.va/roman_curia/congregations/cfaith/documents/rc_con_cfaith_doc_19810401_chiesa-episcopaliana_it.html (accessed January 26, 2011).

83. Cardinal William Kasper, "Mission of Bishops in the Mystery of the Church: Reflections on the Question of Ordaining Women to Episcopal Office in the Church of England" (June 5, 2006), http://www.vatican.va/roman_curia/pontifical_councils/chrstuni/card-kasper-docs/rc_pc_chrstuni_doc_20060605_kasper-bishops_en.html (accessed November 2, 2010).

84. Ibid.

85. Tom Wright and David Stancliffe, "Women Bishops: A Response to Cardinal Kasper," http://www.fulcrum-anglican.org.uk/news/2006/20060721kasper.cfm?doc=126 (accessed October 9, 2010).

86. A more complete argument regarding women deacons is in Zagano, *Holy Saturday*. Subsequent essays include "Women in the Church: The Unfinished Business of Vatican II," *Horizons* 34:2 (Fall 2007) 205–21; "The Question of Governance and Ministry for Women," *Theological Studies* 68:2 (June 2007), 348–67; "The Revisionist History of Benedict XVI," *Harvard Divinity Bulletin* 34:2 (Spring 2006) 72–77; "Grant Her Your Spirit: The Restoration of the Female Diaconate in the Orthodox Church of Greece," *America* 192:4 (February 7, 2005) 18–21 (translated as "Chiesa ortodossa greca: Il ripristino del diaconato femminile," *Adista* [February 26, 2005]); "Women Deacons: Past, Present, Future—An Exploration of the Tradition and History of Diaconal Ordination," in *Re-Imaging God for Today*, ed. Val Ambrose McInnes, OP (Hyde Park, NY: New City Press, 2005) 119–33; "Catholic Women Deacons: Present Tense," *Worship* 77:5 (September 2003) 386–408; "Catholic Woman Deacons?" *America* 188:5 (February 17, 2003), 9–11; "Women of the Church and the New Millennium," in *Themes in Feminist Theology for the New Millennium (II)*, ed. Francis A. Eigo, OSA (Villanova, PA: Villanova University Press, 2003), 128–51; and "Women Religious, Women Deacons?" *Review for Religious* 60:3 (May–June 2001), 230–44.

87. See note 15. For a review of the literature on this subject, see Macy, *Hidden History*.

88. Morrissey, *Papal and Curial Pronouncements*, 26.
89. Congregation for the Doctrine of Faith, for Worship, and Discipline of Sacraments, and for Clergy, "Notification on the Diaconal Ordination of Women" (September 14, 2001). "1. Our offices have received from several countries signs of courses that are being planned or under way, directly or indirectly aimed at the diaconal ordination of women. Thus are born hopes which are lacking a solid doctrinal foundation and which can generate pastoral disorientation. 2. Since ecclesial ordination does not foresee such an ordination, it is not licit to enact initiatives which, in some way, aim to prepare candidates for diaconal ordination. 3. The authentic promotion of women in the Church, in conformity with the constant ecclesial Magisterium, with special reference to (the Magisterium) of His Holiness John Paul II, opens other ample prospectives of service and collaboration. 4. The undersigned Congregations—within the sphere of their proper authority—thus turn to the individual ordinaries, asking them to explain (this) to their own faithful and to diligently apply the above-mentioned directives."
90. The principal Vatican document, *Unitatis Redintegratio*, unequivocally recognizes the sacraments (and specifically Eucharist and orders) of the Oriental Orthodox Churches. In addition, three Joint or Common Declarations by the Catholic Church and the Armenian Church stipulate the same: that of May 12, 1970, between Paul VI and Vasken I, Supreme Catholicos and Patriarch of all Armenians (Echmiadzin, 1955–1995), of December 13, 1996, between John Paul II and His Holiness Karekin I, Supreme Patriarch and Catholicos of All Armenians (Echmiadzin, 1995–1999); and of January 25, 1997, between Pope John Paul II and Catholicos Aram I Keshishian (Cilicia, 1995–present).
91. There is scholarly argument that of Western churches not in communion with Rome, only the Polish National Church holds true apostolic succession and, consequently, valid orders. "La seule Eglise non orientale separée, officiellement reconnue par le Saint-Siege en tant qu'Eglise 'equiparée', est la Polish National Catholic Church (PNCC) aux Etats-Unis et au Canada." Georges-Henri Ruyssen, *Eucharistie et Oecumenisme* (Paris: Les Editions du Cerf, 2008), 254.
92. See, for example, Roberta R. Ervine, "The Armenian Church's Women Deacons," *St. Nersess Theological Review* 12 (2007), 17–56. Ervine writes that, in the opinion of the late Armenian Catholicos Vazgen I, prior precedent for ordaining women as deacons meant the decision to do so was at the discretion of diocesan bishops.
93. On May 27, 1996, German Old Catholic Bishop Joachim Vobbe ordained Old Catholic Deacons Regina Pickel-Bossau and Angela Berlis

to priesthood. Old Catholic Bishop Vobbe is author of a pastoral letter, *Geh zu meinen Brüdern* (Bonn, 1996), which argues the case for the ordination of women.

94. The Old Catholic Church of Switzerland first ordained women deacons around 1991 and priests in 2002.

95. Hana Karasova was ordained deacon in October 2003 by Old Catholic Bishop Dusan Hejbal. Martina Schneibergova, Jana Sustova, "Die altkatholische Kirche hat ihre erste Diakonin," *Radio Praha* (October 30, 2003). "Die altkatholische Kirche in Tschechien hat unter ihren Geistlichen die erste Frau. Über die Weihe der ersten Diakonin durch den altkatholischen Bischof Dusan Hejbal berichtet Martina Schneibergova." Audio, text of report, and photographs are at http://radio .cz/de/artikel/46864 (accessed January 22, 2011).

96. Can. 968. § 1. Sacram ordinationem valide recipit solus vir baptizatus; licite autem, qui ad normam sacrorum canonum debitis qualitatibus, iudicio proprii Ordinarii, praeditus sit, neque ulla detineatur irregularitate aliove impedimento.

97. Pius XII, apostolic constitution *Sacramentum Ordinis* (1947).

98. See, for example, Gryson, *Ministry of Women*; Martimort, *Deaconesses*; Ute Eisen, *Women Officeholders*; Madigan and Osiek, *Ordained Women*.

99. Paul VI, apostolic letter *Ad Pascendum* (August 15, 1972).

100. Some, such as Roman Catholic Bishop Gerhard Ludwig Müller (b. 1947), argue that the documented diaconal ordinations of women were not to the diaconate and were not sacramental, belying the evidence of history as well as the intent of the ordaining bishops. See Müller, *Priesthood and Diaconate*, 42–58. The dismissive tone of Müller's work cannot be overlooked, nor should it be forgotten that he belonged to the International Theological Commission during the final drafting of the document on the diaconate and was named bishop of Regensburg on October 1, 2002.

101. The Catholic Church produces several levels of documents with varying levels of authority. The highest level documents are those of ecumenical councils. Documents issued by curial offices are regulatory but not necessarily legislative and in no way approach the level of conciliar or even papal documents. A declaration is a curial pronouncement "which is an interpretation of existing law or facts, or a reply to a contested point of law or doctrine." Morrissey, *Papal and Curial Pronouncements*, 29.

102. Apostolic epistles, or letters, "contain social and pastoral teachings, but are not legislative texts." Ibid., 13.

103. Canon 749.3. "No doctrine is understood to be infallibly defined unless this is manifestly demonstrated."

104. The International Theological Commission document has been published in French ("Le Diaconat: Évolution et perspectives," *La documentation catholique* 23 [January 19, 2003], 58–107), and in Italian ("Il Diaconato: Evoluzione e Prospettive," *La Civiltà Cattolica* I [2003], 253–336). An unofficial English translation by the Catholic Truth Society has been published in London and Chicago.

105. Nicaea (325) and Chalcedon (451). Chalcedon lowered the minimum age for the ordination of women deacons from sixty to forty. Madigan and Oisek, 121–123.

106. Letter of Pope Benedict VII to Benedict, Cardinal Bishop of Porto 1018: "In the same way, we concede and confirm to you and your successors in perpetuity every episcopal ordination (*ordinationem episcopalem*), not only of presbyters but also of deacons or deaconesses (*diaconissis*) or subdeacons." Madigan and Osiek, *Ordained Women*, 147.

107. A joint Notification issued by the Catholic Congregations for the Doctrine of the Faith, for Worship and Sacraments, and for the Clergy essentially reminded diocesan ordinaries that women were not to be trained as deacons, since they did not envision ordaining them. Cardinal Joseph Ratzinger was among the signers. A Notification is not a legislative document. (See Morrissey, *Papal and Curial Pronouncements,* 36.) "*Notificazione delle Congregazioni per la Dottrina della Fede, per il Culto Divino e la Disciplina dei Sacramenti, per il Clero* 1. Da taluni Paesi sono pervenute ai nostri Dicasteri alcune segnalazioni di programmazione e di svolgimento di corsi, direttamente o indirettamente finalizzati all'ordinazione diaconale delle donne. Si vengono così a determinare aspettative carenti di salda fondatezza dottrinale e che possono generare, pertanto, disorientamento pastorale. 2. Poiché l'ordinamento ecclesiale non prevede la possibilità di una tale ordinazione, non è lecito porre in atto iniziative che, in qualche modo, mirino a preparare candidate all'Ordine diaconale. 3. L'autentica promozione della donna nella Chiesa, in conformità al costante Magistero ecclesiastico, con speciale riferimento a quello di Sua Santità Giovanni Paolo II, apre altre ampie prospettive di servizio e di collaborazione. 4. Le Congregazioni sottoscritte—nell'ambito delle proprie competenze—si rivolgono, pertanto, ai singoli Ordinari affinché vogliano spiegare ai propri fedeli ed applicare diligentemente la suindicata direttiva. Questa Notificazione è stata approvata dal Santo Padre, il 14 settembre 2001. Dal Vaticano, 17 settembre 2001." (Original text).

108. Pontifical Council for Promoting Christian Unity, *Directory for the Application of Principles and Norms on Ecumenism* (March 25, 1993), Para. 122 ff. http://www.vatican.va/roman_curia/pontifical_councils/ chrstuni/general-docs/rc_pc_chrstuni_doc_19930325_directory _en.html (accessed January 22, 2011).

109. In response to a request by the USCCB, Cardinal Edward I. Cassidy (b.1924), then President of the Pontifical Council for Promoting Christian Unity, affirmed that members of the Polish National Church in the United States and Canada could be admitted to Roman Catholic sacraments in accord with Canon 844: "Catholic ministers may licitly administer the sacraments of penance, Eucharist and anointing of the sick to members of oriental churches who do not have full communion with the Catholic Church, if they ask on their own for the sacraments and are properly disposed. This holds also for members of other churches, which in the judgment of the Apostolic See are in the same condition as the oriental churches as far as these sacraments are concerned." "Pastoral Guidelines Concerning Admission of Polish National Catholics to Sacraments in the Roman Catholic Church (Promulgated in a March 13, 1996, Letter to the Bishops of the United States from Most Rev. Oscar H. Lipscomb)," Robert M. Nemkovich and James C. Timlin, *Journeying Together in Christ: The Journey Continues: The Report of the Polish National Catholic-Roman Catholic Dialogue 1989–2002* (Huntington, IN: Our Sunday Visitor, 2003), 82–87.

110. The official French language document is posted on the Vatican website.

111. See Gryson, *Ministry of Women*, 62, citing F. X. Funk, *Didascalia et constitutiones Apostolorum*, 2 vols. (Paderborn: 1905; reprint Turin: 1964, 524, 13–24. The earliest known ordination ritual for a woman deacon is present in the *Apostolic Constitutions*. See Paul F. Bradshaw, *Ordination Rites of the Ancient Churches of East and West* (New York: Pueblo, 1990), 116. See also Ecumenical Patriarchate, *The Place of Women in the Orthodox Church and the Question of the Ordination of Women*, Report of the Interorthodox Symposium, Rhodos (Rhodes), Greece (October 10–November 7, 1988), ed. Gennadios Limouris (Katerini, Greece: Tertios Publications, 1992), 31–32. The liturgical text as reconstructed by Jacob Goar, *Euchologion sive Rituale Graecorum* (Paris, 1647), 262–64, reflects the likely liturgy to be used. Goar reconstructed the ancient formulae of Greek liturgy using seven manuscripts, most probably Barberini, Grottaferrata, St. Mark (Florence), Tillianus, Allatianus, Coresianus, and the Royal Library (France), as follows: "Holy and Omnipotent Lord, through the birth of your Only Son our God from a Virgin

according to the flesh, you have sanctified woman. You grant not only to men, but also to women the grace and coming of the Holy Spirit. Please also now, Lord, look on this your maid servant and dedicate her to the task of your diaconate, and pour out into her the abundant giving of your Holy Spirit. Preserve her while she performs her ministry according to what is pleasing to you, in the orthodox faith and irreproachable conduct. For to you is due all glory, honor and worship, Father, Son and Holy Spirit, now and always and in all ages. Amen." Note that the woman deacon is ordained to ministry (*leitourgia*), Campaign for the Ordination of Women in the Roman Catholic Church "Reconstructed Texts From Seven Manuscripts" trans. John Wijngaards, http://www .womenpriests.org/traditio/deac_gr4.asp (accessed January 22, 2011).

112. "When the question of the ordination of women arose in the Anglican Communion, Pope Paul VI, out of fidelity to his office of safeguarding the Apostolic Tradition, and also with a view to removing a new obstacle placed in the way of Christian unity, reminded Anglicans of the position of the Catholic Church: 'She holds that it is not admissible to ordain women to the priesthood, for very fundamental reasons. These reasons include: the example recorded in the Sacred Scriptures of Christ choosing his Apostles only from among men; the constant practice of the Church, which has imitated Christ in choosing only men; and her living teaching authority which has consistently held that the exclusion of women from the priesthood is in accordance with God's plan for his Church.'" John Paul II, apostolic letter *Ordinatio Sacerdotalis* (May 22, 1994), quoting Paul VI, "Response to the Letter of His Grace the Most Reverend Dr. F. D. Coggan, Archbishop of Canterbury, Concerning the Ordination of Women to the Priesthood" (November 30, 1975); *AAS* 68 (1976), 599.

113. Speaking at an ecumenical congress at Ushaw College, Durham, England, Cardinal Walter Kasper, President of the Pontifical Council for the Promotion of Christian Unity, pointed out that differences within Christianity over moral issues—he specifically noted homosexuality, abortion, and euthanasia "are not on the top of the hierarchy of truths but they are very emotional and, therefore, very divisive." Cindy Wooden, "Ethical approaches make unity appear distant, says Vatican official" *Catholic News Service* (January 13, *2006*). http://www.catholicnews.com/data/ stories/cns/0600225.htm (accessed January 25, 2011).

114. Letter of Rev. Roy Bourgeois, MM, to Congregation for the Doctrine of the Faith, November 7, 2008, as reproduced in *Ekklesia*, http:// www.ekklesia.co.uk/node/8005 (accessed November 2, 2010).

115. Tracy Early, "Ecumenism Undergoing 'Radical Change' in 21st Century, Cardinal Says," *Catholic News Service* (March 17, 2005).

116. Ibid.

117. There are over thirty thousand lay ministers, mostly female, in the United States. This number reflects only those paid lay ministers working over 20 hours per week. In 1990 approximately 40 percent of lay ecclesial ministers were women religious. That number dropped to 28 percent in 1997 and 16 percent in 2005. See David DeLambo, *Lay Parish Ministers: A Study of Emerging Leadership* (New York: National Pastoral Life Center, 2005) 19, 44. In 2005, the percentage of lay women is 64 percent, lay men 20 percent, and women religious 16 percent, primarily working as religious educators (41.5 percent) and general pastoral ministers (25 percent.) US Conference of Catholic Bishops Co-workers in the Vineyard of the Lord (Washington, DC: USCCB, 2005). http://www.usccb.org/laity/laymin/co-workers.pdf (accessed January 26, 2011).

118. Canon 767.1 "Among the forms of preaching, the homily, which is part of the liturgy itself and is reserved to a priest or deacon. . . ." Canon 274.1 "Only clerics can obtain offices for whose exercise the power of orders or the power of ecclesiastical governance is required."

119. The following commentary depends on Phyllis Zagano, "Catholic Women Deacons: Present Tense," *Worship* 77:5 (September 2003), 386–408.

120. "The deaconesses mentioned in the ancient tradition of the Church—as suggested by their rite of institution and the functions they exercised—are not purely and simply the same as deacons." In the original document, "Les deaconesses dont il est fait mention dans la Tradition de l'Église ancienne—selon ce que suggèrent le rite d'institution et les functions exercées—ne sont pas purement et simplement assimilables aux diacres." "Le Diaconat," 107. Translation mine.

121. *Catholic News Service* (United States) first reported that, according to a commission member, the question of whether women deacons could or should be allowed in the Church was left unresolved. The newspapers *La Croix* (France) on October 8 and *National Catholic Reporter* (United States) on October 11 then each correctly reported that the question of women deacons was left open. Zenit news service moved the Vatican press release on October 17; Vatican Information Service (VIS) moved it October 18. See John Thavis, "Theologians-Deacons," *Catholic News Service* (October 1, 2002); John L. Allen, Jr. "The Word from Rome," *National Catholic Reporter* 2:6 (October 4, 2002) http://www.nationalcatholicreporter.org/word/word1004.htm (accessed January 22, 2011), and John L. Allen, Jr., "Draft

Document on Diaconate Leaves Tiny Opening for Considering Women," *National Catholic Reporter* 2:7 (October 11, 2002), 8; "Theological panel rules out ordination of women as deacons; defers to magisterium for a definitive decision," *Zenit* (October 17, 2002); and "Theological commission excludes ordaining women as deacons," *Vatican Information Service* (October 18, 2002).

122. Translation mine. "Pour ce qui est de l'ordination des femmes au diaconat, il convient de noter que deux indications importantes émergent de ce qui a été exposé jusqu'ici: 1) les deaconesses dont il est fait mention dans la Tradition de l'Église ancienne—selon ce que suggèrent le rite d'institution et les functions exercées—ne sont pas purement et simplement assimilables aux diacres: 2) l'unité du sacrament de l'ordre, dans la claire distinction entre les ministères de l'évêque et des presbyters d'une part et le ministère diaconal d'autre part, est fortement souligné par la Tradition ecclésiale, surtout dans la doctrine du Concile Vatican II et l'enseignement postconciliare du Magistère. À la lumière de ces éléments mis en évidence par la présente recherche historico-théologique, il reviendra au ministère de discernement que le Seigneur a établi dans son Église de se pronouncer avec autorité sur la question." "Le Diaconat," 107. The Commission maintains the singular "order" found in *Catéchisme de l'Église catholique*. English language Canon Law (cc. 1008–1054) uses "orders," and the *Catechism of the Catholic Church* (ch. 3, art. 6) uses "holy orders."

123. The seven member subcommittee was comprised of Rev. Santiago del Cura Elena (Spain); Rev. Henrique de Noronha Galvão (Portugal), Chairman; Rev. Pierre Gaudette (Canada); Mons. Roland Minnerath (France); Rev. Gerhard Ludwig Müller (Germany); S. E. Mons. Luis Tagle (Philippines); Rev. Ladislaus Vanyo (Hungary). The 30 men (29 priests) on the ITC at the time included Americans Rev. Christopher Begg of Catholic University, editor of *Catholic Biblical Quarterly*, and Rev. J. Augustine DeNoia, OP, formerly of the United States Catholic Conference of Bishops, now an archbishop and secretary of the Congregation for Worship and Sacraments.

124. A recent editorial in *La Civiltà Cattolica* notes that the work took ten years. "Editoriale: Il Diaconato, Espressione del servizio nella chiesa," *La Civiltà Cattolica* 2003 (March 15, 2003) I, 561–69, 561. A "Note préliminaire" in the published text states that the study of the diaconate was already undertaken by the previous "quinquennium" of the International Theological Commission (1992–1997), but never left the subcommittee, headed by Br. Max Thurian, joined by then Bishop Christoph Schönborn, OP; Bishop Joseph Osei-Bonsu;

Rev. Charles Acton; Msgr. Giuseppe Colombo; Msgr. Joseph Doré, PSS; Prof. Gösta Hallonstein; Rev. Stanislaw Nagy, SCI; and Rev. Henrique de Noronha Galvão. The matter was taken up by the subsequent (sixth) "quinquennium," initially by the subcommittee headed by de Noronha Galvão. *La documentation catholique* 23:59 (January 19, 2003). Cardinal Schönborn, now archbishop of Vienna and bishop of all Austria for the Eastern Rites, is now a member of the Interdicasterial Commission for the Catechism of the Catholic Church, which is also part of the Congregation for the Doctrine of the Faith.

125. de Noronha Galvão's major published work is *Die existentielle Gotteserkenntnis bei Augustin: Eine hermeneutische Lektüre der Confessiones* (Einsiedeln, Switzerland: Johannes Verlag, 1981), his 1979 doctoral thesis at the University of Regensburg. Benedict XVI taught dogmatic theology at the University of Regensburg from 1969 to 1977.

126. Vagaggini, "L'ordinazione delle diaconesse," 151. The suppression of the first Commission study is mentioned in Peter Hebblethwaite, *Paul VI: The First Modern Pope* (New York: Paulist, 1993), 640.

127. The document depends on Piersandro Vanzan, "Le diaconat permanent feminine: Ombres et lumières," *La documentation catholique* 2203 (May 2, 1999), 440–46, and notes. Vanzan reports on the discussions between and among R. Gryson, A. G. Martimort, C. Vagaggini, and C. Marucci.

128. Terrence W. Tilley, "Practicing History, Practicing Theology," *Theology and the New Histories*, Proceedings of the Annual Convention of the College Theology Society, 1998, ed. Gary Macy (Maryknoll, NY: Orbis Press, 1999), 10.

129. "Dans le Motu Proprio *Ad pascendum* (1972) le diacre permanent est considéré signe ou sacrament du Christ lui-même." "Le Diaconat," 107. ("Diaconatus permanens . . . signum vel sacramentum ipsius Christi Domini, qui non venit ministrari, sed ministrare," Paul VI, *Ad Pascendum, Acta Apostolicae Sedis* 54 [1972], 536.) The document tends to move toward an interpretation of the deacon as "sign or symbol" of Christ, which would be in keeping with *in persona Christi* theology of orders.

130. See Phyllis Zagano, "Inching Towards a Yes?" *The Tablet* (January 9, 2010), 10–11.

131. "À l'époque apostolique, diverses formes d'assistance diaconale aux Apôtres et aux communautés exercées par des femmes semblent avoir un caractère institutionnel. C'est ansi que Paul recommande à la communauté de Rome 'notre soeur Phébée, servante (*he diakonos*) de l'Église de Cenchrées' (cf. Rm. 16, 1–4)." "Le Diaconat," 68.

132. See Eisen, *Women Officeholders*, 158–98, at 164.

133. The statement "Il semble clair que ce ministère n'était pas perçu comme le simple équivalent féminine du diaconat masculine," from "Le Diaconat," 71 refers to texts as presented in Gerhard Müller, *Der Empfänger des Weihesakraments. Quellen zur Lehre und Praxis der Kirche, nur Männern das Weihesakrament zu spenden* (Wurzburg, 1999).

134. "Le Diaconat," 105.

135. "Il faut distinguer ce qu'on peut reconnaître comme étant la Tradition elle-même, depuis les originses, et les formes régionales ou liées à une époque de cette même Tradition." "Le Diaconat," 58–59, citing W. Kasper, *Theologie und Kirche* (Mainz, 1987), 99.

136. The document focuses on historical evidence that supports a distinction between deacons and deaconesses, "le deux branches du diaconat," stating that that deacons were chosen by the bishop to do whatever was necessary "beaucoup de choses necessaries" and deaconesses solely served the needs of women. However, since its primary premise was that it is impossible to take local historical facts and create a "Tradition," the same must be applied here. "Le Diaconat," 69.

137. Jean Daniélou, *The Ministry of Women in the Early Church*, trans. Glyn Symon (Westminster, MD: Christian Classics, 1961, 1974), originally published as Jean Daniélou, "Le ministère des femmes dans l'Église ancienne," in *La Maison-Dieu* 61 (1960) 70–96.

138. Daniélou, *Ministry of Women*, 27–29; Daniélou, "Le ministère des femmes," 90–92.

139. *Apostolic Constitutions*, Book VIII.

140. From the library of Cardinal Francis Barberini, and now in the Vatican library, the manuscript is also known as the Nicolai Manuscript, or as the Euchologion of St. Mark. "The detailed rubrics of the mid-eighth-century euchology codex, Barberini Gr. 336 show an almost exact parallelism between the rite for instituting deacons and deaconesses. Both were ordained in the bema, that is, within the sanctuary, inside the templon or chancel barrier, an area of the church from which the laity—and *a fortiori* all laywomen—except the emperor were ordinarily barred. This is especially significant in the light of Byzantine liturgical symbolism, in which the altar symbolizes the divine presence. Only major orders (diaconate, presbyterate, episcopacy) are conferred at the altar within the bema." Robert F. Taft, "Women at church in Byzantium: where, when—and why?" Dumbarton Oaks Papers #52, 28–87, 63. Taft cites S. Parenti and E. Velkovska, *L'Eucologio Barberini gr. 336* (ff. 1–263), Bibliotheca *EphL.* Subsidia 80 (Rome, 1995), §§ 161–64 and *The Rudder (Pendalion)* 372–73, 560. The Orthodox and Byzantine Rite

churches celebrate the feast days of many women deacons, including Phoebe, Macrina, Nonn, Melania, Thesebia, Goronia, Olympias, and Apollonia.

141. See Vanzan, "Le diaconat permanent feminine," 440–446, 442.

142. Also known as Grotta Ferrata, gr. Gb1, the Patriarchal Euchologion or as the George Varus manuscript. Miguel Arranz, *L'Eucologio Constantinopolitano agli Inizi del Secolo XI* (Rome: Editrice Pontifica Università Gregoriana, 1996), 153–60.

143. John Morinus, *Commentarius de Sacris Ecclesiae Ordinationibus* (Antwerp: Kalverstraat, 1695), 78–81.

144. Including the Coislin gr. 213 Manuscript (also known as the Strategios Euchologion); a rite for deaconesses compiled from several manuscripts: Goar, *Euchologion sive Rituale Graecorum*, 262–67; Syriac rituals in *Ritus Orientalium*, ed. H. Denzinger (Würzburg: Typis et Sumptibus Stahelianis, 1864), 229–33; 261–62.

145. "L'imposition des mains sur les diaconesses doit-elle être assimilée à celle faite sur les diacres ou se situe-t-elle plutôt dans la ligne de l'imposition des mains faite sur le sous-diacre et le lecteur?" "Le Diaconat," 71.

146. "As regards the topic of the diaconate, the Commission considers that it is necessary to clarify two points. The first refers to Vatican Council II, which instituted the permanent diaconate in the Latin Church, which used to be considered as a stage toward the priesthood. Moreover, the Council explains that there is only one sacrament of ordination with three stages. How is the diaconate articulated as a stage toward the priesthood as opposed to the permanent diaconate, which in many Churches has already borne rich fruit? . . . 'Diaconate' means 'service,' which is a very common word. And it is in this sense that in the history of the Church there is reference to 'deaconesses.' The problem the International Theological Commission must resolve is to clarify what kind of service is offered by the Church's 'deaconesses,' which does not necessarily imply a participation in the sacrament of Holy Orders." *Zenit* (November 26, 1999).

147. "We determine and ordain: the matter of the holy orders of the diaconate, presbyterate and episcopate is the laying on of hands alone, and the sole form is the words determining the application of the matter, words by which the effects of the sacrament—that is, the power of Order and the grace of the Holy Spirit—are unequivocally signified and which for this reason are accepted and used by the Church." Pius XII, apostolic constitution *Sacramentum ordinis* (1947).

148. Kalsbach, *Die altkirchliche Einrichtung der Diakonissen.*

149. Gryson, *Ministry of Women.*

150. Martimort, *Deaconesses.*

151. For example, Müller in 2000 argued that the office of deaconess was a fourth and minor order in language nearly identical to that of the ITC in 2002: "The office of deaconess is clearly distinguished from the office of the deacons. The diaconal ministry was not performed by women as well; rather there was an ecclesial office held only by women, which, admittedly, was usually mentioned before the office of subdeacon in listings of these ecclesial ministries and thus comes to stand at the head of the ecclesial offices (cf. I Tim 3:11)." Müller, *Priesthood and Diaconate.* (San Francisco: Ignatius Press, 2002), 211. (originally *Priestertum und Diakonat: Der Empfänger des Weihesakramentes in schöpfungstheologischer und christologischer Perspektive* [Einsiedeln, Frieburg: Johannes Verlag, 2000]).

152. Evangelos Theodorou, *Heroines of Love: Deaconesses through the Ages* (Athens: Apostoliki Diakonia of the Church of Greece, 1949); Evangelos Theodorou, *The "Ordination" or "Appointment" of Deaconesses* (Athens, 1954) (in Greek); and K. K. FitzGerald, *Women Deacons in the Orthodox Church* (Brookline, MA: Holy Cross Orthodox Press, 1998).

153. "At a lower level of the hierarchy are deacons, upon whom hands are imposed 'not unto the priesthood, but unto a ministry of service.' For strengthened by sacramental grace, in communion with the bishop and his group of priests they serve in the diaconate of the liturgy, of the word, and of charity to the people of God. It is the duty of the deacon, according as it shall have been assigned to him by competent authority, to administer baptism solemnly, to be custodian and dispenser of the Eucharist, to assist at and bless marriages in the name of the Church, to bring Viaticum to the dying, to read the Sacred Scripture to the faithful, to instruct and exhort the people, to preside over the worship and prayer of the faithful, to administer sacramentals, to officiate at funeral and burial services. Dedicated to duties of charity and of administration, let deacons be mindful of the admonition of Blessed Polycarp: "Be merciful, diligent, walking according to the truth of the Lord, who became the servant of all." Vatican II, *Lumen Gentium* 29, citing *Constitutiones Ecclesiae Aegyptiacae*, III, 2: ed. Funk, *Didascalia*, II, p. 103. *Statuta Eccl. Ant.* 371: Mansi 3, 954. The *Catechism of the Catholic Church* repeats this language in no. 1569: "At a lower level of the hierarchy are to be found deacons, who receive the imposition of hands 'not unto the priesthood, but unto the ministry." Also, "by sacramental ordination the deacon takes on a special 'diakonia,' which is expressed particularly in service to the Gospel. During the rite,

the ordaining Bishop says these words: 'Receive the Gospel of Christ, whose herald you now are. Believe what you read, teach what you believe and practice what you teach.' This is your mission, dear brothers: embrace the Gospel, reflect on its message in faith, love it and bear witness to it in word and deed. The work of the new evangelization needs your contribution, marked by consistency and dedication, by courage and generosity, in the daily service of the liturgy, of the word and of charity." John Paul II, *Angelus* (February 20, 2000).

154. *Ad Gentes* implies that the diaconate shares (rather than cooperates) in the pastoral functions of priests and bishops: "Where episcopal conferences deem it opportune, the order of the diaconate should be restored as a permanent state of life according to the norms of the Constitution *'De Ecclesia.'* (23) "For there are men who actually carry out the functions of the deacon's office, either preaching the word of God as catechists, or presiding over scattered Christian communities in the name of the pastor and the bishop, or practicing charity in social or relief work. It is only right to strengthen them by the imposition of hands which has come down from the Apostles, and to bind them more closely to the altar, that they may carry out their ministry more effectively because of the sacramental grace of the diaconate." Vatican II Decree on the Mission Activity of the Church (*Ad Gentes*), 16. A woman deacon who "shared" such function and authority would *de jure* be in authority over some men, perhaps the crux of the problem.

155. "Le can. 1008 du *CIC* affirme que les trois ministères ordonnés sont exercés *in persona Christi capitis*" and explains in a note "Il a été communiqué à la Commission théologique internationale qu'existe maintenant un projet de révision de ce même canon visant à distinguer les ministères sacerdotaux du ministère diaconal." "Le Diaconat," 106.

156. Zagano, *Holy Saturday*, 64–86.

157. In 2000, Antonio Miralles, of the Pontifical Athenaeum of the Holy Cross in Rome and a consultor to the Congregation for the Doctrine of the Faith and the Congregation for Clergy, said the important question is whether the permanent diaconate as "ministerial participation in the priesthood of Christ, in its dimension of service" was or was not joined later "to the ministerial participation of the priesthood itself, in its strictly priestly dimension." Vanzan, "Le diaconat permanent feminine," 445–46.

158. The *in persona Christi* argument, present in *Inter Insigniores* (1976) and quietly dropped in *Ordinatio Sacerdotalis* (1994), has its own difficulties. For example, "the representationalist view of the priesthood is not the doctrine of the Church, the substance of which is expressed

by the Council of Trent, but rather a language, for the most part conventional and nontechnical, for expressing this doctrine, a language which, when pushed to give a critical account of itself in the light of new questions, has become profoundly questionable." D. M. Ferrara, "In Persona Christi: Towards a Second Naïveté," *Theological Studies* 57 (1996), 65–88, 70.

159. "Même si apparemment il s'agit des mêmes fonctions qu'un fidèle non ordonné exerce, ce qui demeure décisive serait 'l'être' plutôt que le 'faire': dans lactation diaconale se réaliserait une présence particulière du Christ Tête et Serviteur propre à la grâce sacramentelle, à la configuration avec lui et à la dimension communautaire et publique des tâches qui sont exercées au nom de l'Église. L'optique croyante et la réalité sacramentelle du diaconat permettraient de découvrir et d'affirmer sa propre particularité, non pas en relation avec des fonctions mais en relation avec sa nature théologique et son symbolisme représentatif." "Le Diaconat," *La documentation catholique* 23:106 (January 19, 2003).

160. Even prior to the opening of the Council Richard Cardinal Cushing, Archbishop of Boston, called for deacons—and deaconesses—who could serve the Church "save through the purely sacerdotal functions." While he focused on the lay apostolate rather than on the specifics of diaconal ordination, Cardinal Cushing's clarity is prescient. "Summary of the Address of His Eminence, Richard Cardinal Cushing at the Meeting of the Society of Catholic College Teachers of Sacred Doctrine, April 3–4, 1961," in *Proceedings: Society of Catholic College Teachers of Sacred Doctrine 1961* (Brookline, MA: Cardinal Cushing College, 1961), 12. I am indebted to Prof. Sandra Yocum Mize of the University of Dayton for pointing out Cardinal Cushing's comments.

161. Vanzan, "Le diaconat permanent feminine," 440.

162. "L'ordinazione delle donne al diaconato, almeno," Sandro Magister, "Vade retro, Concilio," *L'Espresso* (February 17, 2000). Others assumed to support the notion at the time were Timothy Radcliffe, OP, then Master of the Order of Preachers; Cardinal Karl Lehmann, Bishop of Mainz; John R. Quinn, retired Archbishop of San Francisco; and Cardinal Pierre Eyt, Archbishop of Bordeaux, who died in 2001. Basil Cardinal Hume, who also supported women deacons, died a few months before this Synod.

163. From the official church calendar published by the Armenian Patriarchate of Turkey: "Mother Hrip'sime Proto-deacon Sasunian, Born in Soghukoluk, Antioch in 1928; Became a Nun in 1953; Proto-deacon in 1984; Mother Superior in 1998. Member of the Kalfayian Order,"

Oratsuyts' (Istanbul: Armenian Patriarchate, 2001), 254, trans. Fr. Krikor Maksoudian.

164. "Bartholomew said that there were no canonical reasons why women could not be ordained deacons in the Orthodox Church." National Conference of Catholic Bishops, "News about the Eastern Churches and Ecumenism," no. 5 (February, 1996) 1, reporting from *Service Orthodoxe de Presse*, "Genève: visite du patriarche oecuméique en Suisse," no. 204 (Javier 1996), 3. Two years later, Bartholomew wrote a warm letter as preface to K. K. FitzGerald's important study *Women Deacons in the Orthodox Church.*

165. Pamela Schaeffer, "Dueling Catholics Conferences Enliven Lincoln" *National Catholic Reporter* May 30, 1997). http://natcath.org/ NCR_Online/archives2/1997b/053097/053097e.htm (accessed January 26, 2011).

INDEX

Bruskewitz, Fabian W., (*continued*)
  juridical authority of, xii, 25, 31,
    37–43, 89, 90
  relationship with bishops, 38–39, 51
  relationship with Vatican, 55, 89, 90
  sacramental authority of, 5
  and women, 5, 14–19, 22, 35–36,
    38, 41, 46, 132
Burke, Raymond L., 31
  excommunication of Roman Catholic
    Womenpriests, xiv, 100, 102,
    104
Butler, Sara, 104–5, 146n81, 171–
  72n31, 175n44, 176n48

Call to Action (CTA), 26–43,
  148–49n96
  and Bruskewitz, xii, 4, 14, 19, 23–
    26, 31, 34–35, 37, 39–40, 116
  on married priests, 29
  as forbidden society, 23–24, 34–35,
    37, 39, 40, 42, 43, 144n65
  and *Octogesima Adveniens*, 26–27
  on the ordination of women, 30–34,
    123, 132, 133, 148n94
  and Paul VI, 26
  on role of laity, 4, 26–27, 29, 33–
    34, 39, 42
  and sex abuse, 4, 13
  on sexual issues, 28, 30–34, 64
  and Steichen, 18, 25
Call to Action–Nebraska (CTA-N)
  and "Affirmation of Faith," 21
  and Bruskewitz, xii, 14, 19, 21–26,
    31, 34–41, 43
  and Creed, 21
  and Eucharistic prayer, 21–22, 117
  as forbidden society, 23–24, 34–37,
    40, 144n65
  founding of, 14, 22–23
  and *Octogesima Adveniens*, 27
  and role of a laity, 23, 31, 40–43,
    125
  and sexual abuse, 38–39, 141n34
Canon Law. *See* Code of Canon Law
Castillo Mendez, Luis Fernando, 73
Catholics for an Active Liturgical Life
  (CALL), 14–19, 20, 21, 27, 34,
  41
Chinese Patriotic Association, 70

Chittister, Joan, 31, 36, 151n112
Christus Dominus, 6–7, 138n11,
  143n51, 145n78
Code of Canon Law
  on associations of the Christian
    faithful, 24–25, 149n103
  and bishops, xii, 3, 11, 16, 19,
    37, 40, 86, 90, 93, 114, 129,
    144n67
  on bishops' conferences, 8
  and Bruskewitz, xii-xiii, 19, 23–24
  on clerical marriage, 59–61, 63, 68,
    71, 75, 157n53
  and Congregation for the Doctrine
    of the Faith, 102
  on deacons, 126, 129
  on duty of vigilance by authority,
    24–25, 37
  on excommunication, 29, 100–102,
    168n1
    ferendae sentatiae, 40
    latae sententiae, 39, 153n6
  on exorcism, 58
  on forbidden societies, 24, 34, 40,
    149n102
  on incardination, 153n5
  on infallibility, 89, 91–95, 96–97,
    169n5, 184n103
  Koinótés on, 87
  on lay altar service, 15, 16, 19
  and Milingo, 59–71, 74–75, 78–79,
    84, 157n55
  and Norms, 11
  on ordination, 29, 70, 71, 98, 119–
    20, 122
  on participation of laity, 17, 42–43,
    124, 187n118
  on sex abuse, 11
  and Society of Saint Pius X (SSPX)
    (Lefebvre), 69–70, 78, 84, 85
  on women's ordination, xiv, 29, 86–
    88, 94–95, 97–98, 100–101,
    103, 105, 119–20, 126, 135,
    161n93, 171n28
Code of Canons of the Eastern
  Churches, 29, 124, 170n24
Communion
  definition of, xi, 42, 55
  and juridical authority, xii-xv, 2–3,
    8–9, 35, 37, 89–91, 94, 97,

42, 47, 49, 74, 80, 90, 95, 122,
129
on the diaconate,
192–93nn153–154
Society of Saint Pius X (SSPX), xv,
24, 47, 61, 69, 70, 78–80, 106,
144n66, 152n4, 153n9
bishops of, 24, 70, 78, 83
and Bruskewitz, 35, 144n65
founded by Lefebvre, 46
Spiner, Dusan Spiridion, 81, 82, 83,
99, 106, 167n8, 172n34
Stallings, George Augustus, 61–62,
64, 67, 70, 82, 158n61, 158n66,
161n92, 166n130
Steichen, Donna, 18, 19, 25, 33
Stevens, Maryann, 19–20
Sung, Maria, 58–62, 75, 83
Synod
of bishops, on the Bible, 103,
175n44
of bishops, second, 1971, 27
of bishops, twenty-first, on
Eucharist, 2005, xiv, 28, 33,
76–78
of Church of England, 116
of diocese of Lincoln, 17, 23,
34–35
of European bishops, 1999, 131
of Greek-Melkite Church, 77
of *Koinótés*, 86–88
Szabó, Tamás, 29, 75

Thorburn, Timothy, 22, 23, 24–25,
35, 39, 151n112
Tilley, Terrence W., 139n19

Union of Utrecht Old Catholic
Churches. *See* Old Catholic
Churches, Union of Utrecht
Unitatis Redintegratio, 122, 134,
162n97, 182n90
United States Conference of Catholic
Bishops (USCCB), 10
and Bruskewitz, xii, 3, 4, 14, 38–39,
40–41, 43, 142n35
formation of, 5–7
makeup of, 138n9
and Milingo, 64
publications of, 7, 143n50
and sex abuse, 10–13, 38, 139n22,
140n24, 141n30, 142n36,
151n115
statements by, 30, 139n17, 147n86,
152n127

Vatican II. *See* Second Vatican Council
Viri probati, 77
Voice of the Faithful (VOTF), 13, 25,
33, 39, 43, 116, 151n119

Williamson, Richard, 24, 70, 78, 83,
144n66, 153n6
Winter, Miriam Therese, 86
Women religious, 17, 36, 187n117
Sexual abuse of, 68, 160n85
Women's ordination. *See* Ordination of
women to diaconate; Ordination
of women to priesthood

Zagano, Phyllis, 139n19, 153n10,
171n29, 175n43, 177nn52–53,
187n119, 189n130